Critical Stylistics

The Power of English

Lesley Jeffries

palgrave
macmillan

First published 2010 by
PALGRAVE MACMILLAN

Palgrave Macmillan in the UK is an imprint of Macmillan Publishers Limited, registered in England, company number 785998, of Houndmills, Basingstoke, Hampshire RG21 6XS.

Palgrave Macmillan in the US is a division of St Martin's Press LLC, 175 Fifth Avenue, New York, NY 10010.

Palgrave Macmillan is the global academic imprint of the above companies and has companies and representatives throughout the world.

Palgrave® and Macmillan® are registered trademarks in the United States, the United Kingdom, Europe and other countries.

ISBN: 978–0–333–96448–4 hardback
ISBN: 978–0–333–96449–1 paperback

This book is printed on paper suitable for recycling and made from fully managed and sustained forest sources. Logging, pulping and manufacturing processes are expected to conform to the environmental regulations of the country of origin.

A catalogue record for this book is available from the British Library.

A catalog record for this book is available from the Library of Congress.

10 9 8 7 6 5 4 3 2 1
19 18 17 16 15 14 13 12 11 10

Printed and bound in China

'This is perfectly pitched to meet the needs of students in courses such as English functional grammar, discourse analysis, stylistics, advanced composition and critical discourse analysis. Jeffries's book is a long-needed synthesis of linguistic stylistics and critical discourse analysis; it provides excellent background reading for advanced research on such issues as negation, speech and thought presentation, systemic grammar and presupposition'.

– Donald E. Hardy, University of Nevada

We tend to think that politicians, copywriters and journalists can affect us by their use of language, but how does this happen, exactly? Critical Discourse Analysis provides us with general theories for explaining the impact texts can have, considering the social and political contexts in which texts are produced and read. Stylistics provides detailed tools of analysis for understanding how texts work. *Critical Stylistics* combines the strengths of these two approaches to uncover the deep-seated ideologies of everyday texts.

Original and engaging, *Critical Stylistics*

- presents a new amalgamation of stylistics, critical discourse analysis and functional approaches to grammar;
- introduces a comprehensive set of tools to help explain and analyse the power of written texts;
- examines a wide variety of real texts and provides a wealth of practical worked examples.

Perspectives on the English Language is an innovative series of textbooks for the English language student, together forming a wide-ranging course for undergraduate students of English. The basis of the series is a 'core' of three books which together lay the foundations for further study. A set of higher level textbooks builds on these core books by bringing together the latest thinking in a range of topics in English language. Clearly set out and including relevant exercises and questions, they make both the foundations of language and the latest research accessible to a student audience.

Series Editors: Lesley Jeffries and Dan McIntyre

LESLEY JEFFRIES is Professor of English Language at the University of Huddersfield. She was Chair of the Poetics and Linguistics Association from 2007 to 2009 and has written a number of articles and four other books, including *Discovering Language: The Structure of Modern English* and *Textual Construction of the Female Body*.

808.
042
JEF

PERSPECTIVES ON THE ENGLISH LANGUAGE

Series Editor: Lesley Jeffries and Dan McIntyre

Published titles
Siobhan Chapman   Thinking About Language: Theories of English
Urszula Clark   Studying Language: English in Action
Christiana Gregoriou   English Literary Stylistics
Simon Horobin   History of the English Language
Discovering Language   The Structure of Modern English
Lesley Jeffries   Critical Stylistics: The Power of English

Forthcoming
Jonathan Culpeper   The Pragmatics of the English Language
Rob Penhallurick   Studying Dialect

Perspectives on the English Language Series
Series Standing Order
ISBN 0-333-96146-3 hardback
ISBN 0-333-96147-1 paperback
(*outside North America only*)

You can receive future titles in this series as they are published by placing a standing order. Please contact your bookseller or, in the case of difficulty, write to us at the address below with your name and address, the title of the series and one of the ISBNs quoted above.

Customer Services Department, Macmillan Distribution Ltd,
Houndmills, Basingstoke, Hampshire RG21 6XS, England

Contents

Series editors' preface

The first three books to be published in the Perspectives on the English Language series (Jeffries, *Discovering Language*, Chapman, *Thinking About Language* and Clark, *Studying Language*) together formed the first wave of what will ultimately be a comprehensive collection of research-based textbooks covering the wide variety of topics in English Language studies. These initial three books provide the basics of English Language description, theory and methodology that students need, whether they are specialists in English Language or taking only one or two modules in the subject. The idea was that these books would be used differently by such different students, and indeed they have already proved useful to postgraduate students as well as undergraduates.

Now we are beginning the process of adding to the series the envisaged set of higher-level textbooks which will build on the core books by bringing together the latest thinking in a range of topics in English Language. This 'second wave' comprises books written by current researchers in the field, and far from simply providing an overview or summary of work so far, these books are distinctive in making the latest research available to a student audience. They are not 'dumbed down', but are written accessibly, with exercises and questions for the reader to consider where relevant. And for the HE teacher, these books provide a resource that s/he can use to bring out the best in students of all abilities.

The book you are holding will ultimately be part of a large series of topic-based books in English Language, and we are confident that you will find them useful and interesting. Although this series was begun with only one series editor, the rate of production of the second wave calls for more help in editing and proofreading. We look forward to surfing this second wave together!

Lesley Jeffries and Dan McIntyre
June 2008

Acknowledgements

My friends and family, of course, need to be thanked for their patience in the face of yet another long haul to finish this book; Dave for his competitive 'Well I have a book chapter to write too!' which helped me to see it in perspective, and friends who are waiting for me to rejoin the world of reading books, so I become more interesting to talk to – they hope. I would also like to thank Palgrave Macmillan and the excellent in-house editorial team who have been waiting some time for this manuscript, not for the first time, and have been extremely supportive throughout. My colleagues and students at the University of Huddersfield as usual have had to put up with me during the writing phase, and have helped in many ways to improve this book. The Language and Power group of 2008–9 were particular guinea pigs for some of the material and their comments and responses were very useful in revising the text. Most of all, I owe a great debt of gratitude to Dan McIntyre, colleague and friend, who as co-editor of this series had to take on the editing of this book and did so thoroughly and with good humour. He has certainly saved me from worse embarrassment, but any errors or infelicities of style remain my own.

Introduction

This book introduces a set of tools, which, whilst not complete, are nevertheless more comprehensive than any provided in the literature on CDA and other similarly politically motivated linguistic studies. More importantly, since there are no doubt other possible tools which others will propose, there is a rationale behind the toolkit which I hope will make sense to others working in this field.

When I started studying linguistics, it was a conscious reaction to what I perceived as the vagueness and lack of tools of analysis of literary studies. Having found that stylistics provided me with the vocabulary I needed to describe literary effects, I wanted to apply similar tools to questions of power and ideology in language. I discovered CDA and thought that this would provide the framework that I was looking for, but was dismayed to find that the main practitioners of this field were often more interested in the contextual (and thus necessarily somewhat vague) features of powerful language, and were less concerned than me to provide a reasonably broad range of tools which would help to explain how texts are in a position to persuade the reader to alter or adapt her/his ideological outlook to match that of the text.

This is not to say that the contextual analysis provided by most CDA is not valuable, but it seems to have been adequately and effectively covered by others more competent than me in that area. This book provides only a small amount of discussion of the socio-political reasons why certain texts have power to influence us, and the reader is pointed towards relevant literature to follow up this line of enquiry.

Significantly, many of the CDA texts (see Chapter 1) do provide a short account of some tools of analysis, but there is a tendency to use only those tools that can be accessed relatively easily by non-specialists (i.e. those with little linguistic knowledge) and there is also a tendency to assert that there is no rationale by which a set of tools can be developed to any degree (see pages 12–15), which results in charges of CDA lacking (linguistic) theoretical rigour and thus being somehow lesser in significance than the primary fields of the discipline.

The most useful book I have found to teach the kind of thing I am after is Simpson (1993) which is ostensibly about the language of literature, but gives a better sense than many books of how to approach the question of where ideology lies within all texts. This, of course, reflects the fact that stylistics, originally a straightforward application of linguistic description to literary texts, has developed into a fully fledged and multifaceted field in its own right, and has taken on board progress in all areas of linguistics and literary studies as well as psychology and other fields, in its quest to describe the workings of text, both literary and non-literary.

One of these developments of stylistics in recent years has been the rise of what is often known as 'cognitive stylistics' (Semino and Culpeper 2002) or 'cognitive poetics' (Stockwell 2002). This opening up of stylistics to consider the reader's (or hearer's) construction of meaning, in addition to meaning as it might be decoded from the page, also has something to offer to a more practically oriented version of CDA. Thus, whilst we might use schema theory and deixis to explain the way in which a reader constructs an understanding of a novel, play or poem (see, for example, Semino 1997 and McIntyre 2006), such tools can also help us to explain the process by which readers may be ideologically affected by reading *non*-fiction. That such a process exists is generally accepted by CDA practitioners, and explained in socio-political, rather than cognitive ways. Here, we have the opportunity to complement such explanations with hypotheses about why and how this might happen linguistically speaking.

So, here are the challenges for this book:

- To provide both a more comprehensive set of tools and also a rationale for why they might indeed be a set.
- To give the reasonably advanced student of English Language or Linguistics (i.e. those who at least understand the basics of English grammar and semantics) a sense of how to go about studying the power of texts written and spoken in English.
- To provide an explanation (albeit not yet susceptible to scientific proof) of the cognitive processes which may result in readers being affected by a text's ideological structure.

One further word of explanation may be needed here; to justify the choice of title for this volume. Whilst the ideological focus meant that 'Critical' was inevitably to be included, the choice of 'Stylistics' was more difficult. Clearly the development of CDA in recent years has been away from textual analysis. This book could therefore not honestly be labelled CDA without confusing some readers, and possibly angering some of the proponents of the more socio-political CDA analysts. However, I do consider myself to be working within the broader sub-discipline of CDA, albeit at the micro-analysis end of the spectrum, and with no intention to invalidate the more global kind of work which is more common in this field. In the end, the term 'stylistics', seemed most appropriate because it indicates that this book is more linguistically oriented than much other CDA work. In addition, since I have never considered stylistics to be limited to literary style, the broader definition of style, which focuses on the choices a text producer makes, seems entirely appropriate here. Thus, the producer of any text, though perhaps in cultural terms restricted by background education and so on, is nevertheless also subject to the pressure of choosing the exact terms in which s/he frames the text. This choice, it seems to me, whether made consciously or unconsciously and at the whim of dominant pressures, is always ideologically loaded and may also be ideologically manipulative. These are the things about style that fascinate me, and I hope to show the reader how to get close to the mechanisms by which ideology is thus threaded through our language use.

1 The Background to Critical Stylistics

1.1 Introduction

As I finish writing the text for this book, a number of things are happening in the news which remind me constantly how important ideologies are in the world. This morning on the radio there was one news item recounting the fact that a teacher of a class of seven-year-olds had told them that it was their parents, not Santa, who leave the presents by their beds on Christmas morning. The parents were, apparently, furious, and the school felt it was obliged to discipline the teacher. I personally had conflicting reactions to this story, as I might also have felt irritated if I had been a parent of those children, though I also found it interesting and a little disturbing that the employers had been forced into disciplining a teacher for telling the truth. I told this story to a class of final year undergraduates during the day, and their collective intake of breath made it sound as though I had been telling a tale of horrific depravity. One of the students, a father, said he would have 'smacked' her (or some such violent notion) and when I discussed the same story with a very nice café proprietor I know quite well, she also said she would have 'whipped' the teacher for ruining her children's belief in Santa.

In this story, what appears to be happening is that the ideology of childhood in twenty-first-century Britain, which incorporates innocence, pleasure, protection and myths of kind old men who give you presents, is more important than the truth. This is not to condemn such an ideology outright, though I recall feeling faintly uneasy when I first introduced my own children to the idea of Father Christmas, because I was conscious of it being a lie. What this story shows us is that truth is not an absolute value, even in a society where we profess that it is. Rather, there are negotiations around ideology which take place in relation to each issue that arises. Moral dilemmas of when to tell the truth, an untruth or something slightly less than the truth are common.

Even more complicated is the question of what is the truth and how do we recognize it.

This latter problem has been on my mind for a few months now as the world goes from 'credit crunch' to 'slowdown' and into recession. I am aware that my own values are at odds with the prevailing ones, since I do not really accept that economic growth is the only way for the human race to pursue progress. Even so, it has been extraordinary to hear how the commentators on this financial crisis constantly take for granted that the very thing that caused the problem (overspending on credit) is also the same process we 'need' to stimulate the economy back to economic growth (which is assumed to be a good thing). The extent to which world economies and all the complex machinery of government and business depend on something called 'confidence' in the market is a worrying fantasy reminiscent of our childlike faith in the goodness of Santa. Somehow, we are aware that the world we have created is an illusory one, and the 'teacher' in the form of a recession is telling us the uncomfortable truth. But how we long to return to the safety of a world where the myth of economic growth would bring us all the toys we desire.

So, ideas, and in particular those ideas that are shared by a community or society which are termed *ideologies*, are a very important aspect of the world that we live in, and they are, of course, communicated, reproduced, constructed and negotiated using language. This book concerns the ways in which language, as used in specific texts, can help to embed ideology in our outlook on the world.

1.2 Critical Discourse Analysis

In an edited collection of articles about the language of the nuclear arms debate Kress (1985) defines the field he and others were developing as follows:

> There is now a significant and large body of work which enables us to see the operation of ideology in language and which provides at least a partial understanding of that operation. Some, perhaps the major, problems remain. I take these to be around the question 'what now?' Having established that texts are everywhere and inescapably ideologically structured, and that the ideological structuring of both language and texts can be related readily enough to the social structures and processes of the origins of particular texts, where do we go from here? (Kress 1985: 65)

The answer to this question in practice was that the field became ever more interdisciplinary, in its attempt to understand the context of production of texts, and the ideological implications of this context. Also, in attempting to address the question of the role of the reader in constructing ideological meaning, the field turned to cultural theorists and literary scholars, who had been thinking about such things since the so-called 'death of the author' (Barthes 1977).

However, one of the propositions of Kress's extract above appears to me to have been accepted at face value by those involved in the field and this is that *there is now a significant and large body of work which enables us to see the operation of ideology in language.* Certainly, there is some such work, and to some extent both the ideology itself and how it operates in texts have been investigated. However, the impetus for this book is the sense that what we have in the way of examples of critical analysis of texts is rather patchy in its coverage of linguistic structures and has not yet developed a full methodology – or methodologies – which students can easily try out for themselves.

The aim of this book, then, is to give the reader a clear set of analytical tools to follow in carrying out the critical analysis of texts, with the aim of uncovering or discovering the underlying ideologies of the texts. There are many other books on the market which explore the relationship between language and power, and many of these will be recommended at various points. Most of them, however, have a different focus from this book, and are often primarily concerned with the socio-political contexts in which texts are produced and read or the context in which language choices are made. Though I am also interested in these things, my experience of teaching students to approach texts critically is that they need some *specific tools of analysis* to get a clear sense of how texts may influence the ideological outlook of their recipients. Therefore, what I hope to provide here is a set of tools that can be used either individually or as a set to establish what a text is *doing*.

In order to explain what I mean by this, we can make use of Halliday's division of the functions of language into three metafunctions. Halliday (1971) saw the main functions of language as being 'ideational' (how language represents the world), 'interpersonal' (how language mediates between people) and 'textual' (how linguistic items make the discourse as a whole function). The tools of analysis presented in this book may be seen primarily in the context of the first metafunction, as explaining how language represents the world. Thus, texts may 'name' things, 'characterize them', hypothesize about alternative realities amongst other things, and these notions of what texts do are *fundamental* to the approach being presented here.

Of course, the question of how language represents the world may be innocent, in the sense that it is simply the author's sincere attempt to portray what s/he sees in linguistic form. Many text types may be seen in this light, including literary texts and all sorts of more mundane informational texts. However, it should be made clear at the outset that *all* texts are ideological.

Before introducing the tools of analysis in detail, it is worth spending a short time on some of the fundamental concepts and theoretical assumptions of Critical Discourse Analysis (CDA) and dispelling a few persistent myths.

CDA has provided extensive discussion (e.g. Fairclough 1989 chapter 3) on the nature of social meaning, and how discourse is one of the factors in the reproduction of social inequalities and dominant ideologies (see below). What is meant by *discourse*, of course, is often contested, but most linguistic approaches to the subject accept that there is a broad definition which has a linguistic text (spoken or written) at the centre, but includes the contexts of production and reception as well as the broader social context in which a text may occur or be brought into play. In this book, I am not using *discourse* more generally to mean 'the kind of language used in relation to a particular topic or in a particular setting', though this is often how it is used in cultural and literary studies, and increasingly in some kinds of CDA.

The contention of much discussion in CDA and related literature is that there are dominant groups whose ideologies are bound to be reproduced in the media and other texts, and in this way ideologies are continually reasserted to the point at which they become naturalized (see below) and become seen by the population at large as being common sense, and thus in some sense intrinsically true. Fairclough himself distinguishes between power *in* discourse, which is intended to address how power relations are acted out in the process of communicating, and power *behind* discourse, which addresses the institutional or otherwise accepted power relations between communicating participants and how these affect the communication that takes place.

This latter kind of power, arising from socio-political relationships which exist independently of language, will not be addressed in any detail in this book, though it is taken for granted as one of the underlying conditions of many of the texts being analysed and interpreted in this book. I would encourage the reader to consult other CDA texts (e.g. Caldas-Coulthard and Coulthard 1996, Fairclough 1989, 1992, 2000, Fowler 1991) for discussion of such power, and in particular the established power of the media, though it is important to bear in mind that all text producers have the *potential* to produce hidden ideologies in an attempt to persuade or manipulate, and that the techniques of embedding of ideology introduced in this book are common across the whole range of communicative situations in which we find ourselves on a daily basis. The difference in access to public media is one that is a highly political issue and concerns some of the scholars in this field particularly (see van Dijk 1996). Here, I am concerned with teaching ways of analysing the texts that do make it to the public stage, and thus explaining how they can influence readers/hearers beyond the fact that they see the light of day at all.

I would caution, however, against the view that what this book is doing is returning to an outdated view of how meanings arise from texts. I totally concur with the following statement from Fairclough (1992: 88–9):

> While it is true that the forms and content of texts do bear the imprint of (...) ideological processes and structures, it is not possible to 'read off' ideologies from texts.

He goes on to say that the ideologies pertain to whole discourse events, and thus the interpretative process as well as the textual content itself. This is, of course, true to the extent that readers may agree/disagree with or feel indifferent to ideological assumptions, but I think it *is* possible to separate out some of the ideologies that a text *constructs* (or reinforces) and the assimilation of those ideologies (or their rebuttal) by readers. Thus, it is surely likely that the ideologies of a far right political group such as the British National Party will be 'present' in their propaganda, and that these will be evident to both their supporters and to their opponents. That both groups agree on what these ideologies are does not necessarily mean that both groups will be swayed equally by the text itself. Nevertheless, the presence of extreme views on immigration and race, for example, might have some kind of effect on any reader, even if only for the time that s/he is reading.

1.3 Ideology and rhetoric

It is important to make clear at the outset that ideology is seen by most discourse analysts and linguists as an unavoidable fact of all discourse. Unlike its use in the popular press and some political environments, we do not use the term *ideology* to refer only to ideas that are motivated by political aims or selfish intentions. This is not to say that all ideology is equal; clearly some ideology *is* potentially harmful, some may be a force for good, and some is simply culturally restricted or a question of choice. There is not, however, any possibility that any discourse is free of ideas, and thus of ideology.

The important issue for us is that language can carry ideologies, either explicitly (*I hate foreigners*) or implicitly (*Those horrible foreigners are back again*). It is common, but often implicit in analytical contexts, to take for granted that we are most interested in the less obvious ideological encoding, *because* it is more insidious. This is explored further in the next section, where naturalization is explained.

The popular image of the power of language is one associated with Rhetoric, which is the power of deliberate persuasion The study of rhetoric in classical times was considered vital to the education of a cultured person (i.e. a man) and it was seen as a very accomplished art alongside music, drawing and so on. We are still affected by great speakers, as can be seen by the response to the speeches of Barack Obama during the 2008 election campaign in the United States, but we should not consider the deliberate structuring of arguments to make a case (i.e. rhetoric) to be the same as the weaving of ideologies throughout all aspects of the language of texts. There may be some features of texts that can be described and explained with reference to both rhetoric and CDA, but the latter includes many features that are not only hidden, but may also be unconscious on the part of the text producer. This does not necessarily detract from their potency and may even enhance it, but it does distinguish it from rhetorical features that are usually intentional.

1.4 Naturalization

One of the most important concepts underlying CDA is the notion that some ideology may be 'naturalized' to the extent that it becomes 'common sense' to members of the community. For example, the idea that children should be looked after and are not required to work 13-hour days in factories is now a very common ideology that has been naturalized in the United Kingdom for many years, and as a result seems to us to be self-evident. However, to those Victorian families who relied on children's wages and to those families in the developing world who do so today, this ideology would perhaps be surprising.

Notice that I am not arguing that this is in any sense a 'bad' ideology to hold. The point is simply that it is not an absolute or given moral standard, but reflects a particular socio-political view of how children should be treated. To take a different example, which we may be less inclined to agree with when it is made explicit, much of the media in present-day Western society take for granted that it is good to be very thin if you are female. When it is put like that, we may react against it, but much of our experience of publications depicting the ideal female figure confirms this ideology, and if we are honest, we have trouble rejecting it in our own minds, particularly if we are female.

Ideology, then, may be very evident in some contexts (such as in totalitarian regimes, where it is usually explicit) but we may find it more insidious in some ways when it is simply repeated endlessly in many different forms in all sorts of texts, to the point where it becomes naturalized as self-evident or common sense. There is, presumably, an inverse relationship between the extent to which an ideology is naturalized in a particular community or society, and the extent to which it is consciously 'used' by a text producer. No one would accuse a journalist of ideological bias if s/he described the killing of an old lady by an intruder as 'wicked' but to say the same of the practice of euthanasia, which is in the news as I write, would be to take sides in a clearly controversial debate in British society at the current time. The main social ideology about killing people may be that it is bad, unless it is at the request of the person concerned, but there are also, of course, sub-social groupings where it is a badge of honour to kill, as I heard on the news this morning in relation to gangs of youths in north London.

1.5 Members' resources and schema theory – changing and confirming prejudice?

The discussion of naturalization leads us neatly to the question of whether such naturalized ideologies are shared by everyone in a society or whether there are variations amongst people within the same social grouping.

CDA has used terms like MR (members' resources) to refer to the background assumptions and experiences that make up the foundation of our everyday lives.

> It is an important property of productive and interpretative processes that they involve an interplay between properties of texts and a considerable range of what I referred to in Chapter 1 as 'members' resources (MR) which people have in their heads and draw upon when they produce or interpret texts – including their knowledge of language, representations of the natural and social worlds they inhabit, values, beliefs, assumptions, and so on. (Fairclough 1989: 24)

Though the notion of MR is rather open-ended, it presumably includes those types of knowledge of the world that cognitive stylisticians such as Semino (1997: 18) have described using models provided by schema theory:

> a schema is a portion of background knowledge that contains generic information about different types of events, situations, people or objects.

Schema theory is used to describe the way in which human beings may structure their experience so that they can relate new communications and texts to existing expectations and ultimately to their established ideologies. This means that, for example, the schema for Santa is one that involves a man in a red suit who manages to gain access to people's homes and places presents next to the beds of good children on Christmas Eve without waking them. For adults the schema will also contain the knowledge that this is a myth alongside the notion that it is one that is seen as literally true by children under a certain age and that adults collude with.

One of the uses that schema theory has been put to in stylistics is the explanation of how readers interact with the ideologies in a text. Thus, Cook (1994) argues that literature tends to challenge readers to consider whether they might change their basic schemas and Semino (1997) likewise argues that the reading of poems can be schema-changing. Though Cook and Semino do not apply the same ideas to other, non-literary, texts, it seems clear to me (Jeffries 2001) that texts such as those attempting to teach (e.g. textbooks like this one) as well as political campaigning materials and other propaganda are all aimed at changing the schemata of the reader. To the extent that the reader's schemas reflect the dominant ideologies of their society, it may be the case that some texts reinforce those ideologies, rather than challenging them and changing them. All such effects of texts are of interest to us in this book.

1.6 The place of this book in the CDA context

Fairclough (1989: 26) distinguishes three 'dimensions', which he also calls 'stages' of CDA:

- *Description* is the stage which is concerned with formal properties of the text.
- *Interpretation* is concerned with the relationship between text and interaction – with seeing the text as the product of a process of production, and as a resource in the process of interpretation (...)
- *Explanation* is concerned with the relationship between interaction and social context – with the social determination of the processes of production and interpretation, and their social effects.

The impression I get from the CDA literature generally is that the main area of interest for many scholars working in this field is the third – the process of explaining how texts fit into the socio-political landscape in which they are produced and read. This work draws as much on social theory as on linguistic insights and is extremely helpful in the global task of contextualizing any linguistic analysis that is carried out. I think it is also true to say that it is production, rather than reception, that has received most of the attention of CDA analysts to date, with reception being theorized in general terms in relation to the proposed MR, but with little evidence-based research into the reception of actual texts so far. This is an area that could be fruitfully pursued in the future.

My interest, as a stylistician or text analyst is in the first and second of Fairclough's 'stages' (though I don't see them as sequential as implied by the word 'stage' and I don't think Fairclough intended this either). If we are to understand the precise ways in which texts may transmit, reinforce or inculcate ideologies in their readers, we need to understand a great deal more about the process of interpretation than we currently know. One area of development that may be helpful in theorizing this process is the rise of cognitive stylistic theories which have focused mainly on the interpretation of literary texts in the past, but which may have insights to offer the critical linguist too. This aspect of the application of stylistics to critical analysis of texts will be addressed where relevant in later chapters of this book.

The student beginning to study texts in the spirit of critical linguistics may be forgiven for wondering what it is s/he should actually *do* in studying the ideologies of a text or set of texts. Though the context of production and reception can be described, this is not primarily a *linguistic* activity, and because many books and articles on CDA are written with the non-specialist in mind (though possible specialists from other fields such as cultural studies or media studies may read them), there is a dearth of analytical advice available. Fairclough (1989: 110) acknowledges the incomplete nature of his analytical advice:

> The present chapter is written at an introductory level for people who do not have extensive backgrounds in language study...The set of textual features included is highly selective, containing only those which tend to be most significant for critical analysis.

He then introduces a range of features, by listing ten questions that the analyst may ask, organized under three headings, Vocabulary, Grammar and Textual Structures, which reflect the traditional 'layers' of linguistic analysis. These questions, which include 'What experiential values do words have?' (110) and 'What interactional conventions are used?' (111), do not obviously address the ideological relevance that answers might provide, though examples given later in the chapter illustrate some of the potential for ideological interpretation of the analysis. There is no sense given, either, of what might have been left out, for the sake of the non-specialist perhaps or, because there was perceived to be no potential for ideological meaning.

Chapter 5 of Fowler (1991) is supposed to be a methodology, or at least provides a list of tools. His comment on these tools does not make clear which ones he rejected as irrelevant to the task in hand:

> My attitude to linguistic tools, then, is essentially eclectic. (...) the best model for examining the connections between linguistic structure and

social values is the functional model developed by M.A.K. Halliday and his colleagues, and that is my basis; but I will simplify and alter Halliday's rather forbidding terminology when it suits my purpose, and add terms and concepts from other models when they will do a particular job better. (69)

Fowler's later statement that 'critical linguists get a very high mileage out of a small selection of linguistic concepts such as transitivity and nominalisation' (Fowler 1996: 8) attracts criticism from Widdowson (1998) who accuses CDA of a lack of rigour and suggests that for CDA analysts:

Analysis is not the systematic application of a theoretical model, but a rather less rigorous operation, in effect, a kind of *ad hoc* bricolage which takes from theory whatever concept comes usefully to hand. (Widdowson 1998: 137)

The tools Fowler presents are as follows:

- Transitivity
- Some syntactic transformations of the clause
- Lexical structure
- Interpersonal elements: modality
- Interpersonal elements: speech acts.

Notice that Fowler introduces the interpersonal metafunction as a characteristic of the last two tools of analysis, without making clear how he sees the metafunction of his other tools. It is probable that he assumed them to be ideational, though it is not entirely clear here. I will address the question of the metafunctions at various times in this book, but I think it worth reiterating here that I see all of the tools of analysis presented here as primarily ideational in conception, even those which, like modality, are seen in Hallidayan approaches as being interpersonal.

I am in favour of eclecticism (see Jeffries 2000), but it is hard for me to sense the order in Fowler's suggested list of tools and certainly it feels lacking in comprehensive coverage of linguistic features. I suspect it is even harder for a student of language to see why these features are the only ones/the most important ones, and certainly they seem to be 'random' in the modern sense of that word. For non-specialists there may be similar problems, or they may take it on trust that these *are* the features of language. Perhaps the problem is that the 'tools' tend to be ultimately grammatically defined, instead of starting with the function itself, whether that is to assess the representation of 'reality' as seen through the model of transitivity, or whether it is the consideration of how texts present alternative (hypothetical) 'realities' through the use of modality, negation and so on.

A more satisfying methodology for analysing texts to expose ideological structures is to be found in Simpson (1993). Although much of his book concerns ideology in literature, there is nevertheless a great correspondence between it and the issues raised about non-literary texts. I have found Simpson's account of the modal system in English, his version of transitivity, and his account of pragmatic analysis the most useful for students trying to carry out critical analysis of texts. He also makes a connection between these three apparently unrelated linguistic systems by focusing on the point of view which they present, and the one that the reader is therefore invited to take up. Nevertheless, the same questions apply to Simpson as to the other texts mentioned above. Why only these tools of analysis, and what else might be used to approach the question of ideology in text? To be fair, Simpson does also address questions of space and time, the presentation of speech and thought and some of the psychological models of narrating consciousness that have been discussed by stylistics. These, together, form much of the basis of the tools in the present book, and I would not want to claim that I have 'invented' the tools as a whole. But Simpson presents some of these topics as 'preliminary' – perhaps because they have been adequately addressed elsewhere. I prefer to address here all the tools as equally relevant to the description of the ideological basis of texts, with the explicit purpose of making them equally available to the reader wishing to carry out his/her own analysis.

So, my model, for the purposes of this book, is one that tries to assemble the main general functions that a text has in representing reality. In other words, to provide tools to analyse the different ways in which texts allow/ ask us to conceptualize those topics they are addressing, and to provide some means of accessing this representational practice through the linguistic features that are already well-described in very many semantico-grammatical theories and models. I think that the corrective given to text-based analysis by CDA has been very useful and the contextualization in production and reception terms has helped us to avoid the conclusion that texts have either transparent or stable meaning. However, it is important not to lose sight of the fact that there is a level at which texts organize the world we experience, and that this is demonstrable in the words and structures of the texts them-selves. What the world then makes of these meanings, whether ideologically significant or not, is the question which Fairclough's second 'stage' of ana-lysis – interpretation – addresses, and one which will also be addressed inter-mittently throughout this book.

Thus, the representation of women's bodies in a particular text, for example, may be proven to be intrinsically based on the 'slim is good' ideology, but the way in which this is interpreted by the reader may well depend on their gender, bodily satisfaction, political outlook and so on, and indeed some readers may have simultaneous or consecutive conflicting reactions (Jeffries 2001), depending on their psychological state and the prominence of the various Member's Resources at any one time.

1.7 The tools

For the reasons given above, I am concentrating in this book on giving the aspiring critical analyst a set of tools which on one level at least seem to function in a similar way to each other, and which cover not only the ground suggested by Fairclough, Fowler, Simpson and others but also include new tools which seem to me to work (at least semantically/pragmatically) in a similar way to the more traditional tools such as transitivity and modality. I make no particular claim of comprehensiveness, though I would like to think that this model has at least a sense of coherence and that it would be possible for others in the future to add further tools of this kind without abandoning the basic model. What the tools need to do, it seems to me, is to answer the question of what any text is 'doing'. Thus, I would argue that the tools in the following chapters answer this question in the form of a present participle:

- Naming and Describing
- Representing Actions/Events/States
- Equating and Contrasting
- Exemplifying and Enumerating
- Prioritizing
- Assuming and Implying
- Negating
- Hypothesizing
- Presenting the Speech and Thoughts of other Participants
- Representing Time, Space and Society.

These participles are not intended as a way of dumbing-down the technical language which linguists tend to use, and the rest of this book will use – and explain – technical language wherever it is useful. But the point of these tools is that they are not essentially technical, but conceptual. Readers will immediately have an idea of the kind of information which they address, and can relate the more technical aspects of the tools back to this label as a way of orienting themselves when the difficulties of analysis get confusing. Another reason for using these labels is that they do not equate in a one-to-one fashion with any particular lexical or grammatical feature, though many of them may well have stereotypical or 'normal' features associated with them.

The easiest way to illustrate this lack of form-function mapping is through the presentation of modality in English. Whilst it is uncontentious to say that English modality is delivered largely through the modal auxiliary verbs (*may*, *might*, *should* etc.), there are other lexical ways of achieving the same result, such as modal adverbs (e.g. *probably*, *certainly*) modal adjectives (e.g.*probable*, *definite*) and modal main verbs (e.g. *think*, *believe*). More peripheral, but just as modal, are the uses of certain types of intonation pattern (e.g. rising intonation with declarative clauses) and body language (e.g. shrugging or raising of eyebrows) to deliver the same modal effect as the modal verb itself. The tools introduced in Chapters 2 to 11 will vary in their formal range, but they all seem to be somewhere on the borderline between the formal and the functional aspects of language.

To summarize, this book is in a tradition of bringing the best of stylistics and critical linguistics together, and I find myself agreeing with the aims found in Simpson (1993: 8):

> this book sets out to deliver an integrated programme in stylistic and critical linguistic analysis. The 'package' offered is a general model for linguistic criticism. A common thread running through the entire book is, of course, the preoccupation with point of view in language, whether this be the ideological viewpoint adopted in a newspaper report or the more localized 'psychological' point of view exhibited by a work of narrative fiction. A guiding principle behind all of this is the premise that a particular style represents certain selections from a pool of available options in the linguistic system. By developing a particular style, a producer of a spoken or written text privileges certain readings, certain ways of seeing things, while suppressing or downplaying others. (...) The purpose, in other words, is to probe under the surface of language, to decode the stylistic choices which shape a text's meaning.

Like Simpson, then, I am concerned with stylistic choices, and the textual analysis which can illuminate the choices that a text producer has made, whether consciously or not. This is not a recipe for understanding the full impact of a text on a reader, because the background and experience of the reader will inform that impact. However, it is worth repeating that texts do indeed have some ideological content which may influence the reader (or not) in a range of ways, and the tools in this book are provided to help the reader discover that ideological content.

Naming and Describing 2

2.1 Introduction

This chapter sets the pattern for the following chapters, each of which will introduce a linguistic feature, with related tools for analysing the ways in which texts represent the world with ideological consequences. Each chapter (2–11) will give an overview of its argument and then explain the technical aspects of the feature with examples, to be followed by a summary of the potential ideological effects of that particular textual function, some exercises for the reader to try, and a short review of other relevant literature, which can function as a guide to further reading.

This chapter explores the various ways in which English texts could be said to 'name' the world, which is different from asking the question of how the *English language* names the world. Answering the latter question would lead us into areas of lexical semantics such as the way in which English labels certain semantic fields and raises an implicit comparison with the different ways in which other languages may do so. The question we are considering, in contrast, is how individual texts (and implicitly their authors) may choose from the regular resources of the language in representing a view of the world.

As with all the linguistic features explored in this book, the issue of how texts use the resources of the language seems to beg a rather large question, which is 'what are these resources?' In each chapter, there will be a section on 'form and function' which will explore the relationship between a theoretically stable system of language forms and meanings and their flexible use in particular ideological ways, which may require a simple choice between two or more 'normal' English features but alternatively could mean choosing to add to the stable system or flout its normal rules.

In the case of naming, there may be a perfectly acceptable choice between two or more ways of referencing the same things. For example, the name of someone (e.g. *Lisa Heywood*) might alternate with another 'innocent' way of referencing the same person (e.g. *my sister*). On the other hand, there may be a more biased view possible with a further naming practice (e.g. *the best singer in the school*). In addition, there are other possible ways of referencing someone which might be seen as more unusual morphologically and thus semantically and lexically and these may have ideological significance in certain contexts (e.g. *robo-sister*). Note that all such inventiveness in English is dependent on us knowing the 'normal' rules of morphology and being aware of other words using morphemes such as *robo-*. We are only able to interpret a new form on the basis of analogy with older forms.

This chapter, then, looks at three important ways in which naming can create ideological meaning in English texts. These include the relatively straightforward case in which a noun is chosen out of the available alternatives; the question of what other information is included within the boundaries of the noun phrase or noun group and the way in which processes and actions which are standardly described in English by verbs may be converted into nouns by a process called nominalization with certain ideological consequences.

2.2 A linguistic model of naming

In order to fully appreciate the topic of naming in ideological terms, it is helpful to understand a little about the structure of the English nominal. Readers who feel confident in their understanding of this subject may wish to skim over this section, and those who feel that they need more than is offered here may wish to refer to Jeffries (2006: 104–16).

We can think of a sentence or utterance as being founded upon two vital and mutually dependent parts which are labelled *noun phrase* and *verb phrase*, or *noun group* and *verb group* depending on the system of grammar that you are accustomed to.[1] In the most straightforward representation of the world through language, these two elements of the sentence will represent *entities* in the case of noun phrases and the *processes, actions and so on* in the case of verb phrases.

Now there are *many* exceptions to these rules, and we will see below how some of these can have interesting ideological effects. However, it is a necessary paradox of the way that human language works that it depends on an idealized system of rules, often talked of as a 'code', but at the same time it also has the ability to allow flexibility in the use of the code. Many of the tools of analysis in this volume are situated precisely at the point where the code and its flexibility meet and so it is important for readers to understand what the 'stereotypical' English sentence structure is like, to understand what is happening to meaning – and thus to ideology – when things are changed.

So, in this chapter we are concerned with the part of the sentence that typically 'names' an entity. This is the noun phrase or nominal group. It often functions as the grammatical Subject or Object of a Predicator (verb), and is therefore semantically most likely to be seen as either the initiator of the action, often called 'Actor' (where it is the subject of an active verb) or the recipient of the action, often known as 'Goal' (where it is the object of an active verb). Here are a couple of simple (invented) examples:

	S	P	O
2.1	The prime minister	reduced	benefit payments.
	Packages	raise	anxiety.

Note that the nominal parts of the sentence (S and O here) can be expanded with more premodifiers (often adjectives) and post-modifiers (prepositional phrases or relative clauses):

	S	P	O
2.2	The new, energetic prime minister	reduced	child benefit payments to the rich.
	Suspicious packages in brown paper	raise	levels of anxiety in postal workers.

These expanded noun phrases, despite having a lot more information in them than the originals, are still essentially naming devices, and the modifications simply contribute more in the way of unique identifiers of the entity, rather than proposing some kind of transaction or relationship between them and the head noun, as they would in a full clause treatment of the same material:

2.3   The prime minister is new, is energetic and has reduced child benefit payments. Child benefits were previously paid to the rich.

The packages are in brown paper and are suspicious. They raise levels of anxiety. The anxiety is in postal workers.

We will see below that the main ideological importance of noun phrases is that they are able to 'package up' ideas or information which are not fundamentally about entities but which are really a description of a process, event or action. In other words, the distinction between entities and processes is made less clear, and a process can be presented as being more like an entity.

Naming is a broad descriptive term covering a number of linguistic practices, including:

- the choice of a noun to indicate a referent;
- the construction of a noun phrase with modifiers to further determine the nature of the referent (see also 'describing');
- the decision to use a 'name' rather than, for example, express as a (verbal) process (see 'nominalization' below).

The next sections will deal with each of these practices of naming in turn, though they often coincide in individually attested examples of naming.

2.2.1 Choice of nouns

If we think of naming in everyday terms, we may think about the kind of choice that someone makes for example to call a small individual portion of bread *a roll*, *a bap*, *a breadcake* or *a teacake*. These variations in naming are regional and representative of British English. That such naming implies textual choices may not be evident to the speaker who grows up in a particular place until and unless s/he comes across speakers with different dialects and this may produce nothing more than general interest unless differences in dialect become the source of discrimination or prejudice.

Another kind of choice in naming has more obvious ideological potential. That is the choice of a word with pejorative or ameliorative connotations. In other words, where a choice of word not only makes reference to something, but also shows the speaker's opinion of that referent. For example, the choice between saying that someone gave you a *smile* and that they gave you a *leer* is one between a neutral and a negative evaluation of the facial expression being described. We will look more closely at such connotations in Chapter 7, but here is another illustration of the kind of choice that is meant:

2.4   He lived in a Victorian terraced house with original features.
2.5   He lived in a museum.

Though Example 2.4 is more informative out of context, and the qualifying phrase 'with original features' is usually indicative of approval, a speaker or writer may choose Example 2.5 in preference, to indicate a more negative view of the same referent – and a slight disapproval of the lack of modern fixtures and fittings in the house concerned. Clearly, the second choice here is metaphorical, and may require a little more in the way of processing by the hearer/reader to decode its relevance. This is not our concern here (though see Chapter 5 for more on metaphor) but we may hypothesize that this kind of metaphorical reference provides opportunities for producers of language to include ideological content which may be less evident than in a more literal use of naming conventions. Goatly (2007: 40) argues that conventional metaphors do just this:

> However, misleading though the labels may be, there is a very important distinction to be made between the original and the conventional and the literal in terms of language processing. Metaphors demand longer reading times than their non-figurative counterparts (Noveck et al. 2001). And unconventional metaphors show more right-hemisphere brain activity in fMRI brain scans (Ahrens, Liu, Lee, Gong, Fang and Hsu 2006). The relative ease with which conventional metaphors and literal language are processed suggests the possibility for considerable latent ideological effects.

If, as I would suggest, the pejorative use of *museum* is conventional as a metaphor, there may be less attention paid to the ideology (old = bad) than would be the case with a novel metaphor.

2.2.2 Noun modification

Although the choice of a noun itself can, as we have seen, be ideological, much of the remainder of this chapter will focus more on ways in which the nominal part of English clauses and sentences may use syntactic and morphological techniques to name referents and produce ideological effects. The basis of this approach is that the nominal component (noun phrase or noun group) does not form the *proposition* of the clause or sentence, but instead labels something that is thus assumed (technically, *presupposed*) to exist (see Chapter 7 for more on assuming). It is probably worth taking a moment or two to consider what is meant by this difference. The proposition of any clause can be seen as the assertion that the clause is making about the relationships between the named entities (person, place, thing). The verb is thus essential to the proposition because it tells the recipient how the nominals (nouns and noun phrases) relate to each other. A simple sentence like *Janie ate the last biscuit* takes for granted that there are entities known as *Janie* and *the last biscuit*, but asserts that they have a particular relationship in which one eats the other. This is the proposition of the sentence. The way in which this basic truth about sentences in English can be exploited for ideological or other effect is by putting the processes/actions and so on into a nominal structure, and thus no longer asserting them, but assuming them. Thus, the sentence *Janie's eating of the last biscuit was a scandal in her father's eyes* would change the focus from the eating, which is now part of a nominal (*Janie's eating of the biscuit*) to the question of this action being (*was*) a scandal.

As a result of the 'normal' structure of English clauses, nominals are less susceptible to debate or questioning than other clausal elements, particularly the verbal element. In other words, the nominal parts of English clauses and sentences are 'packaging up' something that is named by that nominal element, and the reader or hearer is not encouraged by such a structure to question the relationship between the parts of that structure.

Take, for example, the following noun phrase:

2.6   the long and winding road that leads to your door.

The head noun here is *road*, and it is modified (premodified) by a determiner and two adjectives (*the long and winding*) and qualified (post-modified) by a relative clause (*that leads to your door*). This noun phrase 'feels' unfinished to a speaker of English because we are asked to assume the existence of such a door (see also 'presupposition' in Chapter 7) and we want to know what the door will do, or in the case of the Beatles song it comes from, what it will *not* do:

2.7   the long and winding road that leads to your door will never disappear.

Now in Example 2.7 we have a full clause with a Subject (i.e. the noun phrase we have already seen), a Predicator (*will disappear*) and an Adverbial (*never*), which just happens to interrupt the verb phrase. The proposition of the sentence is effectively represented by the relationship between the Subject, the Predicator and the Adverbial. In other words, what this sentence is asserting (because it is a declarative sentence) is that a certain door will not disappear, and that this situation will continue indefinitely.

The explanation of this clause's proposition looks less self-evident when we consider that there are also relationships being suggested between the modifier, the head noun and the qualifier – all within the Subject noun phrase. When they are in the noun phrase, the relationships are taken for granted, but these relationships can be expressed differently, by making them the main proposition of a clause:

2.8   the road is long and winding (noun phrase modifier moved to complement position).

2.9   the road leads to your door (qualifying relative clause moved to main clause).

In Examples 2.8 and 2.9 we now have one of the modifications of the head noun expressed not as modification, but as a proposition, so that the recipient is aware that the information content of the clause is precisely that of the relationship between the door and its features (*long and winding* or *leads to your door*). These features are now much more accessible to debate – one could for example respond that one has seen longer or windier roads, or that it only leads to the village and not right up to the door. Such debates are not really on offer with Example 2.7, where one could question other things, such as what is meant by *never* and whether all roads disappear in time, but not whether the road is long and winding or whether it leads to your door.

We may now have spent enough time on an example from a song lyric, but the same kinds of issues arise in every noun phrase in English, and whilst many of them are uncontentious because they are no more than the effect of using the language economically, or refer to self-evidently existing referents (e.g. *the weather last Monday*), there is also huge potential for *ideological* packaging which could encourage the recipient to accept ideas that ought to be open to debate or questioning.

2.10   The committee said it was 'astonished' by the lack of evidence of any work that Freddie had done in return for the £45,000 in salary plus pension payments he had been paid.

This report, about a Member of the British Parliament who is alleged (at the time of writing) to have paid both of his sons public money for little or no work, tells the reader what the committee 'said' (in writing, presumably). This reported discourse (see also Chapter 10) includes a noun phrase within the Adverbial prepositional phrase beginning with 'by':

2.11   the lack of evidence of any work that Freddie had done in return for the £45,000 in salary plus pension payments he had been paid.[2]

The original version of the sentence (Example 2.10) has a proposition which asserts that the committee and the statement had a particular relationship which is defined by a *Verbalization process* (see Chapter 3 for more on types of process). Thus, the proposition asserts that the committee *said something* and gives a version of what that something is. There is therefore nothing here that can be easily contested apart from whether or not the committee has indeed 'said' they were astonished at these things. If we try the same technique with the noun phrase here, as we did with the song lyric, we can see that there are other relationships which are not put into propositional form in the original, but which could be spelled out more clearly:

2.12   There is a lack of evidence of Freddie's work.
2.13   Freddie was paid £45,000 in salary plus pension payments.

We should note here that one of these potential supplementary propositions is more contentious than the other. It is presumably a matter of record that the young man was paid £45,000, but the lack of evidence that he did any work to earn this sum is less easily demonstrated. Whilst it certainly feeds the prevailing public mood of suspicion and mistrust of politicians to believe it, the important thing that we can note here is that the writer, whilst purporting to be reporting what a committee has 'said', only uses quotation marks for the word 'astonished', leaving the noun phrase picked out in Example 2.11 above to merge the voice of the committee with that of the journalist. We will return in Chapter 10 to the use of reported speech and writing as an ideological tool, but note here that the construction of the noun phrase itself contributes to the ideological impact of the sentence.

Here is a clause from a different text type: a political website. You may wish to consider the noun phrase structures within it before reading on:

2.14   Oh dear. What will the doomsayers say now? How will they explain away yet two more scientific studies that clearly contradict the global warming orthodoxy?

What we have in the third sentence of Example 2.14 is a question asked about how *they* (the doomsayers) will explain away the assumed content of the following noun phrase:

2.15   yet two more scientific studies that clearly contradict the global warming orthodoxy.

We will consider the issue of the presuppositions that are triggered by 'yet' and the noun phrase itself, in Chapter 7, but here it is worth considering that what we are being asked is how something will be 'explained away'; that something being the noun phrase in question. The noun phrase has the head noun *studies* which is modified by *scientific* and *two more*, so the question of their credibility is not up for discussion (they are, after all, *scientific*) and they are not the only ones (*more*). Possibly still more problematic for the reader is the post-modifying relative clause (*that clearly contradict the global warming orthodoxy*). Relative clauses form part of the noun phrase they qualify, and in our terms are therefore not part of the proposition of the sentence, but are 'given information' and thus not open to easy questioning. Consider what would happen if this were transformed into a full clause:

2.16   two more scientific studies clearly contradict the global warming orthodoxy.

This version allows the reader to question whether the studies do indeed contradict the theory of global warming, and if so, whether this contradiction is 'clear'. Note that even this version contains a noun phrase that is not really open to question: *the global warming orthodoxy*. The use of the word *orthodoxy* in this context has negative connotations of extreme and inflexible views held by the prevailing authority. It may be that even when this item was posted there was general acceptance of the theory, and it certainly is the case as I write, though the theory is now known as 'climate change' rather than 'global warming'. What is implied by the negative connotations, however, is that this theory is misconceived and unquestioningly accepted, allowing the story of the 'scientific' studies to undermine it further.

2.2.3 Nominalization

Whilst we have been concerned so far with aspects of naming that are built into the structure of the noun phrase by way of the modification, there is also potential for packaging certain ideological content *in the head noun itself*. Critical Discourse Analysis points to nominalization as a process which is often a significant choice in the production of texts, because it is a morphological process which seems to work against the simplest form-function relationships in English. Thus, if the nominal element in a clause has the primary function of naming the *participants* in an event, action or process, we would expect the head noun of the nominal elements in a clause prototypically to refer to a person, place or thing and for the verb phrase to indicate the kind of process that is taking place between these participants. In an invented example such as

2.17   The British invaded Iraq.

we have two participants identified in the noun phrases (*the British; Iraq*) and they are connected by the verb (*invaded*) which relates the Subject or Actor (*the British*) to the Object or Goal (*Iraq*). Because this relationship is the main one in the clause, the recipient is entitled to question, debate or comment upon the process of invading (Did they? Are you sure? Wouldn't you say they had been invited? And so on). Nominalization of the verb would make this whole sentence into a noun phrase:

2.18   The invasion of Iraq by the British.

This is no longer a complete clause, and would presumably then be completed in some other way, such as *was a terrible mistake* or *was an unavoidable necessity*.

What is noticeable here is that, when we turn a *process* into a *nominal* (i.e. a verb into a noun) just as when we use the passive voice (*Iraq was invaded by the British*), we are syntactically able to discard the Actor (*Iraq was invaded*) and this results in a noun phrase which looks superficially much more like the common type of noun phrase such as 'the sound of music', 'the puddle of water' and so on:

2.19   The invasion of Iraq.

At this point, the producer of a text may also wish to introduce some evaluative elements by means of adjectives modifying the head noun (Example 2.20) and prepositional phrases or relative clauses qualifying it (Example 2.21):

2.20   The *illegal/appalling/inspired/disastrous* invasion of Iraq.

2.21   The invasion of Iraq *with such dire consequences/which went so wrong/ which saved the Iraqis from a dictatorship*.

Examples 2.20 and 2.21, being still no more than noun phrases, and not complete clauses, are 'packaging up' information that might otherwise have been the content of a proposition, and thus made more clearly open to debate as in the following:

	S	P	C	
2.22	The invasion of Iraq	was	illegal/appalling/inspired/ disastrous.	

	S	P	O	
2.23	The invasion of Iraq	had	such dire consequences	
		P	C	
		went	so wrong	
		P	O	A
		saved	the Iraqis	from a dictatorship

The following ideologically contrasting examples demonstrate the use of morphological nominalizations of this kind and their potential for ideological effect:

2.24   Shell Nigeria remains committed to minimising the impacts of its operations and activities on the environment. As in previous years, we continued efforts aimed at improving our environmental performance as part of our contribution to sustainable development. We improved our environmental stewardship and programmes in spite of the challenging operating environment. However, due to the lack of access to fields in our western area of operation, we were unable to assess and clean up the spills in this area caused by militant group activities.

http://www.shell.com/home/content/nigeria/news_and_library/
publications/2007/environmental_performance/dir_report2006_
environmental_performance.html

2.25   In the Niger Delta, where Shell sources 10 per cent of its oil, the company's failure to invest in technology results in 700 million scf/d of gas being
burnt off into the environment, an increase on last year, despite a commitment
to end flaring by 2008. Gas flaring wastes energy, contributes to global warming and pollutes the environment. But gas flaring has become an every-day
feature for the communities in the Delta. Oil spills are also common – with
9,900 barrels of oil spilt in 2003. Oil spills are frequently left rather than
cleaned up, contaminating farmland, water courses and fish supplies.

http://www.foe.co.uk/resource/press_releases/behind_the_shine_the_
real_22062004.html

Example 2.24 is typical of the kind of text that results when large corporate
bodies try to explain their moral position on issues which they are charged
with. In this case, the oil company Shell is claiming that it has a responsible
attitude to the areas where it drills and collects oil. There are a great many
abstract and in some cases rather vague nouns which are used here, although
they all indirectly refer to the actions of the company. They include:

2.26   operations and activities
2.27   environmental performance
2.28   contribution to sustainable development
2.29   the spills in this area caused by militant group activities

What is noticeable about many of these noun phrases is that the nominalizations
are not easily 'converted' back into a verb. Thus, operations and activities, for
example, cannot simply be reworded as 'Shell Nigeria has operated and acted',
since these verbs are clearly rather indeterminate in terms of what actions or
processes they refer to. One could conclude that Shell is therefore not being particularly manipulative, since these nominalizations are extremely common in
English, and they are therefore just using the normal resources of the language.
However, the ideological point may also be made from a more social stand-
point; that the language itself reflects the recurrent avoidance of explicitness
with regard to the detail of what large corporations actually do. Performance
and development are further examples of nominalizations that have become
naturalized in this way, reflecting the packaging of activity into a named entity
in the first case, and a process that is superficially devoid of actors in the second.
Note in the case of our contribution to sustainable development, there is also
the nominalization *contribution* which has no specificity, and could refer to a
rather small, or negligible contribution, though the pragmatic presupposition
(see Chapter 7) is that they have made a considerable effort in this area.

Notice, then, that the point about nominalization of this morphological kind is not just that it enables the producer of the text to leave out all mention of the Actor. In the example discussed above, it is clear that *our* refers to Shell and that they are therefore claiming that their company has been contributing to sustainable development (though who is 'doing' the developing is less clear). The other aspect of nominalization is the lack of dynamism. Instead of a process or action, we have a 'thing', which on the one hand is made more tangible (and measurable) by being given a 'name' and thereby being presupposed to exist, and on the other hand is somehow more vague and difficult to pin down, because the detail is missing. If you were to convert these nouns back into verbs, you would be compelled to give more information. Here is one possible intervention in the first part of the base text[3]:

2.30   Shell Nigeria drills in remote and very poor communities and we sometimes spill oil which affects the local communities and the natural world as a result. We aim to minimise the impacts of our work on the environment. As in previous years, we tried to adversely affect the environment less and we see this as helping the local people in places where we work to develop their communities sustainably.

The verbs *act* and *operate* have been replaced by *drill* and *spill* here, making clear exactly what actions we are talking about. The third sentence, which aims to make explicit the actions behind *we continued efforts aimed at improving our environmental performance* is interesting because it results in an admission that they are indeed harming the environment (*we tried to adversely affect the environment less*).

One of the noun phrases in the base text is particularly interesting as it appears to be blaming the protestors (*militant group*) for the oil spills:

2.31   the spills in this area caused by militant group activities

It may simply be a case of bad drafting, or perhaps they are indeed claiming that it is the protestors that have been spilling oil. Either way, they are presenting the reader with the apparent presupposed truth that the spills are caused by protestors, and are not, as they could have done, presenting a proposition to that effect:

2.32   The spills in this area are caused by militant group activities.

Such a proposition, of course, would be more open to question, which would not suit the company's purpose of showing that they are responsible and it is others who are to blame for the problems.

If we turn now to the Friends of the Earth (FoE) website, and particularly its consideration of the very same activity, we find – perhaps surprisingly – that FoE also uses noun phrases and nominalizations in preference to clauses in places where its purpose might benefit from a clearer apportioning of blame:

- company's failure to invest
- a commitment to end flaring by 2008
- gas flaring
- global warming
- oil spills

In each of these cases, a fuller explanation may be ideologically more suited to FoE's purpose, putting Shell in the actor's role more often, rather than listing the nominalized activities using noun phrases. Here is an intervention in their text, with the changed sections italicized:

2.33   In the Niger Delta, where Shell sources 10 per cent of its oil, the company *has failed* to invest in technology result*ing* in *them burning off* 700 million scf/d of gas into the environment, an increase on last year, despite *the fact that they had committed themselves* to end flaring by 2008 [4]. Gas flaring wastes energy, contributes to global warming and pollutes the environment [5]. But *Shell flares gas so much that it has* become an every-day feature for the communities in the Delta. *Shell also spills oil frequently* – with 9,900 barrels of oil spilt in 2003 [6] – *and often leaves oil spills rather than cleaning them up*, contaminating farmland, water courses and fish supplies.

This intervened version of the text reads oddly in places because we are so accustomed to reading texts, even on the campaigning side of such debates, which adopt the 'corporate' style of language with nominalization and abstract nouns in plentiful supply, and where the responsible actor in a process is rarely named. This style has affected even those campaigning groups which, like FoE, are striving to change the world affected by corporate greed, as they see it. However, it is of course useful to such campaigns to make assumptions about the guilt of companies like Shell, and this is one possible effect of the nominalizations they use.

2.3 Form and function

If we consider the formal features of the textual function of 'Naming' as specified in this chapter, we can see that they typify the form-function slippage that I argued in Chapter 1 was at the heart of the model of textual meaning being developed in this book.

The main formal counterpart to naming is the noun, and we saw in Section 2.2.1 that the choice of which noun to use in referring to someone or something was one aspect of the ideological potential of naming. However, the noun operates within a larger unit, the noun phrase or noun group, in which there is scope for including a great deal of information which may be quite innocuous and factual (e.g. *the last week of my holiday; my sister's oldest friend who died last week*) or may incorporate evaluative or contentious qualifications which define the referent of the noun (e.g. *the ridiculous policies of this inept government; the damaging loss of information which should have been avoidable*).

These nominal units, with a noun at their centre (head noun), are the prototypical way of naming things and people in English, and their internal structure, therefore, is one way of including ideological information within a structure that is not easily challenged. We saw examples of this in Section 2.2.2.

The other way in which naming is of ideological significance can be seen in the examples in Section 2.2.3 which challenge the form-function simplicity of the prototypical arrangement whereby nouns are the class of words which name entities and verbs are the class of words which name processes and actions. In the case of nominalization, what happens is that a prototypical process is named, by making the verb into a noun. This can happen in a range of ways, many involving the addition of morphemes (e.g. *information; dependence*), and some just being used without addition as nouns (e.g. *the talk; the walk*).

So, naming, as primary school children know, is usually (typically) carried by nouns, but we have seen in this chapter so far that this textual practice (naming) may also incorporate relations which are more typically thought of as belonging to propositions that is, clauses. The capacity to name the world is a very powerful one, of course, and we will see in the next section how naming may affect the ideological content of a text.

2.4 Ideological effects

This section will discuss a number of examples of naming in some detail. The formal aspects of the noun phrases will be described as an essential part of explaining what is happening ideologically. The ideological effect will be linked back to the textual features described.

The following example is typical of the kind of tabloid news coverage of public sector (civil servants, health professionals, teachers etc.)

issues including pay claims, resourcing debates and disagreements with government:

2.34   Barely a day goes by without more special pleading coming from a different part of the public sector.

This sentence has a cliché as the main clause (*Barely a day goes by*) followed by an Adverbial (prepositional phrase (PP)) which makes up the rest. The preposition *without* is followed by a noun phrase (NP) which can be analysed in the following way:

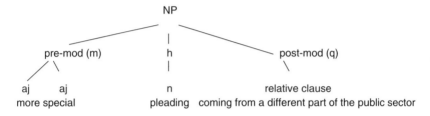

Within the qualifying relative clause, of course, is the prepositional phrase starting at *from* and including the NP *a different part of the public sector*. This NP can be analysed as follows:

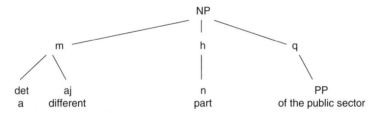

And the PP here also, of course, is made up of a preposition (*of*) and yet another embedded NP (*the public sector*).

So far, this is only analysis of the grammar, but now that we know what is there, we can see what is happening ideologically in this sentence. It is significant that the main clause is an idiom with relatively little in the way of information value – the proposition of the sentence is that there is hardly a day without...etc.

More interesting is the large NP with the smaller one inside it. The first part assumes that there has been special pleading before (by the use of *more*; see also Chapter 7 on presupposition) and uses a nominalization (*pleading*) to turn the activity into a 'thing'. This is followed by the assumption in the embedded NP that there have been earlier complaints by public sector representatives (*a different part*). The sentence is not *asserting* that these things have happened, and nor is it giving any evidence for them – it is simply *assuming* that they are true by packaging them into a NP.

Following Example 2.34, we find a development of the idea that the public sector is the problem:

2.35   But the real story of the credit crunch and the ensuing recession is the suffering being caused to the wealth-creating business sector.

This sentence is a Subject–Predicator–Complement (SPC) clause, with the main verb (*is*) sandwiched between two NP structures. The Subject is made up of a coordinated pair of NPs (NP1 and NP2) and the Complement is a complex NP with post-modification by a relative clause.

Looking at these in detail, we have:

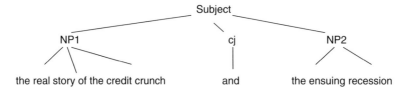

The Subject here is taking for granted the existence (see Chapter 7) of the *credit crunch*, which is itself a simple phrase referring to an immensely complex set of issues of international finance. This first NP has the head noun *story* modified by the adjective *real*, which implies that there may be other (unreal/untrue) stories around. The second NP here is assuming that there will be a recession following the credit crunch, and though this opinion might be based on experience, it nevertheless has the potential for feeding the crisis in confidence that we are told is a factor in the financial markets. Note that I have used the word 'opinion' in the previous sentence, to refer to the view that there will be a recession following the credit crunch. Of course, the whole point about the analysis of naming is that this is not being *presented* as an opinion, or even as a proposition, but is being taken for granted, by being simply *named*. This process of naming something and thereby almost bringing it into existence by that very naming process is sometimes referred to as *reification*.

These two coordinated NPs are then equated, by the copula verb, *is*, with the following NP as a Complement:

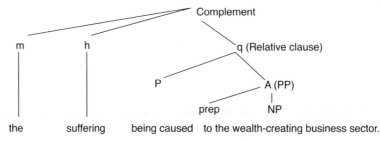

This NP packages up two ideas (ideologies) which are then taken for granted in the same way as we saw in the Subject, by being named, rather than proposed. The first of these is that there is suffering being caused to business, and the second is that the business sector is wealth-creating. Whilst there are undoubtedly difficulties being caused to business in the financial turmoil of 2008–9, the choice of the word *suffering*, which is a nominalization of the verb *to suffer*, and is more usually used in relation to illness and extreme poverty, might be seen as raising the level of emotion, whilst being unavailable to challenge, as it is presented not as a proposition, but a name. Note that the propositional version would be to say that *the business sector is suffering* which although also quite common in these days of media-hype, nevertheless allows us to question whether this is indeed true. The other, more deeply embedded, NP here is *the wealth-creating business sector* which uses the modification *wealth-creating* to characterize the head noun without opening this ideology up for investigation. I have no doubt that it is indeed assumed by many people that wealth-creation is one of the outcomes of business activity, but it is not the only ideology possible, and there are also possible questions about how wealth is defined which could undermine the assumptions present here.

A further sentence in the same text demonstrates the sympathies of the writer still further:

2.36 Small companies and the self-employed have no bottomless pit of taxpayers' money to raid when the going gets tough.

This sentence has a SPO structure, with the Subject being made up of two coordinated NPs (*Small companies and the self-employed*) and the Predicator (verb) being the main verb *have* (note it is not an auxiliary here, though in other cases it often is). The Object NP is the most interesting, ideologically, as it makes a number of assumptions and implications:

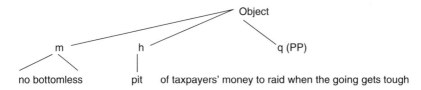

What is implied by this NP, using the negator (*no*) (see also Chapter 8), the modifying adjective *bottomless* and the qualifying preposition phrase (from *of taxpayers'* to the end) is that unnamed others (implicitly the public sector) can resort to public funding when things become difficult. Though the whole sentence is ostensibly about the lack of such back-up funding for business, it is implicitly an attack on the public sector's drain on the public purse.

2.5 Exercises

The following sentences continue the text that was discussed in the previous section. Try analysing the naming practices in a similar way, and compare them with my commentaries, to be found in the Appendix. You do not need to use tree diagrams if they do not help you, and if you need to revise (or learn) the structure of the NP, see Jeffries (2006: 104–16).

2.37   On the contrary, the tax authorities are famed for their lack of sympathy when a business hits cash-flow problems.

2.38   And the big banks, which have been advanced so much public money themselves, are prone to charging rip-off lending rates to business borrowers.

2.39   Entrepreneurs are the life-blood of the economy. Operating without a financial safety net they generate the wealth and employment that keeps UK plc afloat.

2.40   So, at a time when Labour is talking about indulging in another public spending binge, Tory leader David Cameron is right to focus instead on the needs of small firms.

2.41   If Britain wants to avoid a return to the mass unemployment of the early Eighties then paying heed to the essential interests of those who provide millions of people with highly productive jobs is absolutely essential.

2.6 Further reading

The textual practice explored in this chapter is one that, as we have seen, incorporates a number of different phenomena that we have grouped under the label on 'naming'. These include the basic questions of the choice of noun used to refer to a particular person or entity, the question of the structure of noun phrases and what they include and also the question of verbal processes being transformed into nominals in a process called *nominalization*, which has been a long-standing 'tool' of analysis for CDA:

> nominalization: a process is expressed as a noun, as if it were an entity. One effect of this grammatical form is that crucial aspects of the process are left unspecified. (Fairclough 1989: 51)

The careful reader of CDA will find many fairly brief references to nominalization, mostly repeating the same kind of information, but often usefully exemplifying with different cases, which can be useful for the reader.

Here is another explanation, from Fairclough (1992: 183)

> The creation of new entities is a feature of nominalization which is of considerable cultural and ideological importance. For instance, an advertisement for cosmetic surgery has the headline 'Good looks can last you a lifetime!'; 'good looks' is a nominalization (from concrete relational processes such as 'you look good!') which entifies a local and temporary condition into an inherent state or property.

So, one of the consequences of nominalization is that it seems to turn a transitory action or process into something stable, with a label. This is not only ever an issue of ideological manipulation, as Fowler (1991: 79) points out:

> It has often been observed that English is a 'nominalizing' language. By this is meant that it is structurally possible, and actually common, for predicates (verbs and adjectives) to be realized syntactically as nouns: these are called derived nominals. 'Allegation' is derived from 'allege', 'development' from 'develop', etc.

Thus, not all nominalizations will necessarily be suspicious in terms of persuasion or ideological bias, because we use them everyday, and in some genres (particularly political and business-related texts) they are endemic. However, this very tendency, to use words that are inevitably longer, and may be seen as more 'educated' to the extent of being viewed as exclusive, is sometimes seen as being at the root of the mistrust that can be found between the public and those in power, such as politicians and administrative workers. This mystification, sometimes seen as deliberate, is noted by Fowler et al. (1979: chapter 10) and in Fowler (1991: 80) he comments on a further effect of nominalization that is possible:

> If mystification is one potential with nominalization, another is reification. Processes and qualities assume the status of things: impersonal, inanimate, capable of being amassed and counted like capital, paraded like possessions. Fittingly, a self-made millionaire interviewed by the Guardian (5 July 1986) copes with a question about his personal qualities using a string of nouns and derived nominals:
>> (39) My first question was direct. 'What have you got that fifty million other people haven't?'
>>
>> 'Ambition, imagination, drive, energy, determination, courage,' he replied without blushing.

Readers of this chapter who wish to pursue nominalization as a topic in critical analysis of texts are encouraged, then, to search for the many small passages on the topic throughout the CDA literature. What they will not find, except in a recent edition of a journal, *Discourse and Society* (2008, 19.6), is a lengthy and considered assessment of the importance of nominalization for ideological embedding in texts, or any extensive analysis of more than occasional short examples.

The journal mentioned above is a recent addition to the rather sparse treatment of nominalization generally. It is a debate between four members of the CDA community about whether nominalization can and should be avoided by critical discourse analysts in their own writing. This debate need not concern us here, though some readers may wish to follow it up. It is worth noting that one of the assumptions of some of the participants in this debate is that nominalization is in itself a bad thing and liable to lead to confusion and lack of clarity. Others respond that certain areas of human activity, notably science (including the more technical aspects of linguistics) may require nominalization for experts in these fields to be able to communicate easily in a restricted field of knowledge.

We will leave this debate aside here, but it is worth noting that I have not assumed in this book that there is anything inherently good or bad about any linguistic practices, and it is the use to which they are put which is most significant in any one case.

Other aspects of naming commented on in this chapter relate to linguistic features of English which can be followed up in any number of grammar and semantics books by the reader who wishes to know more about the normal workings of, for example, noun phrases or the semantics of English word classes. Here, I will recommend that students may wish to start by reading books in this series which will be likely to use similar terminology to the grammatical terminology used here. This could include Jeffries (2006) for more on the structure of the noun phrase, and Chapman (2006) for some of the philosophical arguments which underlie the questions of how we name things and whether labelling (reference) can be seen as fundamental to human language.

Representing Actions/ Events/States

3.1 Introduction

In Chapter 2 I argued that naming is the linguistic process by which people, places and things are typically identified in language, including the (mainly adjectival) ways in which such entities can be characterized and the ideological consequences of this. In this chapter, we consider a descriptive analysis based on the notion that the verbal element of a clause – also known as the Predicator – is where the actions and processes that take place between these entities are typically represented.

A writer or speaker has the power to choose the words that suit her/his purpose most closely, and this includes the choice of a lexical verb which will present the situation in the way that the author (speaker) desires. The politician who wishes to get votes may choose to describe the economic problems of her/his country as an event (*world markets are falling*), her/his opponent may describe it as an action (*the Honourable Member has ruined the economy*) and a commentator may choose to describe it as a state of affairs (*the world economy is in crisis*). Each of these choices has consequences for the way in which the situation is seen by the reader/hearer and though these may be subtle, and in some cases overcome by the reader with a critical attitude to the language itself, nevertheless, we are all susceptible to the nuances of those who speak to us, whether from a podium or from a news editorial.

3.2 A linguistic model of representing actions/ events/states

At the centre of this book's argument is the view that language has some typical form–function relations which help it to be stable enough to use, but that these relations are also flexible enough to allow meaning to flourish (see Introduction). This chapter will deal with the strand of meaning that relates most clearly to the verbal element of the clause, and stereotypically presents information on what is being done (actions), what is happening (events), or what simply *is* (states). Halliday's transitivity system is the model which most accurately represents this strand of meaning, and in this chapter I will present a version of that model which can be used to describe the choices of verb (Predicator) in any text and facilitate debate on the consequences of those choices. As usual, there are problems arising from the fact that this model, like all of those in this book, sits on the border between form and function or structure and meaning. Though initially confusing for analysts, there is nevertheless more strength in the model as a result of such flexibility.

Perhaps the first thing to explain about this model is its relationship to the 'traditional' grammatical notion of transitivity. In Latin–based grammars, and in some prescriptive grammar books to this day, verbs are described as being either transitive or intransitive. This distinction is based on whether the verb is to be followed by an object (transitive) or not (intransitive). Here are a couple of invented examples to illustrate:

	S	P	O
3.1	The Pope	blessed	the crowds in St Peter's Square. (transitive)
	S	P	
3.2	The Pope	sneezed. (intransitive)	

There are a number of problems with this model, of course, as the following examples illustrate:

	S	P	O	O
3.3	The Prime Minister	gave	me	an ultimatum.
	S	P	A	A
3.4	Nelson Mandela	went	to Cape Town	for the festival.
	S	P		
3.5	The temperature	dropped.		
	S	P	O	
3.6	The waiter	dropped	my soup.	

Example 3.3 demonstrates the type of structure where a verb (*gave*) requires not one but two objects, sometimes known as indirect and direct objects respectively. This means that some verbs (like *give, send* etc.) are 'ditransitive' because they need both objects to form grammatical sentences.

Example 3.4 shows that there are still further classes of verb, in this case, *go*, which require not an object but some kind of adverbial, often an adverbial of place as they are usually verbs of movement. The original transitivity model did not provide labels for these verbs, and did not distinguish between those adverbials which were necessary (*to Cape Town*) and those which were additional (*for the festival*). This example begins to demonstrate a further problem with a purely grammatical model, which is that meaning is also part of the rules of the language, in this case the requirement is that the verb *go* is followed by an adverbial (grammatical) and that this should refer to a place (semantic).

The final problem with the grammatical model of transitivity is illustrated by Examples 3.5 and 3.6, where a single verb is seen as having at least two possible identities in terms of possible grammatical context. Thus, *drop* can either be an intransitive verb, usually with an inanimate subject (Example 3.5), or it can be transitive, usually with an animate (often human) subject (Example 3.6). Like Example 3.4, these begin to show the inadequacies of a model which deals only with the structural aspects of the language, and does not consider the meaningful aspects.

One part of the Hallidayan model of language which has been taken up by CDA analysts as useful for unearthing textual ideologies is his version of transitivity, which is much less exclusively based on structure than the one just described. He saw verb choice as central to each clause, and as dictating many of the other choices that follow. This choice, he concluded, was partly based on the particular view of an event or action (or state) that the speaker/writer wished to convey. Let us consider a simple (therefore an invented) situation:

3.7   A man is cycling down the road, a car passes him, clipping his bike and he falls into the middle of the carriageway. A woman walking by with a dog rushes over to him, and the motorist stops and gets his mobile phone out to ring for an ambulance.

The original man on the bike might declare 'That bastard hit me!' as he lies in agony on the tarmac, whilst the woman may reply 'You fell into his path' and the motorist might say 'You rode into me' or even 'You are an idiot'. Whilst these are different statements, they all relate to one incident, and each one chooses a different kind of transitivity. *Hit* and *rode into* both imply intentional actions on the part of the Actor, who is different in each case, being the motorist in the first and the cyclist in the second. *Fall*, used by the woman passing by is more neutral about whose fault it was, as it does not suggest intention, but may imply an accidental action. In the final example (*you are an idiot*) the motorist uses the verb *to be* (*are*) to show that he does not accept the blame for the accident, but he does so by making a general statement about the character of the cyclist.

These nuanced choices, depending as they do on the verb, but affecting all other aspects of the clause, are what the transitivity model introduced below is trying to address. I will use the version of the model that is set out in Simpson (1993 chapter 4), because it is clear and relatively useable, though it should be clear from the outset that the nature of the form–function relationship in relation to transitivity, as well as our ability to read beyond the surface meaning, means that this is no automatic analytical tool. We will look at examples of analysis in Sections 3.2 and 3.3 where such issues arise, and see how to overcome the problems inherent in the model.

The transitivity model, then, assigns lexical verbs to a number of different categories, according to the kind of process or state they appear to be describing. The following are the main categories:

Material actions are the most prototypical verb, referring to something that is done or happens, often in a physical way, but also in more abstract ways:

3.8   The joint union committee *walked* out of the meeting.
3.9   The government *postponed* their enquiry.

In both of these examples, the participants in the clause are the Actor (grammatical Subject) and the Goal (grammatical Object). The Actors, then, are *the joint union committee* and *the government* respectively and the Goals are *the meeting* and *their enquiry* respectively. Note that the reason for these participant labels is to distinguish the semantic role that such participants play from their grammatical role. The fact that these are independent of each other is evident when the clauses are made passive, and the Actor becomes part of the marginal Adverbial after the Predicator, whilst the Goal becomes the grammatical Subject:

3.10   The meeting *was walked* out of by the joint union committee.
3.11   Their enquiry *was postponed* by the government.

The relationships between the participants remain the same in these passive versions, though the impact of the passive has an added effect which we will discuss in Chapter 7. Notice that the actual activity reported by Examples 3.9 and 3.11 (*postpone*) was probably in truth a language–based activity such as an announcement in a press release, but the choice of verb here does not highlight it as a verbalization process (see below), but a material action. We will return to the question of whether the transitivity categories overlap later.

The material actions in Example 3.8–3.11 are intentional and performed by a conscious being, and these form one subset of material actions, which we will call 'Material Action Intentional' or MAI for convenience. This main category also includes unintentional actions by conscious beings, known as 'supervention', and these will be called 'Material Action Supervention' (MAS) here:

3.12   The baby *fell* out of his pram onto the tarmac.
3.13   The judge *lost* her temper.

In both cases, the process being represented here is one that is beyond the person to control. The baby does something physical that he cannot help, and the judge does something that she cannot help either. The difference in the case of Example 3.13 is that the actual activity is probably verbalization, but the clause describing it uses a verb which downplays the language used by the judge (she might, after all, have thrown something, we do not know) and emphasizes the (albeit metaphorical) loss of control.

The final subcategory of material action verbs is known as 'Material Action Events' (MAE) and refers to the use of verbs with an inanimate Actor, where human agency is either missing or played down. Many verbs are able to be used in both MAI or MAS and MAE contexts:

3.14   The sun *shone*.
3.15   The strike by teachers *challenged* government pay guidelines.
3.16   The tree *fell* on my car.

These examples are all events (MAE) because their Actors are inanimate, though notice that the verb in Example 3.15 (*challenge*) can be used in an MAI context (*The defendant challenged the witness's story*) and the verb in Example 3.16 (*fall*) can be used to describe a supervention (MAS) as in Example 3.12 above.

Although the transitivity model focuses on the verb choice, it nevertheless is a model which encompasses the whole clause, and transitivity categories are at least partly defined by the possible participants that can co–occur with them. In the case of material actions of all three kinds, they all have Actors and may also have Goals:

	Actor	Process	Goal	
	Actor	Process	Goal	
3.17	The chef	stood up.		MAI
3.18	The chief executive	sacked	all his senior managers.	MAI
3.19	My uncle	lost	all his investments.	MAS
3.20	My aunt	collapsed.		MAS
3.21	The lorry	hit	a man on the crossing.	MAE
3.22	The lorry	slowed down.		MAE

These examples, of course, are all invented with the aim of making the model as clear as possible, though examples based on real data will be used later in the chapter to illustrate the importance of transitivity analysis for establishing the ideology of a text. We will also consider, in the next section, some of the difficulties of operating this model when faced with 'real' data. However, at this point I would like to comment on just two of the examples in the list above, numbers 3.17 and 3.22. Each of these examples uses what is known as a 'phrasal verb', where the main verb has a particle attached, looking very much like a preposition or an adverb (up, down) but seeming much more closely attached to the verb than such words would be. Here are the same words used as adverbs for example:

3.23   Can you pass the hammer up?
3.24   She put the book down.

There is an extensive literature on phrasal verbs and many dictionaries specifically list them for the convenience of second and foreign language speakers of English.[1] It is first language speakers of English who are usually less familiar with these verbs, though they will have their instincts available to recognize them as belonging together. Note, for example, that they do not carry separate word stress (see Jeffries 2006: 41–2) whereas those in Examples 3.23 and 3.24 require a stress on both the verb and the adverb.

Verbalization processes (V) describe any action which uses language, and because this means that they have a human Actor, they often seem to be quite close to material actions:

3.25   The President *claimed* that the war was justified.
3.26   He *said* 'No one wanted the dictator to remain.'
3.27   There was no need to worry, the police officer *assured* us.

Though some of these verbs are less clearly verbal than others, they do all involve the same potential set of participants, in this case, a Sayer, which is compulsory, some Verbiage, which is common, but not always present (*She shouted*), and a Target, which is less common, but often possible. Here are Examples 3.25–3.27 again with labels attached:

	Sayer	Process	Verbiage
3.25	The President	*claimed*	that the war was justified.
3.26	He	*said*	'No one wanted the dictator to remain.'

	Verbiage	Speaker	Process	Target
3.27	There was no need to worry,	the police officer	*assured*	us.

In addition to Material Actions and Verbalization, there are two other main categories of process, Mental processes and Relational processes. The Mental process usually refers to what happens within human beings, and they divide into three types. The first is Mental Cognition (MC), such as *thinking, knowing, realizing, understanding* and so on. The second type is Mental Reaction (MR) such as *feeling* (emotionally), *liking, hating* and so on. The third subcategory is Mental Perception (MP) which includes *sensing, hearing, feeling* (literally), *seeing, tasting* and so on The other participants in a clause with a Mental Process verb at its centre are Senser and Phenomenon, as we can see from the following examples:

	Senser	Process	Phenomenon	
3.28	The interviewer	realized	her mistake.	MC
3.29	I	hate	the political system in Britain.	MR
3.30	They	heard	the rumour about Mr Price.	MP

These seem straightforward, and many of them are, but as we will see in the next section, there are examples which challenge the apparent clarity of the model as presented so far.

The final main category of process is the Relational category, which represents the static or stable relationships between Carriers and Attributes, rather than any changes or dynamic actions. These verbs include the copula (*to be*) and other 'Intensive' relations (RI), Possessive relations as indicated by verbs like *have* (RP) and 'Circumstantial' relations (RC) which involve verbs of movement and the verb *be* as well, with the placing or timing of the process being uppermost. Here are some examples:

3.31 The White Paper *is* our attempt to re–balance wealth.
3.32 The students *have* a huge television.
3.33 The largest Sikh community *is* in the north of the city.

Before we continue to look at this model and its use in uncovering ideological content in texts, this is a summary of the transitivity model as we are using it here:

Main Category		Participants		Subcategories
Material Action Processes	–	Actor, Goal	–	Intention
			–	Supervention
			–	Event
Verbalization Processes	–	Sayer, Verbiage, Goal		
Mental Cognition Processes	–	Senser	–	Cognition
		Phenomenon	–	Reaction
			–	Perception
Relational Processes		Carrier	–	Intensive
		Attribute	–	Possessive
			–	Circumstantial

3.3 Form and function

This whole book is, as I have said before, predicated on the belief that language is essentially a finely balanced combination of rules and broken rules, where the fact that there is no one–to–one form–function relationship is the key to many of the most useful and life–enhancing aspects of language, such as the writing of poetry and the use of metaphor in daily life, as well as of the more negative aspects, such as lying and manipulation.

As in other chapters, this section will explore the more creaky bits of the model that I have just outlined above, both to reassure the tentative student that s/he is not necessarily the one at fault when the model seems hard to apply, and also to reaffirm the general point that is illustrated repeatedly throughout this book; that linguistic categories are never watertight, and indeed are often more like reference points on an open field than fenced–off sections with no overlap.

The first point to make about the transitivity model is that it is useful for pointing out how the world is being presented by a text or a group of texts, but in using it, we may often be reminded that most readers/hearers are accustomed to 'reading beyond' the superficial and are well practiced in the art of unpicking the 'real' situation which may lurk behind a manipulative or creative transitivity choice.

Thus, metaphorical uses, such as 'I lost my heart' (MAS) are readily understood as meaning that the speaker felt a strong attraction (MR), despite the words used. Non–metaphorical uses which are nevertheless indicative of other ideologies are also often easily decoded. An employer who emails his staff saying 'offices should not close early on Fridays' is using an Event process to suggest that staff should not be taking Material Action Intentional courses of action and going home early.

Other issues that arise when researchers try to use this model on a range of attested data are the apparent overlaps between categories, or perhaps more accurately the flexibility of some verbs to be used within different transitivity categories.

The case of *feel* is a good example. Whilst we have seen in the last section that it clearly has at least two uses, including mental reaction and mental perception, it also can be used to describe a material action intention process: *I felt along the wall for the light switch*. One option is to identify transitivity categories formally, using their likely participants. If we take the last example, and compare it with other uses of feel, it may be clear what I mean:

	Actor	Process	Circumstance	Goal	
3.34	I	felt	along the wall	for the light switch.	MAI

	Senser	**Process**	**Phenomenon**	
3.35	I	felt	the deep pile of the carpet.	MP

	Senser	**Process**	**Phenomenon**	
3.36	I	felt	afraid.	MR

Example 3.34 is a material action intention, but the Goal is not the usual grammatical Object, but located in a prepositional phrase with an Adverbial function (*for the light switch*). The surface grammar of the Subject does not distinguish between Actors and other participants, like Sensers, and the subtypes of mental process are not distinguished by the participants involved in their clauses, and can only be distinguished semantically as a result. So, the analyst is, as is usual with these form–function categories, not given a straightforward task in allocating verbs to transitivity categories, and this can be frustrating. The reason why the analysis remains worth doing is that it does illuminate certain aspects of the text that cannot be shown at all by conventional grammatical analysis.

Let us consider another potential problem that could confront the novice transitivity analyst. There are a number of verbs, like *agree*, which are not unambiguous members of a particular transitivity category, out of context. The process of agreeing with someone or something is possibly an action, and may perhaps be treated as Material Action Intention, but as we are aware, most agreement takes place verbally and could in some texts be presented as Verbalization, though we are also aware that people may agree silently in their minds, and then it would be Mental Cognition. In order to work out which category is relevant, we need to know what actually happened in the situation being described. Let us see some examples:

3.37	The Board agreed to the Chair's proposal.	MAI?
3.38	She agreed, 'No one should be given a free pass.'	V?
3.39	Deep in her heart, she agreed with what he said.	MC?

In fact, even with context, it is still not always easy to be sure which type of transitivity is relevant. There is a serious theoretical question here, about the extent to which categories of analysis which do not work consistently well are serious categories at all. We might also question whether the ability of a verb to belong to more than one transitivity category necessarily indicates polysemy. These questions may perhaps be answered in due course by those who are working on developing Halliday's vision of a fully integrated Systemic–Functional description of language. However, our purpose in this chapter is not to develop the model of transitivity but to use it for analytical purposes (this will not be true in all chapters, where some are developing new tools).

In order to achieve our goal, the best way for us to use the model is to think of it not as a series of categories with strict boundaries, but to consider the transitivity labels as 'reference points' or 'ideal' exemplars, knowing that many examples we come across will be difficult to categorize uniquely. Thus, *agree* may belong to all three categories listed above, depending on context, but it is just as likely that it sits between them all, and when used without a clear set of participants may simply not be clearly in one or the other category. Thus, a simple clause like *She agreed with him* may be any one of the above, and the context may – or may not – clear up which is intended. Even if we conclude that some verbs may encompass a number of possible transitivity categories simultaneously (e.g. that verbalization is also a material action), the insights provided by this are still useful in understanding the relationship between form and meaning.

In the next section, we will see that such discussions about the nature of the transitivity in any one case will help to establish what ideological underpinnings are encapsulated in the transitivity choices of any text.

3.4 Ideological effects

The following extracts are from an article written by Tony Blair which appeared in the *Times* online in May 2007:

3.40   The absconding of three people on control orders because of suspicion of their involvement in terrorism *has*, once again, *thrown* into sharp relief the debate about terrorism and civil liberty.
3.41   It *is* true that the police and security services can engage in surveillance in any event.
3.42   We *remove* two utterly brutal and dictatorial regimes; we *replace* them with a United Nations–supervised democratic process and the Muslims in both countries *get* the chance to vote, which incidentally they take in very large numbers.
3.43   And the only reason it is difficult still *is* because other Muslims are using terrorism to try to destroy the fledgling democracy and, in doing so, are killing fellow Muslims.

I have italicized the main Predicators in this extract, though I will also comment on the subordinate verbal choices in places. The first sentence (Example 3.40) has a long subject (from the beginning up to *terrorism*) and includes the headword *absconding*, which is a nominalization, and as an abstract noun causes the main verb throw (*has thrown*) to be read as an Event process. The Goal (*the debate about terrorism and civil liberty*) is another long noun phrase, and the result is that most of the sentence consists of packaged–up information with the only question being whether indeed *X has thrown Y into relief* following from the transitivity choice.

The second sentence (Example 3.41) alludes to one of the arguments against some of the newer measures being brought in by government at the time, such as identity cards. This argument is that the police already have all the powers they need to spy on suspects. He does so by using an Intensive Relational verb (*is*) to refer to the status quo, and in doing so, he makes sure that this particular argument cannot be used against him, as he has already mentioned it and accepted that it is true.

Sentence (Example 3.42) uses MAI (remove, replace) to show the actions of the British (and American) government, and gives them the Actor role, though as it is a pronoun (*we*), there is some vagueness about its reference, and whether the people of Britain are also included. The main transitivity choices here, then, make the Allies the proactive 'saviours' of the people in Iraq and Afghanistan, whereas the latter (collected together under the interesting name 'Muslims') only feature as the relatively passive Recipients in a clause where the transitivity choice is a verb of possession (*get*) and as the Actors in a subordinate clause (*which incidentally they take in very large numbers*) which is not only accorded less grammatical priority, but is even introduced by *incidentally*. This rhetorical flourish is typical of Blair's style, and is intended ironically, though one could argue that this does not detract from the view that the *Muslims*, and their capacity for independent action are marginalized in this sentence.

Without going into the complexities of this example, a diagram showing the main and subordinate transitivity choices of this sentence may be helpful here:

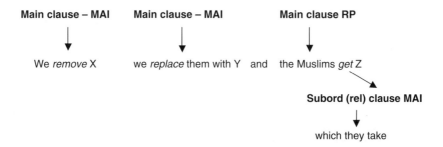

This diagram should help the reader to see clearly how the transitivity choices may work with other textual functions (such as prioritizing – see Chapter 6) to present the reader with clear notions of who is in control, who is a victim and so on

The final sentence (Example 3.46) is based on an intensive relational verb (*is*), with subordinate clauses in Subject and Complement, so that the only proposition of the sentence itself is that the Complement (*other Muslims are using terrorism etc.*) is the reason for the Subject (*the only reason it is difficult still*). This is the only point at which the sentence, then, invites any debate from the reader/hearer, and the transitivity of the subordinate clauses is not up for discussion. These are the intensive relational (*is*) of the Subject, which presupposes *it is difficult still* and the material action of *other Muslims are* using terrorism to try to destroy *the fledgling democracy and, in* doing *so, are* killing *fellow Muslims.* We will see more examples of subordination causing presupposition in Chapter 7. Here, it is the dominance of certain transitivity choices over others which is at issue. A diagram of this sentence, again shows that dominance graphically:

NP Subject (with relative clause IR)	Predicator	Complement (subord clause MAI)
the reason it is difficult still	*is*	Muslims are using terrorism

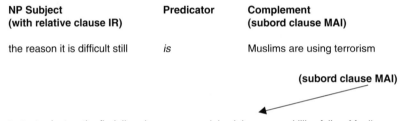

(subord clause MAI)

to *try* to *destroy* the fledgling democracy and, in *doing* so, are *killing* fellow Muslims.

In fact, the highlighted verbs in the subordinate clause labelled above demonstrate that this is actually a clause containing still further levels of subordination, which are not indicated here. The lowest of these levels is the one where he talks of *killing fellow Muslims* which is the strongest of his criticisms of the terrorists, and at this level of structure (i.e. highly embedded) very difficult to argue with. Though the facts may indeed be as he says, and the terrorists as well as the victims be of the Muslim faith, the emotive effect of his naming the terrorists as *Muslims* is very strong. The combination of naming (Chapter 2), transitivity choices (this chapter) and prioritizing (Chapter 6) combine to explain the ideological effects of this complex sentence.

3.5 Exercises

Commentaries on these exercises can be found in the Appendix. As with all the exercises in this book, the answers are not simple, but require discussion and argument.

The following is an introduction to the discussion of capital punishment on the BBC's ethics website (http://www.bbc.co.uk/ethics/capitalpunishment/). Comment on the transitivity choices that have been made here, and what their ideological effects might be. How could you change the transitivity choices, and what differences in ideology would the changes produce?

3.44   The question as to whether or not it is morally acceptable for the state to execute people, and if so under what circumstances, has been debated for centuries.

The ethical problems involved include the general moral issues of punishment with the added problem of whether it is ever morally right to deprive a human being of life.

The following is a passage adapted from accounts of Unidentified Flying Object (UFO) sightings. What do you think is the ideology of the writer? What transitivity choices has s/he made, and do they support the case being made? How could different transitivity choices affect this report?

3.45   Four passengers aboard a Boeing 737 reported a 'wingless projectile', flying underneath the aircraft as they were taking off, whilst on a flight from Gatwick to Hamburg, in June 1991. They informed the pilot, who then reported the incident to the Ministry of Defence and the Civil Aviation Authority. Another report was made the following month by the crew of a 737 that was descending into Gatwick. The crew described seeing a 'dark, lozenge shaped object' zooming by the side of the aircraft. Air traffic control confirmed that they had a 'primary target' on their radar screens and warned another aircraft that was descending behind the 737 to take evasive action. This aircraft had to take a sharp turn to avoid the unidentified object, which appeared to be heading straight towards them, but then turned away.

3.6 Further reading

Transitivity analysis originates in the Systemic–Functional approach to grammar which takes the meaning of all structures in language to be as important as – and indivisible from – the forms themselves. This approach was first set out by Halliday and any approach which refuses to divide meaning from form, as in this book, may be known informally as a 'Hallidayan' type of approach. Halliday's own account of his ideas can be found in Halliday (1994) and there are other very readable introductions to the fundamental notions of Systemic–Functional grammar such as Bloor and Bloor (1995).

Both the fields that underlie this book, Stylistics and Critical Discourse Analysis, have found that a generally Hallidayan approach to textual meaning is the most productive in terms of their aims. It may already be clear to the reader that I do not make a large distinction between these two fields, both of which are interested in textual meaning (depending on which type of CDA you mean) – and the tools that are good for one type of analysis will be good for the other. A number of works have addressed this potentially symbiotic relationship (see, for example, Carter and Nash 1990, Coupland 1988, Fowler 1996), some of the authors (Fowler and Carter in particular) having contributed equally to the two sub–disciplines. Here is Fowler on transitivity:

> A central insight of Halliday's, made very explicit in his most recent book, is that transitivity is the foundation of representation: it is the way the clause is used to analyse events and situations as being of certain types. And transitivity has the facility to analyse the same event in different ways, a facility which is of course of great interest in newspaper analysis. If we see something, says Halliday, 'perceptually the phenomenon is all of a piece'; but when we talk of it, we must 'analyse it as a semantic configuration' – that is, we must represent it as one particular structure of meaning. Since transitivity makes options available, we are always suppressing some possibilities, so the choice we make – better, the choice made by the discourse – indicates our point of view, is ideologically significant.

Here, Fowler makes clear that although we may attribute to linguistic choices some ideological signification, the question of how consciously or intentionally we make such choices is less clear. Thus, we are unaware of some of our ideologies, because they have become so naturalized in our society that we think they are 'common sense'. When we make transitivity choices which reflect such naturalized ideologies, we may well be unaware of them, but they are nevertheless still there.

In this chapter, I drew on the model of transitivity as set out by Simpson (1993), which brings together the two fields of Stylistics and CDA explicitly, by combining the notion of ideology, which has tended to be the preserve of CDA, with that of point of view, which has often been seen more as a literary–linguistic phenomenon. Simpson (1993: 88) introduces transitivity in the following way:

> It shows how speakers encode in language their mental picture of reality and how they account for their experience of the world around them.

As we have seen in this chapter, there are choices to be made each time we use language to represent the world around us, and it can be instructive to unravel some of those choices, to see what ideologies underpin them.

Equating and Contrasting 4

4.1 Introduction

If texts are involved in constructing some kind of version of the world for us to read/hear, then one of the things that they are likely to do is to tell us what they (or their authors) see as equivalent and what they see as contrasting. Though some aspects of the world may be independent of how we speak or write about them in fact, much of our experience of the world is mediated by language and if we accept the view taken in this book that no language is ideology-free, then we ought to consider how texts structure the world in terms of equivalence and opposition, in case these are ideologies we wish to contradict or be aware of.

Though English is reputed to have more synonyms than other languages,[1] because of its rich history, it is one of the assumptions of lexical semanticists that no two words are in fact identical in every way. Even near-synonyms such as *raise* and *rise* have different grammatical properties, the former being a Material Action (Intention) with a Goal (*She raised her hand in greeting*) and the latter an Event with an inanimate subject (*the stocks rose*) or a Material Action (Intention) with no Goal (*I rose from the chair*). There are also many sets of words in English which have identical referents differing only in their connotations (e.g. *toilet, loo, bog* etc.). Nevertheless, there remain many lexical items which speakers of English would consider pretty much equivalent in meaning, and the large number of dictionaries of synonyms and thesauruses aimed at learners of the language indicates that meaning equivalence is psychologically real for English users.

On the question of antonyms, a similar situation exists. The community of English speakers, including some language professionals, such as dictionary-makers and teachers, assume that there is a clear semantic link between certain pairs of lexical items that we can call antonymy. The efforts of semanticists to define the different kinds of antonymy show that this is in fact a broad conceptual grouping of relationships of opposition. These relationships are alike in relating words which are opposed on one particular semantic dimension, whilst normally sharing all other semantic features. Thus, the opposites *large* and *small* and *buy* and *sell* differ in extent and direction of transfer of goods respectively, whilst sharing meaning components relating to size (all dimensions) and commercial transactions respectively. Though these pairs illustrate two logically different types of opposite (gradable antonymy and converseness), they are clearly seen as doing a similar job in the minds of speakers, which suggests that the opposite meaning is more salient than the differences between kinds of opposition. We will consider the importance of the different subtypes of opposite later.

Let us assume for a moment that the core of English has as part of its lexical system this possibility for words to be semantically similar or semantically opposed, and that these words form part of what speakers of English know about the language. This view will be discussed in more detail in Section 4.3, but for now it will be adequate. The contention of this chapter is that texts have the capacity, frequently used, to set up *new* synonymies and oppositions, sometimes between words that we would *never* relate to each other out of context, and sometimes between phrases or clauses, or even whole paragraphs.

Let us consider some simple examples. As we will see in Section 4.2, there are certain syntactic frames which are likely to set up words and phrases as synonyms or opposites:

4.1   It was X not Y. (setting up opposites)
4.2   It was X, Y. (setting up equivalence)

The reader may wish to try out these frames, using any words they care to choose, to see how the context pulls words into opposition or equivalence. Here are some randomly chosen examples of mine:

4.3   It was car-maintenance, not cake-decorating.
4.4   It was fury, incompetence.

Example 4.3 uses a positive/negative pair of structures to set up an opposition between two apparently unrelated activities, and the competent speaker of English will instinctively start to search for a likely context in which these activities might be seen as opposites. One possibility is that there is a list of evening classes for adults, and some are seen as more serious (*car-maintenance*) than others (*cake-decorating*). There may even be some gender ideology here, with one being seen as more masculine and one as a more feminine (and possibly trivial) pursuit. Notice that underlying such textually constructed opposites, there is often one or more basic and conventional conceptual opposites, such as serious/trivial and/or masculine/feminine in this example.

Example 4.4 is based on apposition[2] and implies some kind of equivalence between the two items in the structure. Note the difference between lists and apposition, where a list (e.g. *fury and incompetence*) would have a conjunction before the last item, whereas apposition simply continues the repeated structure with no such conjunction. Where apposition occurs, the convention is that the items have the same referent. A common example would be in news reporting where the name and the position of a person would be mentioned in adjoining noun phrases, such as *Mr Brown, the Prime Minister*. In Example 4.4, the repeated structure contains an abstract noun, and they are nouns which would normally not be seen as having any similar semantics, *fury* normally being a synonym of *anger* and *incompetence* being closer in meaning (out of context) to *inadequacy*. What the reader is required to do in such a text is construct a context whereby these words may have similar referents, and the most likely explanation is that this sentence is referring to a situation where someone is so angry that they become unable to function properly, or possibly vice versa, that their innate incompetence infuriates them.

In the next section, we will consider the range of structures which can create textual equivalence and opposition.

4.2 A linguistic model of equivalence and opposition

In the previous section, I introduced the idea that texts can create relationships (between words and phrases) that are normally thought of as existing outside the text. Here I will set out the tools of analysis that researchers can use to investigate equivalence and opposition-creation in texts (see Davies 2007, 2008 and Jeffries 2007, 2009 for examples).

The first thing to consider is the range of syntactic triggers which occur in English and create such relationships. There are fewer triggers of equivalence than of oppositions, so we will deal with the smaller category first. In the introduction to this chapter, noun phrase apposition was used to illustrate textual construction of equivalence. Other possible syntactic triggers include parallel structures and relational intensive transitivity choices as we can see below:

4.5   High immigration is dangerous. High immigration is our children's future.
4.6   The worst problem we face is migration as a result of global warming.

Example 4.5 is an attempt in an invented example to show that parallel structures can be used to equate two ideas by placing them in the same position in parallel structures with otherwise identical wording. Here, the Subjects (*High immigration*) and Predicators (*is*) are the same, so that the expectation is that there will at least be equivalence, if not identity in the two Complement positions. The convenient 'accident' of English grammar, that Complements may be either adjectival (*dangerous*) or nominal (*our children's future*) means that we end up with an implied proposition that *our children's future is dangerous*, though this is not stated explicitly.

In examples like 4.6, in contrast, the two notions that are to be equated are juxtaposed more straightforwardly and the proposition of the sentence, because of the use of the copula verb (*to be*), is precisely that the grammatical Complement (*migration as a result of global warming*) is identical to the referent of the grammatical Subject (*the worst problem we face*). The parallel structure, then, has a similar effect but the reader has a little more work to do. *High immigration* is equated first with *danger*, and then with *our children's future*. The result is a logical shift to equating *our children's future* with *danger*, and this becomes the message of the text, albeit slightly hidden.

In addition to straightforward syntactic triggers, the very many ways in which metaphors and similes are constructed is another textual way of making conceptual equivalence:

4.7   This government is like a poodle.
4.8   The decision to bail out the banks is a ray of sunshine in a gloomy season.

Notice that the syntactic trigger for the metaphor in Example 4.7 is identical to that in Example 4.6; the use of a SPC structure with a copula verb to project equivalence between the Subject and the Complement. This is only one way to produce metaphorical equivalence, and there is not room in this book to explore all the other possibilities (but see Goatly 2007 for more on ideology and metaphor). The point we need to note here, however, is that the conceptual effect of such structures is similar, whether or not the reader is obliged to operate interpretative strategies relating to metaphor to understand it. In fact, it may be that the cognitive strategies we use to interpret metaphors in everyday life are the same as those used to interpret textually constructed equivalence, since the same processes (of finding similarities) are required.

In contrast with the creation of equivalence, the construction of opposites is very much more complex, and there is no scope to cover all the potential variants of triggers here, so the main types of trigger only will be covered. It is worth noting, however, that for both equating and contrasting, there is a typical structure which is perhaps most common, but like other textual functions represented in this book, it is not the only way of achieving the effect described. In the case of equating, the copular clause structure (*X is Y*) is most typical, and in the case of creating opposites, negated opposition (*X, not Y*) is most typical. Here are some of the more common syntactic triggers that Jones (2002), Davies (2008) and Jeffries (2007, 2009) have discussed:

Negated opposition	X not Y	Home not dry
Transitional opposition	Turn X into Y	Turn water into wine
Comparative opposition	More X than Y	More stupid than evil
Replacive opposition	X instead of Y	Gold instead of yellow
Concessive opposition	Despite X, Y	Despite her anger, she danced
Explicit oppositions	X by contrast with Y	Steel by contrast with water
Parallelism	He liked X. She liked Y	He liked beer. She liked wine
Contrastives	X, but Y	She was young, but ugly

As with the transitivity model explored in Chapter 3, these should not be seen as categories as such, but as indications that the text is constructing a pair of opposites which may or may not be conventionally recognized. Note that more than one trigger may occur in a single example and some are commonly found together. The examples given above are deliberately short and intended as an aide memoire for those attempting to analyse examples of constructed opposition in texts. Below you will find some more complete, though still invented examples. Attested examples based on 'real' data will be examined in Sections 4.3 and 4.4.

4.9   The management of one company was authoritarian and intransigent. The managers of the other were all 'dress down Friday' and workers' panels.
4.10   The denial of climate change by crackpots is stupid. Denial by governments is hypocrisy at best and evil at worst.

Example 4.9 uses parallel structures (X1 was Y1. X2 was Y2) to compare two management styles which are named as *the management* in the first case and *the managers* in the other. Note that this similarity in the subject position helps to set up the opposition in the complement position, as we are asked to see their essential similarity (they are both sets of managers) but then are told different things about them. Note, however, that the naming itself is also significant here, and the use of a more abstract noun (*management*) in the first sentence contrasts with their more human labelling (*managers*) in the second. The actual contrast being set up here, though, is between *authoritarian and intransigent* styles of managing on the one hand and *'dress down Friday' and workers' panels* on the other. The former of course would more normally contrast with words like *democratic* and *flexible*. Here, though, the idea of managers not being remote from the staff (*dress down Fridays*) and of listening to them (*workers' panels*) are emphasized.

Example 4.10 also uses parallel structures and the copula verb (*be*) to trigger an opposition. However, this time the subject is also contrasted, so we have two sets of opposites being set up

crackpots   vs.   governments

stupid   vs.   hypocrisy ... evil

Note how complex a situation is being created here. Though there is an implicit opposition between *crackpots* and *governments*, whereby we expect the former to do stupid things and the latter to do sensible things, we also read into this text the underlying ideology which is that if governments behave just like crackpots, we might think they *are* crackpots. However, the other opposition, between *stupidity* and *hypocrisy/evil* is there to show that governments are still worse than crackpots, as they know what they are doing. We therefore derive a global opposite from this pair of sentences which puts unconscious stupidity at one extreme and conscious evil at the other. This opposite of course, belies the notion that evil is normally the opposite of good, and stupidity the opposite of intelligence. Here, the world is made up of negatively evaluated things, one being only slightly better than the other. The rhetorical consequence, of course, is that the reader is supposed to conclude that denying climate change is bad, whatever your reason for doing so.

Before we leave the discussion of what a linguistic 'model' of constructed equivalence and opposition would look like, we need to consider the model of opposition that has been developed by lexical semantics over a number of years. This is because the subtypes of opposite that can be identified are also relevant to the creation of ideology. Though there are a number of possible subcategories of opposite identified by lexical semantics (see Section 4.6), here we will deal with the four that are most easily identified as having potential ideological effects when used with created opposition. These are introduced below and illustrated with conventional opposites, though comments about how constructed opposition might also exploit these subdivisions are included where relevant.

4.2.1 Complementaries – for example, alive/dead, male/female, right/wrong

Complementaries are perhaps the prototypical opposite in the sense that they are mutually exclusive in logical terms, so that if you are not X, you must be Y.

Note that this kind of opposition is overused by politicians, journalists and others (e.g. advertisers) who wish to present the world in a simple way ideologically, not only in the use of conventional opposites (*If you are not* with *us, you are* against *us*), but also in the construction of new oppositions (*If you are not* with *us, you are* part of the problem).

4.2.2 Gradable antonymy – for example, hot/cold, long/short, rich/poor

Gradable antonyms are those where the language itself recognizes that there are values between the two extremes, and these are identified by the ability to use intensifiers (*very hot, quite rich* etc.) and by the comparative and superlative forms of the (typically) adjectives that are involved (*longest, poorer* etc.). Note that the 'truth' of many real-world situations (e.g. in conflicts) is probably more gradable than complementary, but the tendency to use complementaries to make a 'good story' is often stronger than the desire to demonstrate the middle ground.

4.2.3 Converses – for example, buy/sell, borrow/lend, husband/wife

Converses are pairs of words which have a different perspective on the same scenario, often either a transaction or a relationship. Unlike complementaries, they are mutually dependent, rather than mutually exclusive. Thus, where there is a *husband*, there must also be a *wife* and when someone is *buying*, there must be someone *selling*. This is a less common type of opposite than complementaries or gradable antonyms, though its potential for created opposites is interesting, particularly if texts (and the people behind them) were able to produce better mutual understanding by demonstrating that what looks like complementarity (either your interests or mine) could be differently portrayed as converseness (both our interests, but from different viewpoints). This may sound not only ideological, but also unrealistically idealist, but the possibilities of constructed meaning should surely be explored to see if it would work.

4.2.4 Directional or reversive opposition – for example, pack/unpack, arrive/depart

The final of the four main subtypes of opposition is one where there are actions which are the reverse of each other. These are less clearly relevant to the construction of ideology in texts, though they are worth recognizing for their potential where evaluation is involved. Thus, the positive evaluative force of words like *build, construct, develop* and their negative counterparts such as *demolish, destroy* and *decay* are clearly part of the ideological textscape of political debate in the world.

4.3 **Form and function**

The analytical tools that have been described here are syntactic, in that they are based on triggers in the structure of the texts, and also semantic/ pragmatic[3] in that the result is an equivalence or contrast of meaning which is temporarily attached to the words or phrases (or even clauses or paragraphs) that are being related in this way. Importantly, there is also a link to more deep-seated conceptual meanings, as it appears to be the case that opposites created textually are normally able to be interpreted in the light of some much more general and often canonical, antonym pair, and that this process is the one that is required of readers to make sense of the text concerned. The process for granting equivalence is less well-understood, though it may well be of the same kind, with the need for readers to establish the nature of the canonical equivalence between the pair of items. Thus, in some cases there will be a causal relationship, in others a relationship of co-hyponymy (both subordinate to the same higher-level concept) and so on.

Like many other tools of analysis in this book, the construction of equivalence and contrast by texts is based on a set of syntactic triggers which is nevertheless open-ended in terms of membership. Some of the eight types of opposition trigger above have a number of possible realizations, as we can see in the following table, and it is not certain that this is a complete list either:

Negated opposition	X not Y; some X, no Y; plenty of X, a lack of Y etc.
Transitional opposition	Turn X into Y; X becomes Y; from X to Y etc.
Comparative opposition	More X than Y; less X than Y.
Replacive opposition	X instead of Y; X rather than Y; X in preference to Y etc.
Concessive opposition	Despite X, Y; X, yet Y; X still, Y etc.
Explicit oppositions	X by contrast with Y; X as opposed to Y etc.
Parallelism	He liked X. She liked Y; your house is X, mine is Y etc.
Contrastives	X, but Y.

The equivalence triggers seem to be fewer in number and narrower in range, but readers may find new ones to supplement this list:

Intensive relational equivalence	X is Y; X seems Y; X became Y; X appears Y; Z made X Y; Z thinks X Y; Z cause X to be Y etc.
Appositional equivalence	X,Y,(Z) etc.
Metaphorical equivalence	X is Y (see above); The X of Y; X is like Y etc.

Though there is a range of possibility here for the physical form of opposition and equivalence triggers, and the analyst needs to be alert to new examples and structures, there remains a *conceptual* coherence to the whole which is that texts are able to promote semantic equivalence (synonymy) or contrast (antonymy) by such a variety of means. This function of texts is hugely powerful, as we will see in the next section.

4.4 Ideological effects

In this section, we will consider some examples which are adapted from texts that have been collected over a number of years. What I will try to show here is what Fairclough would call the 'interpretation' stage as well as the analytical stage of the process of uncovering the ideologies in these extracts.

The first extract describes one of the people allegedly responsible for the success of New Labour in the late 1990s and early twenty-first century in the United Kingdom:

4.11   The 'evil genius' behind the strategy that has *turned the party from unelectable to unstoppable* in 10 years.

The trigger for this opposition is transitional (turn X into Y) and the opposition itself holds between *unelectable* and *unstoppable*, rather than the more conventional *unelectable* and *electable*. So, the text is creating a 'new' opposition which perhaps more than anything is a re-categorization from the mutually exclusive complementary type of opposite, whereby you are either electable or unelectable, to an example of gradable antonymy, where one end of the spectrum is those who are unelectable, and the other end is those who are *bound* to be elected (forever?) – with possible notional midway point(s) being (barely or reasonably) electable:

unelectable – barely electable – reasonably electable – unstoppable

Note that any notion of objective 'truth' does not enter into the creation of this meaning, as there could be a range of opinions about whether this quality (electability) is actually gradable or complementary. What is at issue is what this text is *doing* with this meaning relationship by creating temporary lexical relationships, in this case between two morphologically similar words (*unelectable* and *unstoppable*). The ideological impact of the opposition is inherently negative, as the prefix *un-* inclines us to interpret the words in a negatively evaluative light. If being *unelectable* (and thus put up no effective opposition to a strong government) is portrayed as pathetic, it is presented as even more frightening to be *unstoppable* (and thus form a strong government which can do what it likes). The underlying ideology of the text, therefore, validates the British parliamentary system where the system of government and official opposition is seen as providing protection from dictatorship, and the change in character of the Labour Party is presented as a negative force, whether it is spectacularly unsuccessful, as in the mid-twentieth century, or spectacularly successful, as in later years.

Another extract from commentary on a general election in Britain is as follows:

4.12   ...let the professionals remember that the politicians that the public likes best are *not the aloof ones but the human ones*.

This example, adapted from a news editorial discussing the qualities of (professional) politicians uses the standard negated opposition structure of *not X but Y*, to create an opposition between being *human* and being *aloof*. Any trigger involving negation tends to produce the mutually exclusive kind of opposite, complementarity, where there is a logical relationship between the two parts. As with conventional complementary opposites, the negation of one of the terms implies the assertion of the other. So, just as *not live* means the same as *dead*, and vice versa, *not aloof* here means the same as *human*, with the ideological implication that the 'professionalism' of contemporary politicians is making them more remote from the voters.

A final example here comes from the website of the United States' Space Command:

4.13   The precision and lethality of future weapons will lead to *increased massing of effects rather than massing of forces*.

This sentence predicts the effect of future weapons in a context where the authors (unidentified) are arguing in favour of putting weapons into space. The analysis includes the fact that there is a parallel structure (*massing of X, massing of Y*) as well as the explicit opposition trigger, *rather than*. The resulting opposition is between the two different words in this parallel structure, *effects* and *forces*, which is a rather obscure way of referring to the fact that they are designing future weapons systems to be able to kill people in a war zone remotely (*effects*) without risking the lives of their own servicemen and women (*forces*). The ideology, which may not be unique to the United States, appears to be that it is acceptable to fight a war where one's own combatants are not in equal danger to the combatants of the other side. Whatever you, the reader, think of that ideology, you should be able to recognize that it is not in any sense a 'given' truth. Much of the history of war fighting has been based on the notion that there is 'honour' in a fair fight, and yet there is also a parallel history of developing ever more sophisticated weapons to give one an unfair advantage. Both ideologies, then, are in evidence in human history. What is at stake here is the impact of choosing one over the other, and in particular the choice of dehumanizing the two options in this example, where the killing of enemies is covered by the word *effects*. This nominal choice, of course, is a question of naming (see Chapter 2) and it demonstrates, as we will see frequently, that the textual functions we are investigating in this book very often work in tandem.

4.5 Exercises

These textual functions of creating opposites and synonyms can be understood perhaps more easily by the process of synthesis, as well as analysis of examples. Before you look at the examples for analysis below, try using some of the triggers listed in the previous sections, and putting your own words into the frames. Here are a couple of examples:

Using the equivalence trigger, X is Y, put two nouns into the Subject and Complement positions of X and Y. Examples can be picked randomly, by juxtaposing two noun phrases picked from different parts of a text as in

4.14   Our meetings are the first task.
4.15   The fund-raising dinner was an extremely healthy vote.

Here, the results are local equivalences for an organization between priorities (*the first task*) and *meetings* in the case of Example 4.14 and between *fund-raising dinner* and a *healthy vote* in Example 4.15. The latter probably needs some more interpretation to make it work as an equivalence, since dinners and voting are clearly not literally the same. This leads us towards the metaphorical interpretation of the sentence, where the reader will assume that the dinner was successful and the voting concerned is a 'vote of confidence'. In doing this exercise you may end up with something rather strange (e.g. *The song was a sausage!*) but persevere, and you may find that you create some interesting/poetic and/or ideologically significant equivalences. Try a similar exercise with one of the opposition triggers, such as *X not Y* and adding either noun phrases:

4.16   It was a political disaster, not a game of hide-and-seek.
4.17   The war on terror, not the washing up.

These two sentences would need to be interpreted in some kind of context, but for the sake of the exercise, you have to invent a context in which the opposition would make sense. For Example 4.16, that may be a political embarrassment which the people concerned tried to cover up. For Example 4.17 it may be a question of whether the world's crisis is being taken seriously enough, or whether domestic matters are dominating.

   The following sentences, adapted from a range of sources, each construct some kind of unconventional opposition. Write a paragraph on each one, using the previous section as your model, and commenting both on the technical way in which the opposition is constructed and also on the ideological implications of the resulting semantic relationship. The parentheses after each example give a context in which you might find the sentence:

4.18   I'm not a manipulator, I'm a manager. (spoken by a spin-doctor)
4.19   There is real enthusiasm for Labour. It's not just loathing for the Tories. (written by a political commentator before the General Election in 1997)
4.20   Marina says she hopes for a natural birth, 'though I'll probably start off with whale music and end up with an epidural!' (Reader's story in a pregnancy magazine)
4.21   Publishing 12 indifferent cartoons a few weeks ago was justified. In today's climate, it is plainly wrong. (Tabloid newspaper editorial)

   The following is an extract from the 'I have a dream' speech on civil rights by Martin Luther King. Examine the opposition-creation in this text. What ideological issues are raised by it?

4.22   This is no time to engage in the luxury of cooling off or to take the tranquilizing drug of gradualism. Now is the time to make real the promises of democracy. Now is the time to rise from the dark and desolate valley of segregation to the sunlit path of racial justice. Now is the time to lift our nation from the quick sands of racial injustice to the solid rock of brotherhood. Now is the time to make justice a reality for all of God's children.

   My comments on these examples can be found in the Appendix.

4.6 Further reading

This chapter discussed the textual creation of relationships between lexical items which reflect those recognized by semantics, including synonymy and oppositeness. Whilst there is a reasonably extensive literature on the function and contexts of oppositeness, discussions of synonymy tend to remain within the literature of semantics itself. For this reason, much of what follows refers to oppositeness alone.

Readers unfamiliar with linguistic treatment of the phenomena of oppositeness and other sense relations may wish to begin by reading some of the lexical semantic accounts of it. Good introductory accounts can be found in Lyons (1977) and Cruse (1986), where the complexity of the range of different lexical relationships which tend to be recognized as 'opposites' by non-linguists is laid out in some detail. Note that these accounts are working within the tradition of structuralist linguistics, and the separation between langue and parole is thus taken for granted. This means that lexical items are considered to 'have' meanings, including sense relations such as oppositeness, and the textual construction of meaning, including sense relational meaning, is thus backgrounded. However, to understand the use and creation of opposites in context, it is important to recognize the conventional opposite, and how it may be described linguistically. The process of understanding contextually created opposites, I would argue, is based on the idea that speakers (and hearers) have a default understanding of conventional opposites which informs their processing of new ones. Murphy (2003) is a recent investigation into how the phenomenon of opposition may be accounted for as an aspect of the lexicon.

An approach to opposition which recognizes the cognitive aspects of the phenomenon has been developed by Croft and Cruse (2004) and investigated in Murphy and Andrew (1993). With the increasing interest in corpus studies, as computer techniques become more sophisticated, there have been a number of corpus-based investigations, including Justeson and Katz (1992), Willners (2001) and Jones (2002). These studies have tended to use the corpus approach to consider the textual context of opposites and this clearly moves away from the decontextualized approaches of the lexical semantics mentioned earlier. Jones, for example, studied 3000 sentences from a corpus of newspaper data (from the *Independent*) and considered the syntactic contexts in which conventional opposites appeared. This has proved invaluable work for looking at unconventional and textually constructed opposites, and was used as the basis of a study by Davies (2007), which is discussed below.

Most of the works mentioned so far have been concerned almost solely with exploring the conventional opposites that lexical semanticists described, even where they are looking at how they operate in context. An example of the corpus approach, though without the benefit of modern computing power was Mettinger (1994). His study looked at conventional opposites in context (the context of a corpus of crime novels), though he was aware of the kind of opposition that is created in context, which he labelled 'non-systemic':

> It might be noted that non-systemic semantic opposition has not attracted the attention of many structural semanticists. It would, however, be a profitable field of research for any kind of conceptual approach towards the study of meaning-relations. (Mettinger 1994: 74)

The textual creation of opposites has been recognized, so far, by a small number of scholars, including Jeffries (1993, 2007, 2009) and Davies (2007, 2008) who have mapped out the way in which this textual phenomenon can be set alongside more established tools of CDA such as transitivity and modality, as a way of gaining insight into the potential ideological impact of texts on their readers/hearers. Jeffries (2007: 102) comments that

> One of the most important things a text can do, locally, is to create sense relations such as synonymy or antonymy between lexical items. This will have meaning for the purposes of that text in the first instance, but may have repercussions beyond the scope of the text if similar sense relations are repeated, or if the text has a particularly strong effect, as some advertisements, for example, do.

Let us finish our consideration of opposite construction in context with a return to one of the most enduring concepts of stylistics, one of the disciplines that underlies the model presented in this book. A recent second edition of one of the most influential works in this field includes the following discussion of prominence and deviance:

> We presume a fairly direct relation between prominence (psychological saliency) and deviance (a function of textual frequency). It is reasonable to suppose that a sense of what is usual or unusual or noticeable in language is built up from a lifelong experience of linguistic use. (Leech and Short 2007: 39)

Though Leech and Short go on to say that there is no straightforward correspondence between the rarity of a textual phenomenon and its prominence to the reader, it is nevertheless likely that readers will notice textually constructed opposites of the kind we have considered in this chapter as the comparison moves away from a statistically likely juxtaposition.

Those constructed opposites which are just synonyms for more familiar conventional pairings (e.g. *huge – teeny* as opposed to *big – small*) will be less noticeable to the reader, as well as less challenging to her/his view of the world than those which are more surprising such as *placard* versus *banner*, which Davies (2007) analyses in relation to the professionalism versus amateurism of their producers.

Textually constructed sense relations, including synonymy and antonymy as investigated in this chapter, are an under-examined area of potential for ideological influence on readers, but as those who witnessed President George Bush's statements[4] after the attack on the World Trade Center may be aware, the construction of 'us' and 'them' has been a powerful force in early twenty-first-century world politics.

5 Exemplifying and Enumerating

5.1 Introduction

This chapter considers the potential for ideological effect of the two related textual functions of exemplifying and enumerating. As we will see below, there is sometimes no *linguistic* difference between these functions, and the reader/ hearer will often have to rely on pragmatic inferencing to establish which is relevant in a particular case, though it is also true in practice that readers/ hearers may not always need or wish to distinguish between them. There are, as always, consequences for meaning where ambiguities are allowed to remain, and this is true of the fuzzy boundary between exemplifying, where not all cases of a category are listed, and enumerating, where they are.

A pair of simple examples will probably suffice to make clear what these textual functions involve:

5.1   The whole household turned out to welcome us: Mum, Dad, Uncle Sam and the twins.
5.2   The whole town was there: The Mayor and his wife, the City Councillors and representatives of every trade and business you could imagine.

These examples are very clearly enumerating and exemplifying respectively. The reader of Example 5.1 will not imagine that there is another member of the family who turned out, but has not been mentioned. The reader of Example 5.2 will certainly know that either *the whole town* is an exaggeration, or the list following the statement is only indicative of the range of people there, and not comprehensive. In either case, a small amount of pragmatic inferencing will be needed to establish which of the two functions is relevant, but the answer is relatively clear. Note, however, that the structure of these two cases is identical, a list following a colon which expands upon the grammatical Subject in each case. So there is no reason in structural terms why we should be able to distinguish between them, and there may be cases, like Example 5.3 below, where we are unsure whether all examples of the general category have been mentioned:

5.3   The whole range of utensils was laid out: spoons, forks, knives, bowls, whisks and little measuring spoons.

As we will see in the next section, there are conventions in English which identify some lists as more comprehensive than others, and there are also a small number of explicit markers of exemplification and enumeration, which help to distinguish them in some cases. There is also an interesting overlap in practice between lists and apposition, which was discussed in Chapter 4 as being a trigger of equivalence. Some cases of ambiguity between these functions will be explored in Section 5.4 below.

5.2 A linguistic model of exemplifying and enumerating

It is not surprising to find that English has at least some explicit markers of these two related textual functions. In the case of exemplifying, there are certain phrases which make clear that the larger category is being represented by only a few cases, rather than by each member of the group:

5.4   You may feel unwell. For example, you may have a headache or suffer from fainting episodes.

Example 5.4 demonstrates the kind of exemplification that is common in advice literature, where the nature of the rather vague term 'unwell' is indicated by the examples given. One might, for instance, read this and not be surprised to feel slightly nauseous too, but to have a sudden pain in the ankles would not be expected as a result of reading Example 5.4. The usefulness of this kind of exemplification, where the reader is aware that there may be slight variants on the examples given, is clear: the writer does not need to list all possible variants, which may be difficult and could lead to more confusion where a 'new' symptom occurs in a patient.

However, medicines are obliged by law to list all the symptoms that the company producing the medicine is aware of, and of course this results in not exemplification, but enumeration. Here is a list from a packet of Ibuprofen:

5.5   If you experience any of the following, STOP TAKING THE MEDICINE IMMEDIATELY and tell your doctor: unexplained wheezing, shortness of breath, skin rash, itching, bruising or facial swelling, headaches, dizziness, vertigo, tinnitus (ringing in the ears), fluid retention, visual disturbances, sensitivity to light and occasionally blistering or flaking of the skin may occur. It has been known for Ibuprofen to cause gastro-intestinal disturbances such as abdominal pain, nausea, constipation, diarrhea and occasionally peptic ulcers or bleeding in the stomach, also breathing difficulties in patients with asthma or allergic diseases. Rarely blood in the urine, kidney damage, liver damage or thrombocytopenia (a disorder of the blood which causes bruising) may occur. If you experience any other unusual or unexpected symptoms which persist or are troublesome, consult your doctor or pharmacist.

This list is not only an attempt to be complete, but also acknowledges that there may be other members of the set of symptoms which it has not listed. Note that there is a well-recognized effect of this legal requirement, which is the anxiety that it causes in the patient who reads the list and may anticipate the worst effects of the medicine happening to him/her. I will return to the effects of these textual practices in the next section, but here we need to consider further structural features.

If exemplification can be made explicit by phrases like 'for example', 'for instance' and 'to exemplify', this is less common for enumeration. It is, of course, possible to be absolutely explicit, as in Example 5.6, but more commonly there are vaguer indications that the list is complete, as in Example 5.7:

5.6   This is a complete list of what you need to take with you on the field trip: two pairs of walking boots, five pairs of socks, underwear, two pairs of shorts, one pair of overtrousers, a waterproof coat, sun cream (factor 20+), camera, notebook, binoculars, daysack, water bottle and toiletries.
5.7   You should get hold of the following books:
Davies, H. (1999) *A walk in the park.* London: Oak Leaf Books.
Halliwell, D. (2004) *Fungi in public places.* New York: Brooklyn Publishers Ltd.
Creasey, F. (2001) *Mosses and Lichen on park benches.* Bedford: Benchmark Publishing.

Note that the list in Example 5.6 is intended to be comprehensive, though it is likely that other items will also get packed – mobile phone, reading material, music players etc. In the case of Example 5.7, it does not say that you *shouldn't* read other books, but seems to be a minimum of what is required for a particular course. It is evident, then, that even where enumeration seems to be happening, the resulting list may in fact not be set in stone.

In addition to any phrases or clauses which indicate whether exemplification or enumeration appears to be happening, there is *always* a list involved in these textual practices. The list in English is a reasonably straightforward structure, being made up of a set of similar structures (often, but not always, noun phrases) which are separated by commas in the written language, or identified by level intonation in the spoken language, and which have the conjunction *and* between the penultimate and final items:

5.8   The committee agreed that the staffing group should explore *possibilities for new funding and possibilities for rationalization if no funding is forthcoming.*

5.9   The way to get fit is *eat less, do more exercise and sleep well.*

5.10   The children made a play house in the garden, using *an old blanket to make the roof, some bricks to weigh it down, a groundsheet to sit on and some cushions to create the bedroom.*

Here we have three examples with a two-part, three-part and four-part list in them. They illustrate the structural properties of the list in English as we can see from the table below:

Item 1		Item 2		Item 3		Item 4
possibilities for new funding		possibilities for rationalization if no funding is				
	and	forthcoming				
eat less		do more exercise	and	sleep well		
an old blanket to make the roof		some bricks to weigh it down		a groundsheet to sit on	and	some cushions to create the bedroom

In each case, the items are similar to each other. In Example 5.8, the two noun phrases start with the same abstract noun (*possibilities*) and a prepositional phrase post-modifying them. In Example 5.9, the three items in the list are clauses with an infinitive of the verb (*eat, do, sleep*) and some other clause elements (Object: *more exercise* and Adverbial: *well*). In Example 5.10, the items are noun phrases, in each case post-modified by a subordinate clause:

an old blanket	to make the roof
some bricks	to weigh it down
a groundsheet	to sit on
some cushions	to create the bedroom

Not all lists have identical structures in this way, and the closer the list is to a 'real' list – or an enumeration, as in the example from the medicine packet above, the more likely it is that the structures will vary to suit the different items in the list.

So, lists in English are fairly straightforward in formal terms, but the pragmatic effects of the different (two-, three- and four-part) lists are rather different. The examples above illustrate the commonest pragmatic meaning of such lists. Two-part lists often overlap with the textual construction of opposites (see Chapter 5), and the two items in the list may well contrast with each other, as in Example 5.8 where the two outcomes of the committee's work are mutually exclusive (they will either get more money or not and the result will be job security or not).

Three-part lists are very frequently symbolic of completeness. Commentators (e.g. Atkinson 1984) recognize that having lists of three indicates that all possibilities have been covered, and the reader/hearer is invited to conclude that the list is, symbolically at least, comprehensive:

> Whatever the nature of the speech act, political speech or casual conversation, the three-part list is attractive to the speaker and listener because it is embedded in certain cultures as giving a sense of unity and completeness: 'on your marks, get set, go!' is the traditional way to start a race; omit either of the first two components and the runners are unlikely to respond. Beard (2000: 38)

Example 5.9 is a typical case, where a magazine article with advice on keeping fit may produce a three-part list of this sort, though of course a different or longer set of items might well have done just as well. There is a slight ambiguity between the symbolic and the 'real' three-part list, but it is likely that the reader/hearer will conclude that it is symbolic if there is no indication to the contrary.

Four-part lists, and indeed any list with more than four items, are taken to be literal and usually *explicitly* complete in contrast with the default tendency to view three-part lists as *symbolically* complete. Thus, the items that the children used to construct their play house in Example 5.10 are taken to be the complete list, and the details are indicative of this being a 'real' list, whereas three-part lists often sound much vaguer, and may end with a catch-all item as in Example 5.11:

5.11   The main practical considerations in insulating your home are *the construction of your walls, accessibility of the roof space and other similar building-related issues.*

Note that here there could have been a five-, six- or seven-part list if the writer had felt inclined to go into more detail, but instead, there are two specifics and a general item, which makes the advice more apparent than real. This is very common in popular journalism where the advice given on anything from childrearing to face-lifts is often less definitive than it could be.

5.3 Form and function

Unlike some of the tools in this book, the analysis of enumeration and exemplification is more structurally defined and thus easier to identify in many cases. However, there are, as we have already seen, some interesting possibilities for interpretation in pragmatic terms, which will be explored in Section 5.4 below in relation to their ideological potential. Here, we will explore a potential *structural* ambiguity, which means that the textual practice of listing may be at times difficult to distinguish from the construction of equivalence via apposition.

Apposition, you will remember, is the juxtaposition of two (or more) words, phrases or clauses usually with similar structure, which perform the same syntactic function. Here are some examples of apposition of different kinds:

5.12   *My aunt, the Countess of Buckinghamshire*, is coming to tea.
5.13   The music is *sublime, heavenly*.
5.14   They wanted *to sleep all day, to refresh their tired bodies*.

Example 5.12 illustrates the most common form of apposition, between noun phrases having the same referent. In this case, the noun phrases are both functioning as the Subject of the clause. In Example 5.13, we have a grammatical Complement function being fulfilled by a pair of adjectives which, because they are listed, and do not have a conjunction (and) between them, would be likely to be interpreted as referring to the same meaning, albeit with slightly different emphases. Thus, *sublime* and *heavenly* are intended to be seen as one item, and the reader/hearer may well conclude that the writer/speaker is trying to find the appropriate words to describe the music. In Example 5.14 the subordinate clauses likewise are presented as equivalent (see Chapter 4) rather than additional to each other.

This, then, appears to be quite clear. Listing without a final conjunction after the penultimate item is not enumerating or exemplifying, but apposition. However, there are some cases where enumerating and exemplifying do not use the final conjunction either, and there are also cases where the co-referentiality of the two parts of an apposition is not absolutely plain. At these points, the reader will no doubt bring all her/his experience to bear upon the case in question, and the resulting interpretation could be that there is some appositional meaning, but combined with a hint of exemplification or enumeration.

We will consider one example here to illustrate, but there will be further illustration in Section 5.4 below. The following example is drawn from the famous speech by Martin Luther King on 28 August 1963, to the assembled marchers for civil rights in Washington DC:

5.15   With this faith we will be able *to work together, to pray together, to struggle together, to go to jail together, to stand up for freedom together,* knowing that we will be free one day.

What the rhetorical style of Dr King demonstrates is the strength of the list as an emotional trigger. Example 5.15 has a five-part list of things that he is anticipating the marchers can do together towards the freedom he seeks. Note, however, that the items on the list are not entirely distinct. Thus, going to jail or praying may both be one aspect of the 'struggle', and standing up for freedom is surely a summary of all the others. His list, then, is less a list than a repetition of essentially the same idea (solidarity) in different words. This is similar to the literary device sometimes labelled 'elegant variation' in stylistics.

5.4 Ideological effects

Probably the biggest ideological issue relating to enumeration is the very fact that it overlaps structurally and semantically with exemplification, and that the boundaries are not always clear. Where there is a simple list and it is evident that it is complete, there is no real danger of the reader being misled. Very many everyday texts, such as instruction leaflets have such lists:

5.16   Check all bolts, screws, legs and castors regularly to make sure they haven't loosened.

In Example 5.16, there is no question that this list is complete, or that there may be other members of the group because it is only indicative. The fact that it is a four-part list, and that it is included in the instructions for a bed-settee, imply that it is seriously meant, and intended to be comprehensive. There are, however, conditions where the reader may be less sure of these facts. These include the kinds of general advice and guidance that are provided in magazines, as we see in Example 5.17:

5.17   It is thus possible to improve long-term facial contours, for example, by augmenting the cheekbones, the chin, the jaw-line or any other area that lacks definition.

Jeffries (2007: 123) comments on the fact that this list of exemplification ends with a ' "catch-all category" to cover anything that might not have been mentioned individually':

> The reader who is considering facial surgery may read this list and check off the different areas of the face in relation to her own. The final item in the list makes it more likely that each reader will relate to the text personally, as they work out which parts of their own face might come under this description.

More significantly, perhaps, the ubiquitous three-part list seems to imply completeness, without being comprehensive, and often appears to supplant real content, particularly in contexts where positive image-making is seen as important. The introductions to most political texts, whether government websites or campaigning materials, seem to favour the three-part list especially. Here are a couple of examples drawn from a government ministry website:

5.18   Communities and Local Government's vision is to create great places where people want to live, work and raise a family.

Whilst the sentiment is not particularly contentious (what political party would claim differently?), there is nevertheless a force to such three-part lists that goes beyond their contents. Although one could think of other things that make up a contented life, such as pursuing leisure activities or networking with local people, the catch-all 'live' and the fact that the list has three parts together indicate that there is a completeness about the statement that defies argument. This is the party that will make *everything* alright is the implication. The election of Barack Obama to be President of the United States as I write this section provides a range of examples of the three-part list in his victory speech, and each time he uses one, he reaps the expected applause. His thanks to his wife are just such a list: *the rock of our family, the love of my life, the nation's next first lady* and this rounds off a section of the speech in which he uses fewer rhetorical devices as he thanks his team one by one. The rousing nature of the reference to his wife, of course, is a step back into the theme of his victory, and is followed by a more rhetorical section of the speech.[1]

Example 5.19 is more detailed, and not taken from an introductory statement, but from the body of a text. It nevertheless has a similar effect to Example 5.18:

5.19   *The tightening of the credit market, uncertainty in the housing market and slower economic growth* are all going to have impacts on the challenges facing deprived areas and the potential for achieving the transformative change through regeneration.

This statement is emphasizing the difficulty that government and others face when trying to regenerate deprived areas during a financially difficult period. The description of the financial crisis is made in the form of a three-part list (my italics), though there could have been fewer or more items to cover more or less the same intended meaning, since *the housing market* is responding to *tightening of credit* and *slower economic growth* could be unpacked into more elements, including rising unemployment, lower consumer spending, falling exports and so on. The point is that such complex political situations as the 2008 financial crisis could be parcelled up into any number of items on a list, but political rhetoric almost always decides to go for just three. This may well be because the psychology of human beings favours three in a list, but whatever the root cause, the three-party list tends to produce a 'symbolic' rather than a real list.

5.5 Exercises

Look at Examples 5.20 to 5.24 and consider the enumeration/exemplification/listing issues that they raise. Start by describing what they contain, using the commentaries in the previous section as your model. Then consider whether they raise ideological issues for the reader, and what kind of issues these are. Generic contextual information is given in parentheses after each example.

5.20 The role of the organization is to assess on a comprehensive, objective, open and transparent basis the scientific, technical and socio-economic information relevant to understanding the scientific basis of risk of human-induced climate change, its potential impacts and options for adaptation and mitigation. (A scientific organization's website)

5.21 local and regional agencies should use existing planning powers to bring partners together to tackle the underlying economic causes of decline by tackling worklessness, promoting enterprise, and giving people the skills to progress. (A government ministry's website)

5.22 We humans are by and large pretty obsessed with how we look and take any measures available to ensure we *appear as good as possible* at all times. Such measures can be as simple and everyday as a new hairstyle, new clothes, make-up, tattoos and so on. (A website advertising cosmetic surgery)

5.23 We would all like to be part of a safe, prosperous and healthy community. A community where everyone has the right to the same opportunities, freedom and respect. Somewhere we can be proud of. (A government ministry's website)

The following is a more extended passage from the home page of the Communities and Local Government Office of the British government in 2008. Write an analysis and interpretation of the enumeration and/or exemplification that is to be found in this text, and the potential ideological effects of these.

5.24   Communities and Local Government is working hard to create thriving, sustainable, vibrant communities that improve everyone's quality of life. To achieve this we are:

- building more and better homes – and reducing homelessness
- improving local public services
- regenerating areas to create more jobs
- working to produce a sustainable environment
- tackling anti-social behaviour and extremism.

Communities and Local Government sets policy on local government, housing, urban regeneration, planning and fire and rescue. We have responsibility for all race equality and community cohesion related issues in England and for building regulations, fire safety and some housing issues in England and Wales. The rest of our work applies only to England.

(http://www.communities.gov.uk/corporate/about/ 27/10/08)

Finally, consider another passage from the 'I have a dream' speech by Martin Luther King. The italicized part looks like a list. Is it a simple enumeration? What are the issues raised by this listing?

5.25   And when this happens, when we allow freedom to ring, when we let it ring from every village and every hamlet, from every state and every city, we will be able to speed up that day when *all of God's children, black men and white men, Jews and Gentiles, Protestants and Catholics,* will be able to join hands and sing in the words of the old Negro spiritual, 'Free at last! free at last! thank God Almighty, we are free at last!'

My comments on these examples can be found in the Appendix.

5.6 Further reading

This chapter does not lend itself to recommendations to read further in a particular defined field. Rather, because it draws on a number of concepts which arise from different linguistic sub-fields, it is a question of creative reading, using indexes of more general linguistic texts to find references to the phenomena described here. A few pointers to particular reading that may be of interest are supplied below, though it should be noted that conceptualizing the process of textually enumerating and/or exemplifying as an aspect of textual meaning is not something that I am aware of having been discussed ideologically, except by implication where commentators on the potential influence of political speech-making, such as Atkinson (1984), draw attention to phenomena such as the three-part list (and indeed binary opposites), without always considering the linguistic aspects of such phenomena.

The difference between listing and exemplifying in particular is one that I have not seen discussed elsewhere[2] though the former is explained in formal terms in many books on grammar. The difference in functional terms between listing and apposition (which relates to the construction of synonyms – see previous chapter) is touched upon in Jeffries (1994), though in relation to poetry and not in connection with ideology. However, the question of how the reader interprets an apparent list, and when s/he will be inclined to see the members of a list as (possibly metaphorically) having identical referents, is relevant to our concerns here, particularly in relation to the potential for indirect meaning that it allows.

For the sake of completeness, it is important to consider the ways in which texts not only create equivalence and difference, as we saw in the previous chapter, but where they imply incompleteness and completeness of members of a category as we saw in this chapter. This area appears, however, to be under-investigated at the present time and even the three-part list has not yet been subject to a thorough investigation of the kind made possible by corpus stylistic analysis.

Prioritizing 6

6.1 Introduction

This chapter will consider the syntactic possibilities for prioritizing some information or comment over other, building upon existing knowledge of information structure, transformational options and subordination in English.

The English clause has an information structure which generally puts new and important information into the final position in a clause, so that the reader/hearer has a sense of where to look for the salient information when reading/listening. In the following example, the assumption is that the reader is already aware of someone called Simon, and that the new information is therefore the new car, which is in the Object position in the clause. Note that although there is a further clause element (Adverbial), this is an optional clause element and is not normally the carrier of the *most* important new information in the clause.

S	P	O	A
6.1 Simon	saw	a new car	on his neighbour's drive.

We will look into the information structure of the English clause a little more in the next section, but here, I wish to introduce the other main parts of this tool of analysis, transformation and subordination.

Though transformation is a concept mostly associated with the model of grammar arising from the work of Noam Chomsky (1957, 1965),[1] some of its more fundamental insights have found their way into most descriptions of English, and as a result, for example, it is now quite difficult to imagine active and passive sentence pairs, for example, as being anything other than a transformation of each other. Examples 6.2 and 6.3 illustrate:

6.2   The government reduced unemployment benefit.
6.3   Unemployment benefit was reduced (by the government).

Here, we have two sentences which appear to be saying more or less the same thing, though the first is an active sentence, and the second uses a passive version of the Predicator (*was reduced*). The difference between them partly relates to the information structure discussed above, as the focus of Example 6.2 is on the final clause element (*unemployment benefit*) and that of Example 6.3 is focused on the predicator itself (*was reduced*) as a result of the final element (*by the government*) becoming an *optional* adverbial. Perhaps more importantly, the transformation from active to passive allows the Actor in this material action intention (MAI) clause (see Chapter 3) to be erased, so that the responsibility for the action is hidden from view. We will see more examples of this kind in Section 6.4.

The final part of the model that we need to introduce here, to consider issues of prioritizing in texts is the potential for subordination in English syntax. This, of course, is not unique to English, but here it is English that we are concerned with. There is not room here to consider the whole complexity of subordination in English (though see Jeffries 2006 for some of the main types of subordination and Quirk et al. 1985 for a comprehensive account). But to summarize, English has the capacity to include subordinate phrases and clauses at all levels, and to more than one level of subordination. This will be illustrated below, but the ideological point to make here is that the lower the level of the subordination, the less amenable the structure is to scrutiny and/or objection or disagreement by the reader/hearer. In some cases, this inaccessibility goes as far as causing a presupposition, as we will see in Chapter 7, but even where no presupposition exists, the emphasis of the proposition is inevitably on the higher-level clause elements.

Let us consider a single example with multiple levels of subordination:

6.4   I despise your immigration policy which would prevent the families of legitimate residents from entering the country to visit grandchildren and help out during illness or difficulty.

This sentence has a main structure of SPO, and the largest part of it is contained within the Object (from *your* onwards). This Object is a noun phrase, which contains a number of subordinate clauses as shown in the following tree diagrams:

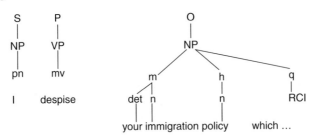

This first diagram shows the structure of the highest level in the sentence, with the Object NP containing a relative clause beginning at *which*. The first of the lower levels looks like this:

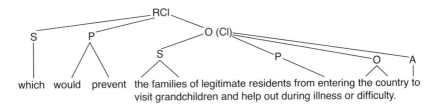

Notice that although this sentence is very complex syntactically, it is nevertheless quite easy to follow as a reader/hearer. This is partly because English is a predominantly right-branching language, and the subordination at each level normally depends on the last main clause element, which as we saw above is the one which carries the focus of the sentence. The reader/hearer is usually therefore in the position of already knowing the full main structure of a sentence before subordination is introduced. Note the difference in difficulty of interpretation if the subordination occurs in a relatively unusual position within the first clause element:

6.5 *Your immigration policy which would prevent the families of legitimate residents from entering the country to visit grandchildren and help out during illness or difficulty is despicable.*

Here, the subject of the sentence (italics) is the long noun phrase that featured as the Object in the original version, and the reader is obliged to grapple with the subordinated elements before knowing what the role of the noun phrase is going to be, which is revealed when the verb phrase is reached. This makes the process of interpretation much harder, and is normally avoided, unless some particular purpose, such as a symbolic or aesthetic purpose, is served.

6.2 A linguistic model of prioritizing

In the introduction to this chapter, we saw that there are three main ways in which the English language may prioritize elements of its structure. These are by exploiting the information structure, the transformational possibilities or the subordination possibilities of the language.

Although we will treat these as separate systems within the structural potential of English, they clearly have the potential to overlap in their effects, not least because the transformation of a sentence will often result in a different element being in focal position and because one may choose to subordinate different elements, also resulting in different information structure.

Note that the textual function of prioritizing presupposes that the writer/ speaker has choices about how s/he constructs sentences, and that these choices may be, in some basic sense, equivalent to each other. It is also worth mentioning here that the choice about whether to include a particular piece of information is a choice which, though different in substance from the topic in this chapter, is nevertheless related in effect to the issues of ideology that we will discuss in Section 6.4.

There is no room to present a full model of English grammar here, which is what is needed for an effective application of this tool of analysis. The reader may consult other books (e.g. Carter and McCarthy 2006, Jeffries 2006, Quirk et al. 1985) for further help with her/his knowledge of the grammar of English. What will be presented here are the main ways in which prioritizing may take place in English, with a number of examples.

Analysing the information structure of a sentence depends on recognizing the main clausal elements of a sentence, and knowing which is the last *compulsory* element, as it carries the focus. Here is a summary of the seven basic clause structures in English:

S	P	
The sun	*shone*	

S	P	O
They	packed	*the car*

S	P	C
It	was	*full*

S	P	A
The luggage	was	*in the boot*

S	P	O	A
I	took	all my books	*to Cornwall*

S	P	O	O
My mother	sent	me	*a cheque*

S	P	O	C
It	made	me	*solvent*

Note that the final clause element in these sentences (italics) is the focal point, if we assume neutral intonation (see Jeffries 2006: 63 for an explanation of contrastive stress). Remember also that the Adverbial elements in the above are compulsory, but additional Adverbials would not change the default focus of the sentences, as they would be optional:

S	P	A
The sun	*shone*	brightly

S	P	O	A
They	packed	the *car*	at midnight

S	P	C	A
It	was	*full*	by half past

S	P	A	A
The luggage	was	in the *boot*	when they left

S	P	O	A	A
I	took	all my books	to *Cornwall*	last summer

S	P	O	O	A
My mother	sent	me	a *cheque*	for my birthday

S	P	O	C	A
It	made	me	*solvent*	for once

It is quite easy to change the focus of the sentences using simply intonation, and there may be some readers who were silently 'reading' these last examples with a contrastive intonation pattern resulting in a change of focal point to the last (optional) Adverbial. It is worth taking some time to practice recognizing neutral and contrastive intonation to distinguish between them. Note that one possible way of making a priority change is precisely to use intonation, so researchers working on speech data are well advised to acquire a facility in intonation transcription. In a neutral rendering of the sentence, the main emphasis, including the main pitch movement (tone), will be placed on the head of the final obligatory clause element. These are highlighted in italics above.

Any change from this, for example, putting the main pitch movement on a different headword in a different clause element, will result in contrastive stress, whereby there is an implication that another particular situation is being denied. Here are some examples, with the contrastive stress being put onto one of the available options in case, and with a (in parentheses) context-ual hint as to the 'other' option in each case:

S	P	A		
The sun	shone	*brightly*		
(It didn't rain).				

S	P	O	A	
They	packed	the car	at midnight	
(I didn't have to do it)				

S	P	C	A	
It	was	full	by *half* past	
(Not twenty past as predicted)				

S	P	A	A	
The *luggage* was		in the boot	when they left	
(Not the body which was found there later)				

S	P	O	A	A
I	took	*all* my books	to Cornwall	last summer
(Not just the ones I needed for research)				

S	P	O	O	A
My mother	*sent*	me	a cheque	for my birthday
(She normally comes to see me)				

S	P	O	C	A
It	made	*me*	solvent	for once
(As opposed to my brother, who is normally the one with money)				

In addition to the stress/intonation changes in focus, the information structure in a sentence can also be changed structurally, using a process known as 'fronting' or a structure called a 'cleft sentence' (see Jeffries 2006: 152–3). Fronting is the process whereby any main clause element can be put towards the beginning of the sentence, making it the theme of the sentence, and relatively speaking assumed to be 'given' knowledge, whereas the remainder of the sentence is moved along to the right, and a different focus emerges. Here is an example based on one of our example sentences from above:

A	P	S	A
In the boot	was	the luggage	when they left

Note that the Adverbial that has moved in this case is the obligatory one, and the resulting structure is a little awkward and requires a swapping of the Subject and Predicator. However, it does successfully change the focus onto the Subject, assuming that the stress and intonation are the default pattern. In contrast, the moving of an optional Adverbial does not alter the information structure:

A	S	P	A
When they left	the luggage	was	in the boot

The other main way of altering information structure in English sentences is to use a cleft structure, which takes one of the clause elements from the basic sentence and places it into focal position after either 'It is ...' or 'It was ...'. These structures, using an 'empty' Subject pronoun (*it*) and the copula verb (*be*) allow all the focus to be placed onto their Complement position, and place the remainder of the original sentence into a relative clause post-modifying the noun in the Complement:

S	P	C
It	was	my *mo*ther who sent me a cheque for my birthday
It	was	a *cheque* that my mother sent me for my birthday
It	was	my *birth*day that my mother sent me a cheque for

Notice that the only clause element that *cannot* become the focus of a cleft sentence is the Predicator, though some of the others can sound rather strained at the point where the relative clause tries to fit in all the remaining information. The default intonation/stress pattern reinforces the focus, of course, with the tonic syllable falling in the head of the Complement noun phrase in each case (italics in the above).

What we have dealt with in discussing information structure overlaps to a certain extent with the question of transformations in English. It is noticeable, for example, that in the explanation of both fronting and cleft sentences I theoretically base them on the notion of some kind of underlying sentence, which the fronted and cleft structures are derived from. This insight, that sentences may share some kind of 'deep structure', is one of the more famous of the impacts of the Chomskyan 'revolution' in thinking about language.

Chomsky (1957, 1965) changed the structuralist way of thinking about language from a static to a dynamic model, whereby the grammar of the language was seen as a process occurring in the brain of the speaker, which developed utterances on the basis of a set of rules not unlike those which drive the processes in a computer. One of the kinds of rule that he hypothesized was the transformation, seen as a high-level rule operating on already well-formed sentences but supplying the final forms of structures which shared an underlying deep structure.

Probably the most famous of these transformations is the passive transformation, which was developed to reflect the insight that active-passive sentence pairs seem to be saying the same thing at some level, though with superficial differences:

6.6   The government accepted the law on detention.
6.7   The law on detention was accepted by the government.

These sentences, and many like them, are seen as having a deep structure which looks rather like the active one of the pair (in this case Example 6.6) and which changes to a passive by the use of the passive form of the verb phrase (*was accepted*) and a change in the order of the Actor and Goal (to use participant names from the transitivity model – see Chapter 3) so that the grammatical Subject of the passive sentence is now *affected* by the action of the verb, rather than *enacting* it. The Subject of the active sentence now becomes part of an optional adverbial and is thus not only disposable, but also lacks the default focus which attaches only to the compulsory elements. We will see in Section 6.4 how this facility may affect the ideological impact of texts.

Though the passive transformation is clearly important in ideological terms, there are many others which have similar potential impact, though they are less frequently mentioned outside the world of theoretical grammar. We will look at just one further transformation here, and refer the reader to the literature on Transformational Generative (TG) grammar (e.g. Radford 1988) for further transformations as potential candidates for prioritizing effects.

The adjectival transformation rests on the insight that there is some kind of relationship of meaning between adjectives that occur within the noun phrase as a premodifier to the head noun, and those which occur in the Complement of a clause. Here is a pair of such structures:

6.8   The man is old.
6.9   The old man.

Most English speakers would probably wish to agree that these structures are related, although the latter is not a complete clause, but a noun phrase. One possible strategy which the premodifying adjective allows is for the resulting noun phrase to be downplayed in relation to the rest of the clause:

6.10   The old man stole my dog.

Notice that the question of whether the man is indeed old no longer crops up with Example 6.10, though it is the central proposition of Example 6.8. Whilst this may not seem significant in relation to such invented examples, it becomes more so when the topic is a matter of life and death as in:

6.11   The terrible beatings were reported in the news.

Here, the proposition is about the reporting and not about the beatings being terrible, which is presupposed by the definite noun phrase (see Chapter 7). The underlying structure, according to transformational grammar, would be a proposition like:

6.12   The beatings were terrible.

The *ideological* impact of this deep structure is rather different, then, from the transformed version. Note that in information structure terms, the focus in Example 6.11 is on the reporting (the prepositional phrase on the news is optional) and in Example 6.12, the focus is on the claim that they were terrible.

The final aspect of prioritizing we will consider here is the question of sub-ordination. Rather than making the question too complex by attempting to demonstrate a range of different types of subordination, we will consider just one case, and show how different textual choices will inevitably change the priorities of the sentence as a result. Here are two sentences with noun clauses each containing different aspects of the same information:

6.13   The MP was honest, which the voters could see.
6.14   The MP told the voters that he was honest.

There are some minor differences in vocabulary here, but the main difference is that the question of whether the MP is honest is the main proposition in Example 6.13 and subordinated in Example 6.14. The tree diagrams below demonstrate the difference:

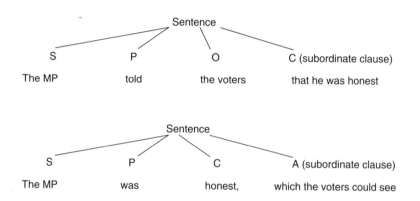

Note that putting something at a higher syntactic level may mean that it is more important, but it also is likely to make it more susceptible to questioning, so that text producers who wish their ideas not to be questioned too closely may well make something quite uncontentious the main proposition of their sentences, as in Example 6.15:

6.15   The politician gave an interview to the press to defend himself.

Here, the politically sensitive issue which is whatever the politician is accused of is subordinate to the main clause reporting the factual information about him giving an interview. The reader is thus invited to focus slightly more on the fact of the interview than on his defence and/or the accusations against him. The way in which such an example would 'play' ideologically in a real situation would depend on the details of the situation, though it is worth noting one of the alternative possible versions of similar information:

6.16   The politician defended himself in an interview to the press.

The difference is subtle, but the focus has changed from the interview to the defending. This version may well appeal more to someone reporting from a position antagonistic to the politician concerned.

6.3 **Form and function**

The 'tool' with which this chapter is concerned is, as are the others, a primarily conceptual one, and is accessed through a range of different structural (formal) analyses which share the idea that some parts of an English utterance/sentence may be more prominent than others. This may be phonological (intonation and stress) but may also be grammatical and can be approached through various descriptive tools which were developed for grammatical purposes, and not primarily discourse analytical aims. The result is what may seem like a rag bag of analytical approaches, but the reader should keep in mind that they can all be used to ask the question 'how else could this same basic information have been conveyed?' and the related question 'Are there ideological effects of making the choices that we see in this text?'.

In addition to drawing upon a disparate set of descriptions, the question of priorities overlaps with many, if not all, of the other tools of analysis in this book. Taking the adjectival transformation for example, we find that the question of whether an adjective is premodifying the noun or complementing the subject is part of the question of how something is named or characterized (see Chapter 2) and may also result in a presupposition (see Chapter 7).

This is not a weakness of the model itself, but it does cause some procedural problems for analysts and may be confusing for students at the outset of their studies into language and power. The problem is one of categorizing, and explaining a multidimensional issue in linear fashion as an essay or project report (or textbook) requires. However, if we see the tools of this book not as categories but as a set of constraints and pressures on textual choices, we can see that each utterance or sentence in a text may well be under more than one of these pressures at once. It may be, then, that any example we discuss will require us to call upon a number of the tools to explain the effect it has in the context of its use. Some of the examples in Section 6.4 (and similar sections in other chapters) illustrate this tendency.

Let us consider for a moment the nature of the textual function being described in this chapter. It concerns the relative significance given to the different participants in an utterance by their placing in particular roles or their positioning at higher or lower levels of structure. This can result in them being 'packaged' into a noun phrase, spelled out in a main clause or embedded in a subordinate clause or phrase. The transitivity choices made as a result, and the nature of the presuppositions and implicatures that arise, are all connected to each other.

6.4 Ideological effects

Because there is so much overlap between the tools of analysis in this book, I will not discuss in this section the presuppositions that may arise as a result of placing information into a subordinate, rather than a main clause. This will be covered in Chapter 7. Instead, here I would like to pick up on other important ideological effects of prioritizing, which may come about as the result of repetitive textual choices, but may simply be inherent in the structural choices of a single sentence. Here is an example of a sentence adapted from a website supportive of the Republican candidate for the 2008 US Presidential election:

6.17   Senator McCain gave Americans specifics on how he will work to increase jobs, establish energy independence, and lower health care costs, while Barack Obama showed he was unable to give Americans the straight talk and straight answers they deserve.

Of course, a full analysis would comment on the naming processes (*Senator McCain* is given his title, but Barack Obama – also a Senator – is not) and on other issues such as the positive *gave* used of McCain and the negative *was unable* used in relation to Obama. Here, however, I would like to focus on the prioritizing of the sentence's structure. The main clause is as follows:

Subject	Predicator (verb)	Indirect Object	Direct Object
Senator McCain	gave	Americans	specifics…costs

The clause relating to Barack Obama at first looks like a parallel structure, which might appear to give the candidates equal weight, but it is actually a subordinate clause, following the subordinator, *while*. Not only that, but the parallel part of the clause, *give Americans the straight talk and straight answers they deserve*, is still further embedded as subordinate to *showed* and *was unable*. In tree diagram form, the embedding is clear, as can be seen below. Note that for reasons of space some of the sections of the example have been shortened (particularly the direct object in the main clause). None of the main structures have been affected, however.

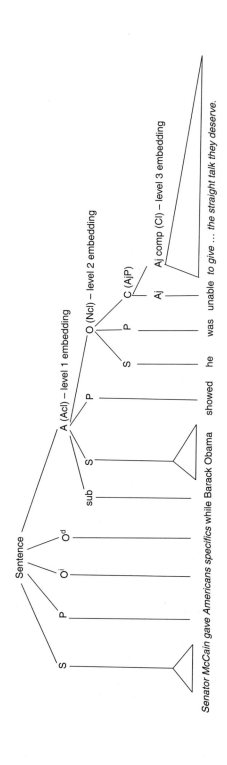

Sentence

S   P   O^i   O^d   A (Acl) – level 1 embedding

sub   S   P   O (Ncl) – level 2 embedding

S   P   C (AjP)

Aj   Aj comp (Cl) – level 3 embedding

Senator McCain gave Americans specifics while *Barack Obama* showed he was unable *to give ... the straight talk they deserve.*

The two potentially equivalent clauses here are highlighted in italics, and it shows that the one concerning McCain derives from the highest level of structure, the main clause, whereas the one concerning Obama is three levels of embedding down from the main clause. Whilst very many of the subordinate clauses we encounter in daily life arise from nothing more than the need for economy of expression, there are nevertheless occasions when it is worth investigating the correlations between subordination and power, to demonstrate the indexical relationship that can be built into texts with ideological intentions. Note that other consequences also arise from this particular example, such as the presupposition that Obama was indeed *unable to give Americans the straight talk…they deserve*. This is a result of following the 'factive' verb *show*, which requires that its complement will be true. These issues will be discussed in Chapter 7.

The other illustration to be discussed in this section relates to the passive transformation as a means of ideologically slanting the information being given. Example 6.18 is a version of one of the reports of the inquest into the shooting of a Brazilian man on the London underground in 2005.

6.18   Earlier at the inquest, a senior detective said he could not 'recall' whether images of the real suspect, Osman, *were discussed* at a dawn briefing before Mr de Menezes' death. Det Insp Merrick Rose said surveillance of the 21 July would-be attackers on a Lake District trip the previous year *was talked about* at the meeting. But he could not remember if images of Osman *were mentioned*.

The passive verb phrases in this report are highlighted in italics. Notice that this example should also be investigated in relation to the reporting of speech and thought (see Chapter 10) since there is some doubt about the faithfulness of the reported speech to the original words of the detective. However, it is likely that the reporter has used passive verb forms where the speaker used them, and in each case the Actors are lost in the transformation to passive, so that we are not given a clear sense of who *talked about* the would-be attackers and who may (or may not) have *discussed* or *mentioned* images of the *real suspect* Osman. The implication of these passive verb phrases is that Detective Rose is trying to remember what others said – or did not say – at the time. However, the structure would allow for it to be he himself that was the proto-speaker and the passives could therefore be a claim that he did not remember what he – or others – said at the meeting concerned. Such vagueness is helpful in avoiding confronting some of the outstanding issues in relation to a mistaken identity which had such terrible consequences.

The value of taking a transformational approach to these clauses is that the reversal of the transformation brings us up clearly against what is missing from the clauses:

- he could not 'recall' (X) discussing images of the real suspect, Osman,
- he said X talked about surveillance... the previous year at the meeting,
- he could not remember if X mentioned images of Osman.

It is, of course, true that human beings often fail to remember details of discussions they have had at an earlier time, and yet the discussion being reported here is so important, and led to such a significant mistake, that the exact question of who said what not only has importance now, but also ought to have been salient to the police officers at the time.

6.5 **Exercises**

The following extracts are versions of texts concerning police accountability, repossession of homes, debt management and injury claims respectively. They have been changed in some details, to make the analysis clearer. Think about how they have prioritized different parts of their content over others, and write commentaries explaining their structure, perhaps by pointing out some of the alternatives. Then comment on the ideological significance of the prioritizing choices that have been made.

6.19 What this also relates to is the tradition of the police being allowed to collaborate on crafting a story, a commonly agreed version of events, whereas members of the public would be questioned separately to establish facts and veracity of testimony. So with the police proving themselves to have no superior morals or professional standards they should have to follow the same rules of investigation that are applied to everyone else.

6.20 Remember that a large number of properties get repossessed because the borrower was just too frightened to fight it, not because they could not afford to pay back the debt.

6.21 If your financial circumstances change for the better or the worse, you may adjust payments in the debt management programme accordingly. This will give you the chance to regain control of your finances.

6.22 We are the most experienced personal injury specialists in the UK and have helped hundreds of thousands of people by putting them in touch with our nationwide network of specialist personal injury solicitors who will work hard and fast to win your case.

The Appendix gives example answers to these questions.

6.6 **Further reading**

The reader who wishes to make a study of the effects of prioritizing in texts will need first of all to be a confident user of a grammatical model. Although there are differences of emphasis and effect, the main models of English grammar which may be useful here are those offered by the Survey of English Usage which have an emphasis on the formal properties of English sentence structure, and the more functionally oriented models arising from Hallidayan approaches to the form-function dyad, which however, also rely on fundamentally similar structural descriptions of English clauses, albeit with an emphasis on the meaning potential of these structures.

In the first instance, if readers are already competent users of the standard (mostly formal) model of clause structure as exemplified in Quirk et al. (1985) and Huddleston and Pullum (2002) and in this series in Jeffries (2006), then this will be a good starting point for exploring the relative importance allocated to different aspects of the information in a sentence or utterance. Readers beginning from this more formal end of the spectrum will then need to add into their considerations those aspects of information structure and focus that Hallidayan approaches tend to start with. A good place to begin reading on information structure from this functional perspective is Butt et al. (2000) chapter 6, which takes a thematic view of how we organize information into clause structure, though it does not take an ideological perspective on the thematic decisions that text producers take. Among those CDA researchers who employ thematization as an analytical tool is Fairclough whose 1992 book includes the following:

> Looking at what tends to be selected as theme in different types of text can give insight into commonsense assumptions about the social order, and rhetorical strategies. Consider, first, commonsense assumptions. The 'unmarked' choice of theme in a declarative clause (a statement) is the subject of the clause; this is the choice made if there is no special reason for choosing something else.

The construction of information in clause structure is a complex, but rewarding area of study for those wishing to see beneath the surface of the linguistic form, and map out the apparent priorities of the text producer. The contention is, of course, that recipients of texts are potentially influenced by the priorities of the producer.

Implying and Assuming 7

7.1 Introduction

This chapter will take us part-way into the field of Pragmatics as well as drawing on some of the concepts that we have already seen in other chapters. In some ways, it is central to the concerns of the book, because Pragmatics is more about what is implicit in language than what is explicit, and it is clear that one of the main powers of language in general and English in particular is the ability to use assumption and implication to make ideologies appear to be common sense. This process of naturalization was introduced in Chapter 1 as one of the most important features of the way that texts can influence people's viewpoints, and we will see examples of this in Section 7.4, as we have already seen in earlier chapters.

What speakers/writers assume or imply is powerful, then, because these ideologies are *not* structured into the main proposition of the utterance/sentence, and are therefore less susceptible to scrutiny or questioning. The following (invented) examples demonstrate this tendency:

7.1   The selfish tendencies of Thatcher's politics have not diminished in the Blair years.
7.2   Most right-thinking people realize that abortion is wrong at any time.
7.3   Gordon Brown would probably do very well on Strictly Come Dancing.

In these examples, we have two presuppositions (Examples 7.1 and 7.2) and an implicature (Example 7.3). The next section will explain the difference between these. Later sections will also include more examples with different structures. Here, though, the presuppositions are the result of a definite noun phrase in Example 7.1 (*The selfish tendencies of Thatcher's politics*) and the clausal complement (*that abortion is wrong at any time*) of a factive verb (*realize*) in Example 7.2. Thus, the question of whether Thatcher's politics were indeed selfish is not up for debate in Example 7.1, as the main proposition (and thus the main question that can be asked) is that (whether) such tendencies have diminished since 1997. In Example 7.2, the presupposition that abortion is wrong is not available for discussion, as the main proposition is that most people *realize* this 'fact'. In Example 7.3, the implicature that is implicit in the apparently straightforward statement depends on cultural knowledge, in this case that Gordon Brown is an (currently) unpopular prime minister, and that Strictly Come Dancing is a very popular TV show in which celebrities are taught to dance by experts and are voted for by the public each week. Additional knowledge about this show might also inform the implicature, because there is usually an overweight, ageing and uncoordinated celebrity whom the public decide to vote for to keep him/her on the show. Gordon Brown is ageing and overweight, and cannot get the opinion poll votes of the public, so the implicature is that his best way to become popular is to make a fool of himself on the dancefloor. The notion of doing very well, then, is ambiguous, and the joke of the sentence is that he would probably do extremely badly in dancing terms, but very well in terms of the rules of the competition.

7.2 A linguistic model of implying and assuming

The two concepts of assuming and implying are well-recognized by speakers as demonstrated by the fact that these are labelled in common usage. This might suggest that readers/hearers are well-placed to notice, and possibly to react to, the ideologies which writers/speakers try to slip past them in an assumption or an implication. At this point, we should begin to use the technical terminology that linguists generally use in relation to the textual practices of assuming and implying. This is not an empty exercise; the terms are often used to refer to a well-defined set of items or structures, whereas the corresponding term in the natural language is often used much more vaguely.

The term presupposition is used to refer to assumptions that are built into the text, and though they are therefore sometimes seen as semantic, rather than pragmatic, they do remain rather elusive as they are not encoded directly by the text, but are the background upon which it is built.

There are two major kinds of presupposition, existential and logical presuppositions and we will explore here the ways in which they can be recognized. The existential presupposition is fundamental to the way that language works, and not obviously manipulative or persuasive in many instances. We would be unable to communicate with each other at all if we did not make some assumptions about what our interlocutors already know, and it is this shared understanding which is both mundane and potentially manipulative. Here is a mundane example:

7.4   The man I call Dad turns out to be my Grandfather!

In this sentence, explosive as it would be in the speaker's life, there is no manipulative intention, and the two noun phrases make entirely understandable presuppositions that such people (*the main I call Dad* and *my Grandfather*) exist. Perhaps the only ideological assumption here is that we usually trust our parents to be our biological parents in the absence of any contrary evidence. The shared knowledge of the world that the speaker is relying on for the sentence to make the required impact is that our father is not, and cannot be, our grandfather.

If we look at a slightly different kind of topic, we will see that the effect of similar noun phrases can be much more manipulative:

7.5   The Prime Minister we applauded turns out to be the Headmaster from Hell!

Here, both the noun phrases are again presupposed to exist by virtue of being in definite noun phrases, and we are only presented with the proposition that both people (*The Prime Minister* and the *Headmaster from Hell*) are the same.

So, existential presuppositions may be powerful, as we will see further in Section 7.4, but they may also be innocent in ideological terms. They are always the outcome of noun phrases, and these are always definite noun phrases, meaning that they have a determiner which is the definite article (*the*) or a demonstrative (*this, these, that, those*) or a possessive (*my, our, his, her, its, your, their*). Indefinite articles (*a/an*) do not introduce noun phrases containing existential presuppositions (Let us buy *an ice cream*).

Logical presuppositions are harder to identify than existential ones, as they have a set of triggers which, like those of opposites (see Chapter 5), are open-ended. Many examples, however, fall into the following main groups:

Change of state verbs presuppose the earlier state of affairs that has been changed by the process of the verb:

7.6   You have *stopped* snoring since you lost weight.
7.7   They *started* to play tennis regularly.
7.8   He *resigned* from the Board of Directors.
7.9   They *finished* laying the path.

These are just four of an enormous number of verbs which can cause logical presuppositions to arise. The presuppositions in these four examples are as follows (in parentheses):

7.10   You have *stopped* snoring since you lost weight. (you snored before)
7.11   They *started* to play tennis. (they didn't play tennis before)
7.12   He *resigned* from the Board of Directors. (he was on the Board before)
7.13   They *finished* laying the path. (they were laying the path before)

The second type of trigger of logical presuppositions is factive verbs, which are a small group of verbs in English, including *realize, understand, regret, discover*, and some senses of *know*. They are followed by a clausal complement (often, but not always beginning with the subordinator *that*) and it is this clausal complement that is presupposed:

7.14   They *understand that they have lost the battle.*
7.15   Mr Taggart *knew that they were right.*
7.16   The Colonel *regrets killing innocent civilians.*

Here, the presuppositions are the clauses in italics. In the case of *regret*, the clausal complement usually has the same subject as the main clause (in this case, *the Colonel*) and it is therefore ellipted.

The third kind of trigger of logical presuppositions is the cleft sentence, which was introduced in Chapter 6 as a way of changing the default information focus in an English sentence. In addition to this change of focus, the clefting process also introduces a presupposition in the post-modifying relative clausal complement:

7.17   It was Jamie *that broke your vase.*
7.18   It is the cynicism of young people *that is undermining the electoral system.*
7.19   *What the government hid from the people* was the amount of borrowing.

Here, the italicized sections are presupposed to be true, that a vase was broken, the electoral system undermined and things hidden from the people. Note that in Examples 7.17 and 7.18, the cleft sentence uses a 'dummy' subject, *it*, to allow most of the actual content of the sentence to be placed within the presupposed subordinate clause. In Example 7.13, which is a structure often called a 'pseudo-cleft' sentence, the presupposed subordinate clause is in the grammatical Subject position.

Another trigger of logical presuppositions is iterative words, where some earlier or later occurrence of the process is presupposed:

7.20   He lied about his income *again*. (He lied about it before)
7.21   We are going to *rewrite* the whole document. (We wrote it before)

The iterative triggers are often adverbs (*yet, any more*) adjectives (*another*) or main verbs which may have some morphological evidence of their iterative nature (*reassess, revisit, recalibrate* etc.). However, there is no definitive list of either word forms or actual lexical items which trigger presuppositions in this way, so the researcher working in this field needs to be alert to new examples.

The final logical presupposition trigger I will mention here is the comparative structure, where the basis of the comparison is presupposed (the presuppositions are in parentheses):

7.22   Your dog is *as ugly as* a pit bull terrier. (Pit bull terriers are ugly)
7.23   Your argument is *as fallacious as* Clive's. (Clive's argument is fallacious)

Note with this trigger, however, that some adjectives in comparative form, and some contexts, do not produce the expected logical presupposition:

7.24   Sarah is taller than Jessica. (But Jessica is still quite tall)
7.25   Brad is more famous than Angelina. (But Angelina is still quite famous)

This means that individual comparative structures need to be examined carefully for evidence that they do – or do not – introduce logical presuppositions. This may be helped by the main test of a presupposition, which is to negate it and see whether the putative presupposition remains or is cancelled. This test distinguishes presuppositions from implicatures, which *will* disappear if the main clause in which it occurs is negated.

If we reconsider the examples from this section on logical presupposition, we can see that the negated form retains the presuppositions listed when they were in the positive form:

7.10   You haven't *stopped* snoring since you lost weight. (you snored before)
7.11   They didn't *start* to play tennis. (they didn't play tennis before)
7.12   He didn't *resign* from the Board of Directors. (he was on the Board before)
7.13   They didn't *finish* laying the path. (they were laying the path before)

7.14 They didn't *understand that they have lost the battle.*

7.15 Mr Taggart didn't *know that they were right.*

7.16 The Colonel didn't *regret killing innocent civilians.*

7.17 It wasn't Jamie *that broke your vase.*

7.18 It isn't the cynicism of young people *that is undermining the electoral system.*

7.19 *What the government hid from the people* wasn't the amount of borrowing.

7.20 He didn't lie about his income *again*. (He lied about it before)

7.21 We are not going to *rewrite* the whole document. (We wrote it before)

7.22 Your dog isn't *as ugly as* a pit bull terrier. (Pit bull terriers are ugly)

7.23 Your argument isn't *as fallacious as* Clive's. (Clive's argument is fallacious)

There are other triggers which do not fit into one of these categories, and a fuller list can be found in Levinson (1983: 181–5). The reader is advised to be alert to new triggers when analysing logical presupposition, as there may be some not listed yet, and Levinson himself suggests that his list may not be complete, since it depends partly on the definition that one chooses of presupposition.

We will look in Section 7.4 at the ideological impact of presupposition, but here we need to look at the model of implicature provided by Pragmatics and building on the work of Paul Grice (1975, 1978) who proposed the Co-operative model of interaction, with its four maxims:

Maxim of Quality: **Truth**

- Do not say what you believe to be false.
- Do not say that for which you lack adequate evidence.

Maxim of Quantity: **Information**

- Make your contribution as informative as is required for the current purposes of the exchange.
- Do not make your contribution more informative than is required.

Maxim of Relation: **Relevance**

- Be relevant.

Maxim of Manner: **Clarity**

- Avoid obscurity of expression.
- Avoid ambiguity.
- Be brief.
- Be orderly.

There is no space here to hold a full theoretical discussion of Grice's model and its strengths and weaknesses, though the interested reader may wish to follow up this question by reading some of the works referred to in Section 7.6. Readers who are not yet familiar with Grice's model may also wish to read Levinson (1983: 100–18) to familiarize themselves with the main arguments.

Here, in contrast, we simply need to access the main analytical tools of the model, to be able to define the types of naturalization of ideology which are being facilitated by the implicatures in a text.

So, for us to see how a text is working fully, we need to be able to identify not only the assumptions (presuppositions) it is making, but also any implied meaning (implicatures). These are recognizable as cases where the text flouts or violates the Gricean maxims of cooperation, under the assumption that the speaker remains generally cooperative. So, a violation of the maxim of Quality, for example, will result in a straightforward lie if the hearer is not aware of the flouting, but in some other kind of implicature if the hearer is aware that the speaker is not being *literally* truthful:

7.26   The Honourable Gentleman in question is a monkey and should answer the question.

In the context of the British Parliament, this statement would be understood as being the closest to an insult that is allowed under the rules, as anything stronger would probably result in the speaker being banned from the House of Commons for a day or more. In any context to say that a human being is a monkey would result in the conversational implicature that, since both speaker and hearer know that it is not literally true, then there must be an implicature that the person concerned is *like* a monkey in some way (e.g. cheeky or troublesome). Many conversational implicatures are of this metaphorical kind when the maxim of quality is flouted. Most children, at or around adolescence flout the maxim of quantity, for example in answer to the question 'what are you doing this evening?' by answering with either a grunt or a single word answer such as 'dunno' or 'nothing'. Whilst the adults interacting with them know, on some level, that there is a very obvious implicature in the exchange (*leave me alone* or *it's none of your business*), they may also repeatedly make the mistake of reading the implicature as 'I am unhappy' or *I have no friends* and follow it up with more questions (*are you alright?*) which only serve to make the situation worse. So, implicatures are often clear, but may also be ambiguous or vague, and this can lead to misunderstanding. However, in this book we are more concerned with those floutings that lead to a naturalized ideology, and it is these we will explore in Section 7.4 below.

7.3 Form and function

This chapter deals with two textual practices which seem to be superficially similar, but in fact are rather different, linguistically. Presuppositions are text-based, easily defined and verifiable, and cannot be cancelled, even if the sentence carrying them is negated. Here is Example 7.5 again, but in a negated version:

7.5   The Prime Minister we applauded turns out not to be the Headmaster from Hell!

The meaning of this sentence is different and is now much more complimentary to the person in question. However, the two noun phrases still conjure up existential presuppositions, so that *The Prime Minister we applauded* and *the Headmaster from Hell* are still presupposed but are no longer proposed to be the same person.

Presuppositions, therefore, are difficult to deny, once encoded in the text, whereas implicatures are more easily defeased or cancelled. Thus, the MP charged with insulting his colleague in the House of Commons by using the sentence at Example 7.24, might respond by saying that indeed he was a great fan of monkeys and was intending to compliment, not insult. Politicians, of course, find defeasing a useful conversational tactic when they have been caught *implying* something that later turns out to be a vote loser. It is much harder for them if they have been seen to presuppose an unacceptable viewpoint (Example 7.27), and harder still if they have actively proposed that viewpoint (Example 7.28):

7.27   *The Honourable Member, the lying scoundrel,* should answer the question.
7.28   The Honourable Member is a lying scoundrel and should answer the question.

Example 7.27 uses existential presupposition in the appositional noun phrases (italic) to equate the Honourable member with a lying scoundrel. This would be difficult to defease, if challenged, though there is anyway less likelihood of being challenged on a presupposition than on a direct proposition such as Example 7.28 where the proposition of the sentence itself is precisely the suggestion that the Honourable Member is a lying scoundrel.

Here is another example of a conversational implicature which relies on the 'right' circumstances for its effect:

7.29   A man was seen running away from the scene of the crime. A man in his 20s is helping police with their enquiries.

Most experienced speakers of English would recognize this as the usual way that news reporting of criminal arrests occurs. The police are not able to say that someone is a suspect until they have been charged, and the news reporters are obliged not to jump to any conclusions about any arrests that have been made. Nevertheless, in many criminal investigations it is clear that the police have apprehended someone that they think may be guilty, and the news media want to report this fact as soon as they can. They therefore resort to a well-used technique of juxtaposing two sentences where the identity of the criminal and the person arrested are not presented as identical. This is achieved by using an indefinite article in both noun phrases (*a man* and *a man in his 20s*) and the same head noun (*man*), leaving the reader/hearer to conclude that the police suspect this is the same man in both instances. There is also, of course, the euphemism, *helping police with their enquiries*, which most English speakers would recognize as meaning that someone is a suspect, but which does not say so literally.

Whilst it may seem to be the case that presupposition and implicature are linguistically rather dissimilar, it is worth noting that they do not seem so to ordinary users of the language, who equate implication and assumption as both being potentially 'underhand'. It may be significant in this regard that there is another similar category of cases which are variously labelled 'pragmatic presupposition' or 'conventional implicature' (as opposed to conversational implicature) and where there is *both* a textual *and* a contextual element to the textual practice. So, there are a number of textual choices where the experienced reader/hearer would normally draw a presupposition from the text, but where the text itself *could* be read differently. Thus, the conjunction *and* is often read as though it conferred chronological ordering on the two clauses it joins, as in Example 7.29, but this is not necessarily the case, as we can see in Example 7.30:

7.30   I went home and phoned the police.
7.31   I learnt the violin and walked the Pennine Way when I was at school.

These conventional implicatures, then, are triggered by the text, but are not intrinsic to it in the way that presuppositions generally are. Neither are they dependent on the situational context alone to the same extent that conversational implicatures are. They sit, in other words, right on the border between implying and assuming, and may be one of the pieces of evidence that there is indeed no clear cut-off between these two categories which seem so different at first.

7.4 Ideological effects

The precise ideological effects of any case of presupposition or implica-ture will vary with the context and content of the text concerned. What is common to most of these examples is the potential for impacting on the reader/hearer because the relatively 'hidden' nature of these types of meaning makes them less amenable to comment, debate or scrutiny.

Here are three examples of factive verbs creating logical presuppositions in their subordinate clauses:

7.32   Gordon Brown has suddenly realized where his own reforms have failed.

7.33   President Bush regrets his legacy as the man who wanted war.

7.34   Russell Brand has revealed that the recording of the obscene messages left on the answering machine of the Fawlty Towers' actor Andrew Sachs had been toned down before it was aired.

What we *regret, reveal, realize* etc. are taken for granted to be true by the listener, and though these may indeed be accurate, they are nevertheless the text producer's own version of what the three men actually said. In this instance, then, the analysis of presupposition overlaps to some extent with analysis of discourse presentation and the question in particular of how faithful an account of earlier discourse is. The first two examples, however, are not clearly discourse presentation at all, but may be simply speculation as to the thought processes of two powerful men.

The following examples both illustrate the possible effect of iterative triggers of presupposition:

7.35   Thompson insists the BBC will do everything in its power to ensure the breakdown in editorial standards never happens again.

7.36   Stephen King: Another British currency crisis – it's enough to make you feel nostalgic.

In the first example (7.35), the Director General of the BBC tacitly acknowledges that there has been a breakdown in standards by the use of *again*, though it also reinforces the existential presupposition of the noun phrase *the breakdown in editorial standards*. In Example 7.36, the fact that the currency crisis of 2008 is not the first to hit Britain is indicated by the presupposition triggered by *another*, which is an iterative adjective. Whilst these presuppositions are commonly found in all news reporting and commentary, and to some extent are thus relatively unremarkable, we need to remind ourselves that they are there, and that they have an effect on the textual meaning by providing a kind of background commentary on the main story.

Whilst presuppositions are relatively easy to spot after some practice, and the ideological assumptions can then be assessed, the identification of implicatures is less straightforward, as they do not rely on even an open-ended range of triggers or structures, but are based on their relation to the conversational maxims of Grice's Co-operative Principle. The following example has an implicature that the government does have some policies to reduce carbon in the atmosphere, but that they are meaningless ones:

7.37   The government needs to put in place *meaningful policies* to urgently reduce emissions – and to act on them immediately.

The reader will be able to process the surface meaning, which is an exhortation to the government to act, and also access the implicature, which is the criticism that they have ineffective policies in place already. The phrase *meaningful policies* is a tautology, since policies ought to be meaningful automatically, and the phrase therefore flouts the maxim of quantity by saying more than it should. This flags up to the reader that there is something significant in the use of the adjective, *meaningful*, which thereby implies a contrast with the implied policies of the government, which must by contrast be meaningless.

7.5 Exercises

The following examples have either presupposition or implicature adding to the surface meaning of the text. In some cases, more than one. Write a short commentary on each one, explaining what it is that they are assuming and/ or implying, and how you know this. Comment on the ideological effect.

7.38   After yet another of their ideas fails to fly – when will they replace unworkable plans with serious leadership for the long-term good of the country.

7.39   Mr Brown's irresponsible plans are not a way forward. They're a return to the dark old days of spiralling deficits and capital flight that are the hallmark of every Labour government to have ever held office.

7.40   It is a pity that the people who run this country only read newspapers such as the *Times*, the *Guardian* and the *Telegraph*.

7.41   St John's Wort plant as effective as Prozac for treating depression.

7.42   Helen Mirren: why I stopped taking cocaine.

7.43   In addition, the real reason for their development has not been to end world hunger but to increase the stranglehold multinational biotech companies already have on food production.

7.44   Food is not just food, and milk is not just milk. (from an anti-milk campaigning website)

Examples of commentaries on these examples can be found in the Appendix.

7.6 **Further reading**

The best place to read up on the basics of Pragmatics is Levinson (1983), chapters 3 and 4, as well as the introductory chapter where the relationship between semantics and pragmatics is explored. A simpler introductory text is Thomas (1995) and for those who wish to go 'behind' the model and consider the philosophy underlying pragmatics, Grice (1975) is the originator of these ideas, and they are accessibly discussed in Chapman (2006: 99–102, 136–40) and in more detail in Chapman (2005). The reason why pragmatics is of particular interest to us here is that the ideological influence of texts is often assumed to be based more on what is implicit than what is explicit in them. Pragmatics, being the study of language in context of its use, rather than texts in isolation, has a number of helpful concepts to aid the analyst in working out how ideologies might be encoded in texts without being superficially evident.

It may be important, before using the concepts of implicature and presupposition, to understand where they came from, and Levinson (1983: 97) is helpful here:

> First, implicature stands as a paradigmatic example of the nature and power of pragmatic explanations of linguistic phenomena. The sources of this species of pragmatic inference can be shown to lie outside the organization of language, in some general principles for co-operative interaction, and yet these principles have a pervasive effect upon the structure of language. (...) A second important contribution made by the notion of implicature is that it provides some explicit account of how it is possible to mean (in some general sense) more than what is actually 'said' (i.e. more than what is literally expressed by the conventional sense of the linguistic expressions uttered).

Presupposition is not strictly speaking pragmatic, since it has clear origins in the forms of language used, but it tends to be associated with pragmatics because of its implicit nature. Levinson has a chapter on presupposition itself, so he clearly sees the need to include at least some consideration of it within the realm of pragmatics:

> another kind of pragmatic inference, namely presupposition, that does seem at least to be based more closely on the actual linguistic structure of sentences; we shall conclude, however, that such inferences cannot be thought of as semantic in the narrow sense, because they are too sensitive to contextual factors in ways that this Chapter will be centrally concerned with. (1983: 167)

Levinson is comprehensive, but not concerned with the ideological aspects of implicature and presupposition. Simpson (1993) chapter 5 provides both an introductory overview of the pragmatics of implying and assuming and a way of thinking about the ideological implications of these textual functions using the umbrella concept of point of view. Simpson (1993: 121–2) comments on the fact that a great deal of work in this field has focused on language in the face-to-face situation, rather than language which is used between producers and recipients who are separated in time and/or space:

> This 'displaced' communicative situation is none the less amenable to analysis within the parameters of a linguistic model designed largely on face-to-face interaction. Although the direct 'feedback' which characterizes everyday conversation will be missing, media and advertising language still relies on a kind of interaction between producers and interpreters. This is a heavily one-sided interaction in many respects, but it is none the less one where meanings need to be negotiated between sender and receiver.

Simpson goes on to show how the ideas of implicature and presupposition can be used in analysing the ideological implications of texts that are representative of the displaced communication he describes.

Jeffries (2007: chapter 5) demonstrates the kind of analysis recommended in this chapter, as applied to the construction of the female in women's magazines. The following extract (133) illustrates the kind of findings reported there:

> Whilst it is to be expected that articles which purport to be of help to women might address all readers as female, there are also a very large number of presuppositions and implicatures which detail the *kind* of women that they are addressing. Whilst there is no explicit statement of expectation that the reader will have these characteristics, there is, nevertheless, the potential for a normalising effect where the same characteristics are assumed time and again.
>
> Take, for example, the assumptions that everyone lives in a nuclear family, and in particular, that everyone has a mum. Text 5, for example, presupposes just these things, by the mechanism of the same *your* + noun structure that we have already seen:
>   you're also worrying about what *your mum* will say when she does your washing.

The capacity for creating meaning without the reader consciously noticing is one that speakers instinctively recognize. The ability to analyse how this capacity operates linguistically is one that requires careful analysis of implicature and presupposition.

8 Negating

8.1 Introduction

This chapter introduces a textual practice which may have narrative and/or ideological significance. We tend to assume that most texts produce some kind of picture of the world as it is, or even as the speaker/writer thinks it is. However, a great deal of our communicative time is actually spent constructing and interpreting non-existent versions of the world which are created for a great many different reasons. We may be imagining a world that we wish existed (*He doesn't love me*), enhancing a narrative by relating the things that are absent from it (*He didn't reach the bridge in time*) or attempting to persuade someone ideologically (*The world's resources are not infinite*).

The model we will discuss here (and the one discussed in Chapter 9) has the capacity to construct in the reader/hearer's mind a version of the situation which is clearly at odds with the one being otherwise confirmed in the text concerned. Here, 'negating' is being used as a generic term to refer to a conceptual practice rather broader than the simple negating of a verb. Thus, the following sentences all contain some kind of negating element:

8.1   The door is *not* closed.
8.2   There is *no* milk in the fridge.
8.3   *No one* seems to be listening to me.
8.4   There is a *lack* of respect in your attitude.
8.5   The press were simply *absent* that day.

As we will see in later sections, it is the *pragmatic* force of negation which is significant in making the reader/hearer aware of scenarios that are *not* taking place, but presumably might have done in other circumstances. The relatively innocent examples above (8.1–8.5) thus alert us to the possible situations in which the door is closed, there is milk in the fridge, people listen to you and respect you, and the press are present respectively. If these things had not been denied in the first place, we would probably not think of them.

We will take a closer look at the textual practice of negation in the next two sections, but let us pause for a moment to consider, in general terms, why it is of interest to us here. If it allows the speaker/writer to produce a hypothetical version of reality, even though it is marked as being 'unreal' in the case of negation (see also modality in Chapter 9), there is at least the *potential* for a hearer/reader to conceptualize this hypothetical situation. To the extent that it has been conjured up, it may have some persuasive power. This could be negative power, for example, by scaring people as to possible scenarios, or positive power such as might be the case where advertising attempts to persuade people that there could be a better life if they bought a certain product. In pragmatic terms, these constructions seem to produce implicatures by a number of possible means. First, they introduce *more* information than is strictly known about, and to that extent, they create implicatures about what other realities could exist by flouting the Gricean maxim of quantity. As Semino (personal correspondence) suggests:

> in my view, in Gricean terms examples such as 'No man is an island' flout the maxim of quantity, not quality: on the face of it, the negative statement is true but uninformative (the maxim of relation may also be invoked). The same applies, for example, to Blair's famous line (in a 2003 speech): 'I've not got a reverse gear.'[1]

As Semino says, it could be argued that the maxim of relation is the one producing an implicature, because telling your readers/listeners about something that is *not* happening (does *not* exist etc.) appears at first sight to be irrelevant and thus appears to flout the maxim of relation. The recipient of the utterance/text will no doubt try to produce some explanation as to why it is indeed relevant, and this will result in an implicature, which will be positive (you do want to buy the product) or negative (this is the possible result of certain scenarios) depending on content. (See Chapter 7 for more on implicature.)

A quite familiar use of this creation of negated hypothetical text worlds may be found in (at least dramatic representations of) criminal court cases where the prosecutor or defence counsel may use such constructions to plant ideas into the jurors' minds. They may then be instructed by the judge to ignore this part of the 'evidence' (since it is not in fact evidence), but they are well aware, of course, that having produced the image in the minds of the jurors, it will be harder for them to ignore than if they had said nothing. An invented example here, for illustration:

8.6   The defendant says he did not go round to the victim's house in the early hours after drinking in a local bar. He did not shout loudly at her window and did not force the door to the house before attacking her.

The judge may well deem such non-narratives to be out of order in the court setting, and say so, but the damage will already have been done if in the jurors' minds they can see that he has described a plausible scenario to explain all the facts they have been presented with. The use of negation can thus allow text producers to play with the imagination of their recipients.

8.2 A linguistic model of negation

Though the models in this book are different in detail, they share a common feature, which is that they have a typical or central syntactic realization, but may also be realized in an open-ended range of ways that reflect the form-function flexibility of English as a language. In this section, we will consider the main ways in which the practice of negating may be achieved in English texts, and in the following section, we will consider both ideological effect and also the broader range of potential ways of negating.

Negation is typically seen as a grammatical phenomenon in the addition of a negative particle to the verb phrase. This particle is added to the *first* item in the verb phrase (see Jeffries 2006: 100) which will be an auxiliary or if there are no auxiliaries, then it will be the 'dummy' auxiliary verb, *do*:

8.7   This holiday *won't* cost you a fortune.
8.8   The MPs *haven't* admitted their mistakes.
8.9   The people *aren't* objecting to CCTV cameras.
8.10   This law *doesn't* produce the right effect.

In addition to the negative particle, negation can be introduced through pronouns (*none, no one, nobody, nothing* etc.), which replace whole noun phrases or through the adjectival use of *no*, where the negation is a modifier of the noun:

8.11   *Nobody* joined my political party.
8.12   There is *no consensus* in this meeting.

Of course, this is not the whole story and negation can also be built into the semantics of the words we use. This notion, that some words are *inherently* negative, is a difficult one to pin down more precisely, partly because of course we can vary what exactly we mean by negation. But let us, for example, discount for these purposes one of the everyday meanings associated with negation, such as those connoting depressive tendencies (*she's so negative*) and concentrate here on the equivalent to the formal realizations of negation (*not* and *no*) in the case of lexical items which appear to encode either some kind of absence or a lack of action. These may include the following, though this is an open-ended list and readers will no doubt think of many more of their own:

- Nouns: *lack, absence, dearth, scarcity,* and so on
- Verbs: *fail, omit, refuse,* and so on
- Adjectives: *absent, scarce,* and so on

Because of the very nature of the phenomena that we are dealing with in this book, there will probably never be a foolproof way to establish when a linguistic item or feature is representative of the textual practices being investigated. However, there *are* a number of ways to make sure that any analysis you do is as rigorous as possible, including making explicit all the decisions you make in the process and the reasons for them where possible.

Slightly more formal than the semantically negative lexical items, and thus easier to find, are those words in English which have some kind of morphological negation, usually in the form of a prefix. Here is a list of some of the many thousands of morphologically negated adjectives in English:

- incomplete, undecided, uncompromising, asocial, anti-depressant.

Note that the meanings of these negative bound morphemes varies considerably, so that, for example, *incomplete* refers to a process which is not finished, though it may have been started, whereas *uncompromising* does not imply an unfinished process, but rather an inflexible stance which has no half-way position. Notice that in discussing the meanings of these words, it is hard to avoid using other morphologically negated words (e.g. *unfinished, inflexible*). I would suggest that although this range of particular meanings might make one question whether they all belong in the general concept of negating that we are considering here, the popular belief that they all belong together, much like popular views of opposition, ought to convince us that they somehow share a cognitive frame in recipients' minds and should therefore be treated together.

English of course also has a number of negated nouns (e.g. *inactivity, amorality*) and verbs (*deactivate, disrespect*), though many of these are adjectives in their base form. Being so commonly used and often more common than their positive versions, these seem like rather different creatures from the syntactic and even the semantic forms of negation, but on closer scrutiny, they too conjure up a world that is not:

8.13   This government is *undecided* about almost everything.

Such a comment coming from a popular and confident opposition may well be intended to make the reader/hearer aware of the alternative – the government in waiting that *will* be decisive.

So, we have seen that the negation function can be fulfilled by syntactic, semantic or morphological processes. This concept, which like others in this book, seems to range across formal divisions in English, will be explored in a little more detail in the next section and followed by discussion and illustration of its importance in the ideological underpinnings of texts.

8.3 Form and function

In earlier sections the textual function of negating was introduced, and some of the main textual vehicles for this function were illustrated. Here, we will consider the particular ways in which negating in texts crosses the division between form and function in English.

We have seen that negating has a core form (the negation of verbs) and that this is the prototypical carrier of the textual function of negating. It is a very good example of a conceptual meaning which is embodied in a particular form in the language, but which can crop up in all sorts of other places and at other levels too. Thus, we have seen that negation occurs across morphology (*undone*), syntax (*isn't*) and lexis (*lack*) and in fact it can also be performed by intonation, resulting in an ironic negation, and/or with body language signs such as the shaking of the head or wagging of the finger.

Thus, we are left with the *meaning* of this textual function as the more stable aspect of the form-function dyad, with the potential linguistic or paralinguistic realization of the core meaning occurring in a range from the most typical to the more peripheral.

It is also important to note that one result of the lack of unique form-function relationships is that the same form may contribute to more than one textually created meaning of the kind we are investigating here. Thus, negation has already been seen to play a very important part in the textual construction of oppositional relations (see Chapter 4). In a sense, what is being proposed in this chapter is that a negative construction or lexical item sets up for the reader/listener a particular kind of regular opposition, by conjuring up not only the absence of an occurrence of a process (*the dog didn't bite the postman*) but also a positive version in which the process occurs (*the dog bit the postman*).

What happens in a case where negation and opposition work together is that the text itself creates not only the presence-absence kind of opposition that we have been seeing so far in this chapter, but also tells the reader what the absence itself produces as its positive counterpart:

8.14   The decision to introduce ID cards was a gamble, not a principle.

In Example 8.14, then, we have not only the negator (not a principle), but also an explanation of exactly what it meant in this particular case for the principles to be lacking – that the government were effectively taking chances with the electorate's support. Any analysis of textual negation needs to take account of both the pragmatic context of the negation, since it can have a range of effects on meaning, but may also need to account for the overlap with construction of opposition as we have seen here.

8.4 Ideological effects

The effect of negation on ideology is seen regularly as it is so common throughout the language. Whilst many examples of negation are not significant in ideological terms, there are nevertheless many where the very mention of the situation *which does not exist* is enough to put into the mind of the reader a different world where that situation is reality and this can have a range of potential effects. The following examples illustrate this:

8.15   Scientists warn that there *may* be *no ice* at North Pole this summer.

8.16   *No murders* took place at the care home at the centre of a child abuse investigation, the new police chief leading the inquiry said today.

8.17   *Nobody has to be vile* in order to do business these days; collaboration with employees, dialogue with customers, respect for the environment, transparency of deals – these are the keys to success.

One of the most powerful effects that language can have is to strike fear into the heart of the reader/hearer to make them act or think in particular ways. This effect is managed very well by those trying to make the public (and thus also the politicians) take climate change seriously. Example 8.15 is typical of the kind of scenario which can be hypothesized by the joint use of a modal (*may*) and a negator (*no ice*) to show the possible effects of climate change on a stable feature of our planet (see Chapter 9 on modality). The thought of the North Pole with no ice is so extraordinary that it has a powerful effect on the imagination since we are all so used to the image of the world with ice at both poles.

Example 8.16 reports the lack of evidence that any murders took place at a children's home being investigated by police, but of course the amount of interest in this story was generated because some apparent signs had been found of the possibility that not only abuse but worse violence has taken place. The prurience of news reporting, feeding the public craving for the sensational, is behind this kind of reporting which still manages to place in the minds of the reader an alternative scenario where grisly murders did take place, even when the juiciest part of the story is being denied (*no murders*).

An example adapted from commentary on the changes taking place in capitalism (Example 8.17), uses the negative pronoun, *nobody* to conjure up the type of business practice, characterized as *vile*, which it claims is no longer necessary. Note that the negation here is joined by an iterative trigger, *these days* (see Chapter 7), producing the logical presupposition that business practice in the past has indeed been vile. The two together produce a vivid mental picture of vile businesses and the clear distinction between that and the current practice (listed in the three-part list following) which is presented in a very positive light.

8.5 Exercises

The examples below each contain one or more negated elements. Comment on the ideological effect of these forms in their context, using the concepts of negating as your reference point. What kinds of ideas do these examples have the potential to conjure up in the mind of the reader, and why?

8.18   National Accident Helpline specialise in making no win no fee accident compensation claims easy and straightforward, with no hidden costs.
8.19   Where we have really fallen down is, we have lacked the ability to be relevant to people's lives.
8.20   Nearly £2bn owed by absent parents should be written off as uncollectable, according the organisation that will replace the Child Support Agency.
8.21   The Queen yesterday called the global financial crisis 'awful' – and asked why nobody had seen it coming.
8.22   HBOS and Lloyds TSB last night created a monstrous new banking entity safe in the knowledge that nothing can possibly go wrong.

Sample answers can be found in the Appendix.

8.6 Further reading

Like the textual construction of opposition (see Chapter 4), negating is not a familiar tool of CDA, though there is much written on the form and meaning of negation in grammatical and semantic terms, but its discourse uses are relatively under-examined so far. Readers wishing to examine the basis of negation in English could search in the index of any fairly comprehensive grammar of the language and might start with Huddleston and Pullum (2002) or Quirk et al. (1985). For more detailed analyses and typologies of negative terms, see Horn (1984) and for a study in variation of negating, see Tottie (1990).

Some studies have begun to take account of the role of negation in discourse, and these include Hidalgo-Downing (2002), which, like Nahajec (2009), looks at the role of negating in poetry and Nørgaard (2007) considers its use in focalization in a short story. Pagano (1994) and Ryan (1998) also take a wider view of the role of negation in literature. Though negation is recognized as a trigger for binary opposition in some ideologically sensitive texts, so far it has not been seen as a textual practice in its own right in non-literary discourse, except perhaps anecdotally.

9 Hypothesizing

9.1 Introduction

The previous chapter introduced a textual practice which, it was argued, could influence the reader ideologically in a number of ways by describing what was *not* the case. Here, we will consider the contribution of modality to the ideology of texts, by looking at the *hypothetical* situations that modality introduces. As with negation, though we may tend to assume that most texts reflect the world as it is, many texts in fact reflect the speaker's or writer's view of how the world is or might be, how it ought to be or how they wish it was. This whole range of meaning I am gathering here under the label 'hypothesizing', since even a modal sentence like *I wish it would snow this Christmas* is creating an imagined world in which the clichéd snowy Christmas of Hollywood films takes place. Even the really *certain* kind of modality (*I am sure house prices will rise next year*) introduces an element of doubt as we will see below, and this means that wherever the text producer's opinion about the truth or desirability of a process is expressed, the envisaged situation or process itself is somewhat hypothetical.

We will return to questions of certainty and doubt and their ideological impact later, but let me first introduce the model that we will be using here to talk about hypothesizing alternative versions of reality. This is the linguistic system of modality, which Halliday (1985) includes as one of the main functional systems in his description of language, and which has been used extensively in critical approaches to language. Like negation, modality has a range of possible realizations, which we will explore in more detail in the following sections, but here are some examples with the modal element highlighted:

9.1 The government *might* change its mind on the 42-day limit on detention.

9.2 I *can see* the government changing its mind on the 42-day limit on detention.

9.3 It's *possible* the government will change its mind on the 42-day limit on detention.

9.4 It's a *racing certainty* that the government will change its mind on the 42-day limit on detention.

9.5 No one *doubts* that the government will change its mind on the 42-day limit on detention.

9.6 I *wish* the government would change its mind on the 42-day limit on detention.

9.7 The government *should* change its mind on the 42-day limit on detention.

We will take a closer look at the formal and functional aspects of this textual practice in Sections 9.2 and 9.3, but first we need to think about why it is of interest to us here. We saw in Chapter 8 that negation introduces the possibility of other imagined (non)realities, which may either attract or repel the reader/hearer, and could thus influence them in various ideological ways. Modality is slightly different, because it *explicitly* introduces the viewpoint of the text's producer, and this in itself may have an effect on the recipient, depending on what the recipient thinks of the producer. Thus, those in the powerful position of putting a great amount of information into the public domain, such as large news organizations (e.g. the BBC or a national newspaper such as *The Times*) are often seen as authoritative in having access to 'truth'. Any modal statements coming from respected organizations will tend to be believable because of their status. Similarly, all those in authority, such as politicians, teachers and doctors, may express an opinion about what might be, or should be, and will often be listened to. This general tendency, of course, may be undermined by levels of cynicism in the public mind, and there is a counter-culture which inclines some readers/hearers to disbelieve *everything* said by such authorities automatically. This kind of individual reaction does not contradict the general point that the pervasive power of the media in particular tends to produce complicit readers rather than sceptical ones.

This status-based authority is not connected to the specifics of any text, of course, but the point in relation to modality is that even if the text producer is honest about any doubts (*we think x might have happened*), there is still a likelihood of them being believed. This tendency is not in itself manipulative, but of course it is open to abuse. Thus, the journalist or editor who wishes to implant an idea in the mind of their readers, in the absence of concrete evidence for their story, may nevertheless decide that even a modal assertion, such as *We believe the government is planning a huge rise in taxes* will carry some weight with readers. Such an assertion, being modal, is exempt from legal challenge of course, since all it asserts is what the newspaper *believes*.

We will see below (Section 9.4) that examples of modality can produce imagined hypothetical situations which may affect the reader/hearer over and above the status-based influence discussed here. In the meantime, we need to investigate modality itself.

Epistemic modality, as we will see below, indicates the view of the speaker as to the *likelihood* of something happening/being true etc., but its main effect textually is to construct a potential view of the world that the reader/hearer may adopt or be influenced by. The other range of modal meaning, that of desire and obligation, explores issues relating to the presentation of the speaker/writer's personal opinions. This, like many of the other tools, overlaps with other textual practices, but it is useful to the analyst to be able to locate and separate out the different strands of meaning in each case.

Here we are particularly concerned with the way in which the originator of a text may indicate her/his belief in the certainty or uncertainty, approval or disapproval of or desire for the outcome specified by the text, and the way in which this may influence the outlook of the reader/hearer. We have all known the experience of admiring someone personally and then finding ourselves drawn to agree with their pronouncements on issues that we perhaps have not thought through independently. This is natural, particularly as we grow up, but can become invidious if we unthinkingly take on the attitudes of others because of some generalized adulation we feel for them.

However, there is a great deal in modern life which leads us towards such unthinking acceptance of attitudes and beliefs. For a start, modern life is extraordinarily complex, and we are required to assimilate and understand very large quantities of information just to function on an everyday level. If we add to that the large volume of media-driven information that bombards us daily, and is often produced by a multinational corporation which has only commercial interests at heart then we may see that even the most careful, intelligent and/or resistant reader may find him/herself affected by what s/he reads or hears.

Modality is one conceptual tool of analysis that we can access linguistically and is the one which alerts us to the encoding of the speaker/writer's own personal viewpoint. This is the topic of the current chapter, and it will draw on the modal model developed by Simpson (1993) and also on the semantic concept of connotation, which can help us to see when we are being given a viewpoint and not just a factual piece of information.

9.2 A linguistic model of negation and modality

In this section, we will use the model of modality explored in detail in Simpson (1993) which brought together some of the insights from earlier models of modality into a framework investigating textual point of view. Modality is a classic example of the kind of textual function I am using as tools of analysis in this book, as it has a core form which is the modal auxiliary verb in English and also a range of other ways of producing modality, as well as some peripheral forms which demonstrate the producer's viewpoint without being centrally modal.

The modal auxiliary verb in English is the *first* potential auxiliary in a verb phrase that may contain up to four auxiliaries and a lexical verb, at its longest (e.g. *may have been being followed*). Note that not all English verb phrases have modal auxiliaries (*has been dancing*) or even any auxiliaries (*danced*) though many verb phrases are frequently made up of one or two auxiliaries and a lexical verb (*will be arriving; has been broken*). The modal auxiliaries in English include *will, would, shall, should, may, might, can, could, must, ought, dare* and *need* (though the last two may be on their way to becoming full verbs[1]). These verbs between them cover the modal meanings we will be discussing shortly, and it is important to note that many of them may have more than one of the modal meanings, depending on context, as we shall see.

The meanings of modal forms fall into two main categories. On the one hand, they concern the likelihood (or unlikelihood) of something being the case. Thus, *she might come* will convey the speaker's doubts about it, and *I am sure she'll come* conveys the speaker's certainty. This kind of meaning is known as epistemic meaning, and relates to the range of certainty that a speaker may express, including strong certainty as well as weak certainty. The other main category, which divides again into two subcategories, is that of the desirability of something being the case, which further divides into obligation (deontic modality) as in *You should take more exercise* and desire (boulomaic modality) as in *I wish you would phone your mother*. As mentioned in the introduction to this chapter, modality of all kinds can have the effect of creating a hypothetical or alternative world/situation conceptually for the reader/hearer, and in turn this alternative reality may have a number of potentially ideological effects on the recipient of such texts.

The modal verbs themselves can create a number of different meanings, depending on the context, and sometimes also on the content (other word choices) and the delivery (e.g. the intonation and stress) in the spoken language. Here are a few examples of the range of meaning of the various forms:

9.8 You *may* step down from the witness box now. (deontic modality – permission)
9.9 It *may* be best to wait for the next train. (epistemic modality – medium certainty)

9.10   The troops *must* withdraw before we will talk about peace. (deontic modality – obligation)

9.11   Judging by the military traffic passing by, the troops *must* be withdrawing. (epistemic modality – above average certainty)

9.12   The rain *might* hold off until dusk if we're lucky. (Epistemic modality – medium certainty)

9.13   You *might* have waited for me! (Deontic modality – obligation)

In each pair of examples above, we have the same modal verb (*may, must, might*) occurring in two different contexts and producing different modal meanings. It is a pleasing exercise to try using a modal verb in its most 'natural' usage, and then attempting to make up a different scenario where it might be used with a different meaning. Although there is a clear difference between epistemic and deontic uses of the verbs in the examples given here, there are some possibilities where the distinctions are not so clear. Take, for example, the following:

9.14   I *might* win the prize for best actress!

9.15   You *could* come round and watch a film.

Although the probable strict interpretation of these modal meanings is epistemic in the case of Example 9.14 and boulomaic in the case of Example 9.15, there is some overlap here between what is possible and what is desired. In Example 9.14, then, not only is the modality expressing the potential for prize-winning, but the content may incline the reader to also read it as boulomaic, since it is clearly a desired outcome. In Example 9.15, the force of the modal is to suggest this as a course of action to be taken but it is also likely to be tinged with the epistemic meaning (*it is possible for you to come round* etc.). These categories and subcategories, then, are not absolute, but may be seen, as stated in relation to other tools of analysis, as reference points with clarity in theory, but often overlapping in practice.

Before we look at the form-function issue in relation to modality, let us consider some of the more common modal items in English which are however not auxiliary verbs. The formal possibilities for constructing modal meaning fall into the following categories:

- Lexical verbs – think (I think that she'll come), suppose, wish, hope, and so on.
- Modal adverbs – probably, maybe, definitely, of course, and so on.
- Modal adjectives – probable, possible, definite, sure, certain, obligatory, forbidden, and so on.
- Conditional structures – *if...*, *then...*

Note that, unlike the modal auxiliary verbs themselves, these other modal forms tend to align themselves with one or other of the main modal meanings so that, for example, the individual lexical verbs which express modal meanings fall into those which express epistemic meaning (*think, know, suppose* etc.) and those which are boulomaic (*wish, hope*) or deontic (*expect, require*) in their force. The other word classes and forms also seem to be unambiguous in their modal meaning too, so that the modal adverbs are clearly either epistemic (*possibly*) or boulomaic (*hopefully*) and the adjectives are epistemic (*probable, certain*) deontic (*obligatory*) or boulomaic (*desirable*).

In addition to the modal meaning that presents desires and certainties, the speaker/writer may also let her/his views be known by either explicitly using lexical items of evaluation or words that have positive connotation. Thus, the following sentences, though declarative in nature, also demonstrate a clear viewpoint:

9.16   It is inconsiderate to talk about me to my friends.
9.17   I hate the increasing surveillance in Britain.
9.18   The new manager guffawed in agreement.

Here, we have an apparent statement of what is the case (Example 9.16) but which clearly is the view of the producer of the sentence. There is also an explicit statement of dislike (Example 9.17) using a word (*hate*) which denotes the speaker's viewpoint and a word (*guffawed,* Example 9.18) which indicates dislike through connotation. These expressions of personal evaluation are in some ways more straightforward than other tools of analysis, though they are also difficult to pin down, since they are largely semantic properties of lexical items, and are therefore not open to direct scrutiny, though semanticists have relatively objective ways to examine such phenomena.[2] However, it is certainly worth assessing texts for emotive vocabulary of this kind, and any doubts about the analysis can be dispelled by blind double testing or corpus investigation.

Simpson (1993) combines modality and these evaluative features in his modal grammar of narrative fiction, and produces a model of point of view that we can usefully adopt here. The consideration of whether a narrative is first (Category A) or third (Category B) person has a long tradition in literary study, and in particular in narratology and stylistics. Such categories have been less well-used in CDA, though there is scope for applying the same categories and considering their potential for effect on reader/hearers' ideological viewpoint.

There will follow here a very short summary of the way in which Simpson combines person, modality and semantic aspects of a text to produce these categories, but the reader is also recommended to read the original text for more detail. The full model can be seen below in the figure illustrating Simpson's modal grammar, but first the terms need to be explained.

Category A refers to what is often called 'homodiegetic narration' and is first person viewpoint narration. Category B refers to third person narration and divides into two, the first subcategory is termed the 'narratorial mode' as it has a point of view *outside* the consciousness of any participant in the narrative. The second subcategory is the 'reflector mode' which is also narrated in third person but from *within* the consciousness of a participant in the narrative. Each of these categories and subcategories then divides similarly into three, by the means of a cross-cutting categorization reflecting positive, negative or neutral modality. These modal categories are indicated in the text by the features listed below:

Positive – deontic and boulomaic modal forms, *verba sentiendi*, evaluative adjectives and adverbs, generic sentences.
Negative – epistemic and perception modality, words of estrangement.
Neutral – complete absence of narratorial modality – categorical assertions alone.

We have already encountered the different basic types of modality above, though notice here that texts, according to Simpson, often seem *either* to have a preponderance of deontic and boulomaic modal forms, expressing desire and obligation (positive modality) *or* they are characterized by epistemic and perception modality expressing truth, certainty and observation (negative modality). In addition, positive shading uses *verba sentiendi* (Latin for 'verbs of feeling' such as *hope, wish* etc.), evaluative adjectives and adverbs such as *fantastic* or *unfortunately* and generic sentences such as *Bankers are untrustworthy* or *Men tend to be emotionally immature*. The negative shading of Simpson's model of modality is represented by epistemic and perception modality, including in particular 'words of estrangement', such as *apparently, as if,* and *seem,* which keep the 'truth' of the text at arm's length from the speaker/writer, and have the effect of the producer of the text refusing responsibility for the remaining content.

Finally, neutral shading is the absence of modality, and is therefore delivered mainly through categorical assertions. This shading is of course more typical of journalism, particularly in the narratorial mode, than of fictional narration, and is much stronger in effect than the strongest epistemic modality. One of the overlaps between journalism and fictional narration in stylistic terms is the readers' story text type, which is used increasingly in specialist magazines, such as those on pregnancy, health issues or slimming. These stories purport to be 'real life' stories, and are often written in third person narrative style, but from the point of view of the reader being featured. These are, then,

Category B narratives, and may have positive, negative or neutral shading, though positive shading is most common, showing as it does the opinions and judgements of the character concerned.

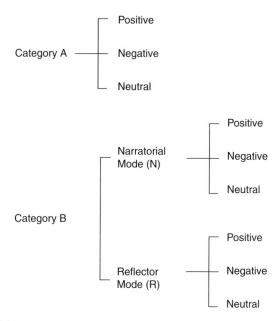

Simpson's modal grammar

9.3 Form and function

In earlier sections the textual function of hypothesizing was introduced, and some of the main textual vehicles for this function were illustrated. Here, we will consider the particular ways in which this function clouds the distinction between form and function in English.

We have seen that modality has a set of core forms (the modal auxiliaries) and that these are the prototypical carriers of these particular textual functions. Like negation, modality is a very good example of a conceptual meaning which is embodied in a particular form in the language, but which can additionally be invoked in a range of linguistic (and paralinguistic) ways. It is primarily delivered by the modal verbs, and then also by a number of lexical means as we saw in the previous section (modal adverbs, verbs and adjectives), but it can also be phonological, using intonation patterns indicating uncertainty or certainty or body language such as the shrug of the shoulders or an enquiring lifting of the eyebrow.

As well as the main modal vehicles already mentioned, Simpson's model sees other semantic groupings of words as contributing to the modality of a text. Thus, in his model, we see semantic categories such as 'words of estrangement', 'evaluative adjectives and adverbs' and *'verba sentiendi'* contributing to the particular modality of a text type.

The topic of this chapter is the linguistic representation of the text producer's meaning, and as we saw in Chapter 8, there is a sense in which the *whole* of this book is about the producer's meaning, since ideologies are embedded in so many aspects of linguistic form and choice. Also, modality itself is often represented as the ultimate example of the interpersonal metafunction of language, according to Halliday's three-way distinction between ideational, interpersonal and textual functions of language (see Chapter 1 for more on this distinction). What we see in this book, however, is that the 'textual' functions presented here are a way of representing the world, and at the same time also represent the producer's *view* of the world as well as being a 'textual' process in themselves. Because negative and positive shading (in Simpson's model) of texts, using epistemic, deontic and boulomaic modality as well as evaluative adjectives and adverbs and so on, is more clearly reflective of the producer's meaning, this chapter is also central to the question of how texts reflect their producers' ideology.

As with many of the textual practices being considered in this book, the representation of speaker/writer's opinions is not a simple one-to-one form-function relationship. Simpson's model is just one of those which have been produced in relation to fictional narratives to try and capture the way in which linguistic text can produce a range of experiences for the reader. The model relies on a range of features, including the modal system, which we have seen was already more complex than just the modal auxiliaries. In addition to different types of modality, the production of viewpoint in text also requires the use of a narrative type A or B (depending on the personal pronouns used) and on the inclusion of *verba sentiendi* and generic sentences (for positive modes). We will see in Section 10.4 how these different narrative modes may crop up in non-fiction contexts, and how they may present the reader/hearer with ideologies that can become naturalized over time and after repetition.

The textual function being described in this chapter, then, covers the range from personal viewpoint expressed in first person narration, through more discreet opinions and viewpoints expressed via an apparently omniscient narrator or viewpoints which may be presented as fact, through the avoidance of any of the linguistic features discussed in the last section. There is no single feature which will unambiguously classify a text as belonging to any particular category of narrative mode and as we will see, a single text may change from one kind of narrative mode to another within a few sentences. In fact, as with most linguistic features of this kind, one might see the categories of Simpson's model as reference points or prototypical modes, rather than absolute categories with clear boundaries between them. This does not invalidate their use as analytical tools, but shows yet again that text is made up of a complex set of features which can be used to describe in some detail the character of texts – in this case the viewpoint which is being constructed. As in all cases we have looked at in this book so far, the categorization of the text is dependent on formal features which may indicate a particular character, but not necessarily allocate it to an absolute category.

Before we consider the ideological effects of modality, it is worth noting the very important but often ignored issue about whose opinions modality is representing. It is not enough to say that all 'modal' forms show the producer's viewpoint, since this is clearly not true in the sentence *John thinks she might come* where the use of the verb think with a third person subject is nothing more than the reporting of a fact, though the same verb with a first person subject (*I think she might come*) is clearly modal. It is not as simple as suggesting that modality needs to attach to first person narration to be interpersonal in the Hallidayan sense, since *She might come* is technically third person, though it demonstrates the speaker's viewpoint. Analysis, therefore, needs to take careful note of other aspects of the text, including any delayed reporting clauses, to ascertain the force of any modality.

9.4 Ideological effects

There is a sense in which *everything* in this book is ultimately about the viewpoint of the producer of a text, and how it may encode – and thus potentially transfer – an ideological outlook which may (but may not) be persuasive, manipulative or even harmful.

This chapter, though, deals with linguistic analytical tools which are in a way less hidden and thus apparently less suspect than many of the others. Thus, a writer/speaker who produces a text which clearly disapproves of something through using negative connotation is being more honest than we might expect and may, ultimately, persuade us more as a result of gaining our respect. However, we may also find ourselves simply accepting some ideologies from media-driven exposure to certain people, whether they are celebrities extolling the virtues of cosmetic surgery or politically motivated newspapers making clear their preferences for closed borders or low taxation. Preferences or certainties, particularly when expressed either very often or by people we generally accept as authorities, are hard to ignore, even if they are less hidden than many of the ideological encodings we have been discussing in this book so far.

Let us revisit the modal model introduced above. As in Chapter 8, where it was claimed that negation brought into play a whole other view of the world, and that this may have consequences for textual ideology, modality also draws on the issues of hypothetical worlds and speaker preferences/certainties, and the focus here is on persuasion by evaluative opinion, as well as persuasion by imagining different possibilities.

Modality, as we saw above, can be divided into epistemic (doubt and certainty) and boulomaic/deontic (desire and obligation). These are most typically produced by modal verbs, but can also be produced by anything from an adverb (e.g. *preferably*) to a gesture (e.g. a shrug). All of these may produce a speaker/writer viewpoint which will be evident to the hearer/reader:

9.19   This law *ought* to be repealed.
9.20   I *wish* my legs were longer.
9.21   *If only* people would realize that abortion is murder.
9.22   The Tories are bound to win the next General Election.

In considering the impact of speaker/writer's viewpoint on recipients, it is worth noting here that the ideology of these sentences is more explicit than we saw in many of the earlier chapters, and is not *necessarily* manipulative as a result, but may simply be the genuinely expressed view of the originator of the text. Thus, a straightforward debate on a law might produce Example 9.19 from one of the participants, an interview with a model or actress (or long-jumper!) might produce Example 9.20 and a statement from a pro-life campaigner may produce Example 9.21, though note that the modality (*if only*) is used with a presupposition triggered by the factive verb, *realize*, here (see Chapter 7 for more on presupposition).

However, there is in addition a potential effect from any or all of these on the reader if s/he is repeatedly exposed to the viewpoints expressed from many high-profile sources and in authoritative publications. Thus, a strong negative response to an unpopular law (Example 9.19) might produce the general ideology that it is bad, even if the issues are not debated in detail. The wish for longer legs by women (Example 9.20) *is* ubiquitous in all sorts of contexts and the modality here produces an implicature that women with long legs are more beautiful, which reproduces this as a general ideological view.[3] The pro-life campaigners who wish to ban abortion repeat their mantra (Example 9.21) connecting abortion with murder repeatedly on the assumption that reinforcement of this view will affect readers and result in more supporters. A more local effect (in 2008) is the view that the Conservative party are bound to win the next election (Example 9.22) in view of the troubles of the Labour government. Though there are reasons why such statements may be made frequently in the press and other media, it is nevertheless their repetition from authoritative sources that make them into a self-fulfilling prophecy.[4]

The effect of modality on ideology varies, depending on the content and context of the text concerned, though there are a certain number of standard effects that can be demonstrated to occur frequently. The following examples illustrate this:

9.23 Why long-haul food *may be* greener than local food with low air-miles.

9.24 *It's obviously true* that American-style free market economics are under something of a cloud, even in such a hothouse of free market trading as Hong Kong – while the mainland Chinese mix of a more statist market economy, with huge accumulated reserves to draw on in such a crisis, *looks* rather brighter.

The examples above (9.23 and 9.24) demonstrate further ways in which the use of modality is powerful in putting over an ideological point of view. In the first case, news articles which challenge the accepted wisdom of the day are always attractive for news producers as they may produce more readers/ listeners. This story concerned the notion of food miles which links the distance food has travelled to the damage this does to the environment and claims that lower food miles is a target we should all have. The argument is made in the article that the situation is more complex and that like-for-like the food which travels is not always more damaging than local food. The reality, of course, is that those who take food miles seriously will usually also link this ideology with one of in-season eating, so that comparing tomatoes flown in from southern Europe with hot-housed tomatoes grown out of season in England is not as sensible as it sounds. However, the introductory sentence, shown here, manages to make us doubt one of the strongest tenets of the environmental campaigners, that local food is best for the planet, by the use of a modal auxiliary which though not as strong as a categorical clause (*long-haul food is greener* etc.) is nevertheless able to summon up this surprising scenario by mentioning it at all.

Example 9.24 shows a different example of epistemic modality as it is strong in its commitment (*It's obviously true that* etc.). Strongly argued epistemic modality appears to make a firm case for the reality of the scenario it is putting forward (here, the loss of influence of American-style free market capitalism). In fact, the article goes on to explain that free market capitalism is not taking as hard a battering as this sentence seems to be claiming, so it turns out to be a way of setting up an article which entrenches the all-powerful nature of the American form of capitalism after all. The ideological impact of using strong epistemic modality here, only to undermine this professed certainty later, is a rhetorical strategy which will ultimately naturalize free-market capitalism as the only option for the world economy.

The question of exactly what effect the particular textual practices discussed in this chapter may have is a further step away from the text itself and may be considered as a contextual effect which we can label 'interpretation' as we have done in the past. So, for example, the use of a positive first person narration (A+ve in Simpson's model) would have one effect (possibly an aesthetic one) in a novel and a different effect (probably an ideological one) if it were a newspaper editorial.

The examples below illustrate a range of positive shading effects in non-fiction texts:

9.25   The International Monetary Fund *should* quickly put together a preventive facility to restore the capacity of countries with healthy macroeconomic accounts to borrow from private capital markets.

9.26   World-class economists – what the political leaders *should* do…

- In the financial sector, leaders *should act* quickly, strengthening and coordinating the emergency measures to staunch the bleeding; in the real sector, they *should use* fiscal stimulus to get the patient's heart pumping again;
- They *should act* immediately to strengthen the ability of the IMF and other existing institutions to deal with the crisis in emerging markets;
- They *should start* thinking outside the box about longer term financial and monetary reforms; and
- Do no harm.

9.27   People of Amble ought to be ashamed of themselves. I live in a busy inner city area of a large city and the neighbourhood attracts lots of volunteers, who willingly, from time to time, go on litter picks and clean up days.

It is worth noting that the question of whether a non-fiction text is Category A or B is not *entirely* dependent on the presence or absence of the first/ third person pronouns. For example, the presence of deontic modality in Examples 9.25 and 9.26 with *no* use of first person pronouns is nevertheless an indication that it is the writer's opinion that is represented in the modal forms, which is relatively normal in political commentary, where the use of the first person pronoun (*I*) is avoided to background the fact that it is opinion and not fact that is being produced. Example 9.27 contrasts with the previous two examples, as it is adapted from a website discussion list, and is clearly meant to be the opinion of a private individual, albeit published in an accessible form for all to see. Note the difference in force of a clearly personal view in the first person, from a private individual and how much more 'objective' and 'impersonal' the collected views of the so-called 'world-class economists' seem in Example 9.26. Of course, we tend to take more notice of those with relevant knowledge and experience, but it is also interesting to see how the style of positive shading in a Category A type narrative, but omitting any mention of the first person which would undermine its force, is one way of making your opinions sound less subjective.

9.5 Exercises

The examples below each contain a modal form. Comment on the ideological effect of these forms in their context, using the concepts of negating or hypothesizing as your reference points. What kinds of ideas do these examples have the potential to conjure up in the mind of the reader, and why?

9.28   Organic farming 'could feed Africa'.

9.29   The consequences of a credit crunch could be dire for both their public and corporate sector. This would ultimately stall the last engine of growth on which the world economy relies. (Experts comment on the situation in emerging markets such as India and China)

9.30   No barbed wire ... it might hurt the thieves, allotment holders told.

9.31   Emperor Akihito of Japan should follow the example of Germany in making a genuine gesture of contrition for his country's wartime aggression in Asia, Lee Myung Bak, the South Korean President, has said.

Sample answers can be found in the Appendix.

9.6 Further reading

The main formal realization of the textual practice of hypothesizing is the modal verb. This aspect of the grammar of the English verb has been the subject of a number of detailed treatments, including Palmer (2001) and Mindt (1995) for example.

Modality as a textual practice, and with a scope wider than the modal verb, has been discussed by stylisticians (e.g. Simpson 1993 chapter 3) as one aspect of the point of view of texts, and recognized by CDA scholars as a potential site of ideological power which is dependent on the authority of the writer or producer. Fairclough (1989: 127) explains:

> Notice that the authority and power relations on the basis of which the producers of this text withhold permission from, or impose obligations upon, the people it is sent to, are not made explicit. It is precisely implicit authority claims and implicit power relations of the sort illustrated here that make relational modality a matter of ideological interest.

Note that most commentators see modality as expressing not the ideational, but the interpersonal metafunction of language:

> As was pointed out earlier, modality refers broadly to a speaker's attitude towards, or opinion about, the truth of a proposition expressed by a sentence. It also extends to their attitude towards the situation or event described by a sentence. Modality is therefore a major exponent of the interpersonal function of language. (Simpson 1993: 47)

Whilst this is generally agreed amongst commentators, I would point out that few linguistic systems work solely on one of the three metafunctional levels of Halliday's model. Specifically, it seems entirely possible, and consistent with the approach of this book, to see modality as another capacity of text to structure meaning, this time in terms of hypothetical situations. This, however, is not the attitude of Fowler (1991: 85):

> Even if the line between the ideational and the interpersonal is fuzzy, it is worth drawing, because there are some devices which are clearly either one thing or the other. The first clearly interpersonal feature to be mentioned is modality.

To see an example of modality used as a descriptive tool to delineate such a textual function, the reader may wish to consult Jeffries (2006: 182–8). Here, the modality of texts in women's magazines is analysed:

> However, the writers of the texts in this study, and the people that they quote, often make the understandable, and very human, assumption that strongly certain epistemic modality as well as hedging with weaker epistemic modality, can give an impression of authority. Such effects can be seen in quotations from the 'experts', such as plastic surgeons, who wish to emphasise their sense of responsibility by distancing themselves from what they might see as bad practice:
>
> - We would *never* remove more than three litres of fat (56)
> - This *may* help for a while (56)
> - Irregularities *can* start showing through (56)
> - you *could actually* see the tracks (56)

The emphatic use of *never* in the first example shows the surgeon protesting his sense of responsibility and the doubt introduced by *may* about some techniques seems calculated to impress upon the reader his own credentials as a reliable and knowledgeable practitioner who will not cut corners.

Similar effects are achieved by the use of epistemic modality in the two final examples, using *can* and *actually*, where the reliability of someone so honest can hardly be doubted by the reader.

The strength and power of categorical, as opposed to modal, utterances, is emphasized by a number of writers. Here is Fairclough (Fairclough 1989: 129) on the topic:

> The ideological interest is in the authenticity claims, or claims to knowledge, which are evinced by modality forms. Newspapers are an interesting case. In news reports, reported happenings are generally represented as categorical truths – facts – without the sort of intermediate modalities I have just illustrated.

So, the power of modality is partly to emphasize the perceived authority of the text producer, and perhaps more insidiously, to cause the recipient to imagine hypothetical situations, whether these are desired or feared.

10 Presenting Others' Speech and Thoughts

10.1 Introduction

In the previous chapter we saw that modality is one of the means of producing an alternative or hypothetical text world that the reader may potentially be influenced into believing, desiring or fearing. Here we will consider the viewpoint of the participants who are discussed in texts but whose words and thoughts are mediated by the narrating voice of the text, whether this is an explicit and personal voice or a supposedly 'neutral' voice of, for example, a news organization such as the BBC.

The power to represent the words and thoughts of others is potentially very manipulative of their ideologies as well as those of the reader. Whilst many texts claim to represent 'faithfully' (i.e. verbatim) the words of others, in fact there is *always* a gap between the original version and any quotation, even if no malice is intended. Not only are hesitations (*-er*, *-um* etc.) and false starts likely to be 'ironed out' in a presentation of others' words, and intonation and paralinguistic features (like facial expression) omitted when speech is turned into writing, but even the choice of which words to quote may be significant (*you have quoted me out of context*) and as we shall see below there are also many possible interpretative possibilities when indirect speech is used. As for thoughts, it is not only impossible to access others' thoughts directly, but it is also always an act of interpretation to put those projected thoughts into linguistic form.

Thus, what appears at first sight a rather mundane and certainly common form of straightforward and neutral reporting, can be as ideologically significant as any of the other textual practices reported in this book. The development of a model of speech and thought presentation was first mooted in relation to literary fiction (see Leech and Short 1981, 2007), and though some other text types have now also been investigated, the model has been developed through a number of versions mostly in relation to its use in literature (though see Short 1988) and with a view to making as complete a model as possible of how we quote others in English texts.

The question of whether/to what extent we may manipulate the words (and thoughts) of others to some kind of ideological purpose has not been widely addressed by the literature on this topic (though see McKenzie 1987 and Roeh and Nir 1990), but it seems very likely that this is one of the main ways in which producers of texts may influence the reader whether intentionally or not. It is not unusual to hear people who are in conflict with each other, whether personally or politically, say that their words have been taken out of context. This effectively means that the words they said have been edited so that the listener does not know what came before or afterwards. This is just one way that text producers have of exploiting their power over the representation of others' speech and thoughts.

10.1   I regret the pain I have caused to my family and friends, but I do not regret telling the truth.

Example 10.1 is typical of the kind of original statement that may be taken out of context. Though headline writers would be entirely within their rights to use 'I do not regret' as a quotation from this example, the originator of the quotation may well feel aggrieved that his sensitivity to others around him is not equally represented. This is just one way in which representing others' words can be manipulated. Below, we shall see some others.

10.2 A linguistic model of speech and thought presentation (S&TP)

In this chapter, we will use the model of speech and thought presentation from Short (1996) though there have been further developments of the model in more recent publications (see Semino and Short 2004), and more work is continuing on the model as I write. Readers who embark on analysis of S&TP may wish to follow up the latest form of the model for their research, though the model presented here will be a good starting point for our purposes.

At the root of this model is the traditional distinction between direct and indirect forms of speech presentation, whereby the direct version claims to present *exactly* the words that were spoken whereas indirect speech presents a 'reported' version of the same speech act, possibly fairly close to the original but with a change of person (from first to third) and a change from present to past tense where relevant. Here is an (invented) example of each to compare:

10.2   He said 'I am innocent'.
10.3   He said that he was innocent.

Example 10.2 demonstrates the use of direct speech, with a reporting clause (*he said*) followed by quotation marks and a sentence that purports to be exactly what was said, using first person pronoun (*I*) and present tense verb (*am*). Example 10.3 in contrast is indirect speech and follows the same reporting clause (*he said*) with a subordinate clause introduced by *that*, a change from the first person to third person (*he*) and from present tense to past (*was*).

This simple example seems to imply that the use of direct or indirect speech is nothing more than a matter of a choice between stylistic variants, with the two being narratorially equivalent, but in fact, the situation is far more complex than these invented examples imply. For one thing, there are other categories of speech presentation in addition to the two described here. We will see these categories below. In addition, the question of faithfulness – how close the words are to the original speech – is not straightforward and can have a range of possible effects on the ideology of the text as we shall see below. Thus, indirect representations of speech can choose to be faithful to the speech act alone (*he asked a question*), the specific proposition being put forward but not the verbatim text (*he asked whether she was lying*) or the actual words themselves (*he asked was she telling the truth?*), and each of these has different potential effects on the reader.

The model of speech and thought presentation which has been developed over a number of years and by different scholars (see Section 10.6 for more details), and in particular by Leech and Short (1981, 2007) and Semino and Short (2004) takes account of these issues by dividing speech presentation into the following categories:

- Narrator's report of speech (NRS):   e.g. *He spoke.*
- Narrator's report of Speech Act (NRSA):   e.g. *He apologized.*
- Indirect speech (IS):   e.g. He said that he was terribly sorry.
- Free indirect speech (FIS):   e.g. *He was terribly sorry.*
- Direct speech (DS):   e.g. He said 'I'm terribly sorry'.

These categories represent a progression from least faithful to the original version at the top (NRS) to most faithful at the bottom.[1]

Notice that although I have tried to use closely related examples through-out the list above, in fact it would be possible to represent the original in a number of different ways as the distance from the originator becomes greater. If we assume that *'I'm terribly sorry'* is a reasonably accurate version of the original, given that we cannot see or hear the actual performance of it, then the IS version may not be as faithful to the words themselves and yet still not change the meaning. Thus, *He said he regretted it* and *He said he felt bad about it* are not all that faithful reproductions of the original, but would not be considered untruthful either. This is often no more than a trivial matter, though it may raise hackles in private conversations when we feel we have been misrepresented. More significantly, if we begin to depart from the verbatim text of someone's speech in public texts where ideology is being reinforced, created or manipulated, we may more or less subtly misrepresent them, with a range of consequences.

The narrator, therefore, has a range of possible ways of coming between the originator of the quoted speech and the recipient. The closer the text is to the left-hand side of this diagram (from Short 1996: 293), the more the narrator is interpreting the original speech.

NRS NRSA IS FIS DS

This can have two main effects, which will have differing consequences for ideology in different situations. First, there is the opportunity, mentioned above, for the narrator to interpret the actual speech by moving away from the 'faithful' end of the range. This may allow for slanting or misrepresentation, partly because, as we saw above, non-verbatim reporting of speech is relatively normal in everyday language use, and the abuse of this facility may go unnoticed. The other main effect is the fact that readers/listeners are aware of the intervention of a narrator and will be sensitive to the distance between them and the original speaker when they encounter indirect speech or anything to the left of it. This could result in a reader/hearer concluding that the narrator is not sure of exactly what was said, or is holding something back. In contrast, the reader may be inclined to believe that direct speech reporting is somehow more reliable than anything more indirect. Most of all, the category which sits between the two, free indirect speech, has the potentially uncomfortable effect of merging the narrator's voice with that of the original speaker, and though this may lead to nothing more than interesting 'voices' in fiction, it can be a significant factor in the effects of non-fiction texts on their recipients as we will see in Section 10.4.

Before we consider the ideological implications of presenting others' words (and thoughts), let us consider the formal features of the different categories of speech representation and compare them with the representation of thought.

- NRS – includes a Verbalization process (*speak, talk, shout* etc.) possibly followed by a prepositional phrase or noun phrase giving the subject-matter of the verbiage. For example, *They discussed the situation in Tibet.*
- NRSA – includes a Verbalization process denoting a specific Speech Act (*apologize, accuse, deny* etc.) possibly followed by a Goal (prepositional

phrase) giving the subject-matter of the speech act. For example, *She apologized for the mess.*

- IS – includes a reporting clause (*he said*) followed by subordinate clause usually introduced by *that*, and containing the Verbiage as a version of the supposed verbatim speech, changing any present tense verbs to past, first person pronouns to third person and proximal deictics to distal ones. For example, *She declared that she would stand as a candidate for the Presidency.*
- FIS – has no reporting clause but consists of a representation of the original speech with tense, pronouns and deixis similar to IS. For example, *She would stand as a candidate for the Presidency.*
- DS – reporting clause with, prototypically, inverted commas containing verbatim representation of original speech, including any first person pronouns, present tense verbs and proximal deictics. For example, *She declared 'I will stand as a candidate for the Presidency'.*

It is arguable that the perceived 'norm' for speech representation is Direct Speech, because it purports to be as faithful to the original as possible, with little narrator intervention (Leech and Short 2007: 268). This norm is proposed on the basis that since speech is an external phenomenon, DS gets us closest to faithful representation of this. In terms of their formal features, a parallel set of categories can be applied to the representation of thought, though the norm in this case (at least for fictional narration) is thought to be Indirect Thought presentation (IT), since it is an internal phenomenon, and cannot be directly scrutinized (Leech and Short 2007: 277–8).

				norm ↓
NRS	NRSA	IS	FIS	DS
NRT	NRTA	IT	FIT	DT
		↑ norm		

This difference of norms can be attributed to the fact that the representation of thought is clearly only approximate, because we have no direct access to others' thoughts, and even our own thoughts may not have a clear linguistic form. Thus, to say *He thought 'I must get out of here fast'* (DT) is taking a liberty as narrator to put into words the thoughts that the character is supposed to be having. No one reading or hearing this sentence would be under any illusion at all that this is somehow faithful to the 'original' thoughts, and indeed it has the implication that the narrator is intervening quite heavily. In contrast, to assert that *He thought he should get out of there fast* (IT) is to make it clear that the narrator is somehow trying to represent what the original thinker thought, without any particular claim to faithfulness of language. Note that in the fictional context, where an omniscient narrator is assumed, there is no particular oddity in understanding that the narration will get inside the heads of the characters. It is one of the many aspects of the 'suspension of disbelief' that we accept in that range of genres (novels, short stories etc.). In contrast, and significantly for our purposes here, the assumption that a narrator of non-fiction, whether personal or institutional, can access the thoughts of others is clearly not generally accepted. Thus *The Prime Minister thinks that the economy will recover* is a statement which may well be found in news commentary, but it will almost always be accompanied by some evidence for this view, or the implied 'ownership' of this view by a particular person or group of people. Note that if successful, a text which manages to imply privileged access to the thought processes of those who are powerful in society will have a very strong potential effect on its readers. We will return to these topics in Section 10.4, but first let us consider the formal features of the representation of thought.

- NRT – includes a Mental Cognition process (*think, consider* etc.) possibly followed by a prepositional phrase or noun phrase giving the subject-matter of the Phenomenon being thought about. For example, *He thought about the war.*
- NRTA – includes a Mental Cognition process denoting a specific Thought Act (*imagine, decide* etc.) possibly followed by the Phenomenon of the Thought Act. For example, *She imagined the scenario after the bomb had exploded.*
- IT – includes a reporting clause (*he thought*) followed by subordinate clause usually introduced by *that*, and containing the Phenomenon as a reasonably accurate imagined version of the thoughts expressed as language, but changing any present tense verbs to past, first person pronouns to third person and proximal deictics to distal ones. For example, *He thought that he had seen enough of that horror.*
- FIT – has no reporting clause but consists of a representation of the original speech with tense, pronouns and deixis similar to IT. For example, *He had seen enough of that horror.*
- DS – reporting clause with inverted commas containing verbatim representation of original speech, including any first person pronouns, present tense verbs and proximal deictics. For example, *He thought 'I have seen enough of this horror'.*

Below, we will consider some of the differences between speech and thought presentation in non-fiction contexts. First, let us see how this tool of analysis fits into the general approach to textual meaning that is being proposed in this book.

10.3 **Form and function**

Whilst this model of speech and thought representation has been presented in a number of versions (see Section 10.6 below) as having a set of categories, into which any individual example will fit, the truth is that they are more like idealized categories, prototypes or reference points than absolute categories. This, we have seen, is true of very many linguistic features of the kind we have examined in this book. Though there are some reasons why analysts have to make decisions about category membership, such as the need for clear tagging decisions when using electronic corpora, it is nevertheless important to recognize the overlapping features of these categories because therein lie some of the possibilities for ideological influence.

The free indirect speech category, for example, sits between indirect and direct speech, and already has some of the features of both, as we saw above, but in fact, there are more possible positions on the cline between these two than is represented by FIS alone. Let us consider one set of examples to illustrate:

10.4   He said 'I am the best person to lead the country out of recession in current economic climate.'

10.5   He said that he was the best person to lead the country out of recession in the prevailing economic climate.

10.6   He was the best person to lead the country out of recession in the prevailing economic climate.

Example 10.4 is a DS representation, 10.5 is IS and 10.6 could be seen as FIS. Note that Example 10.6 illustrates a potential problem for analysis of FIS, because there is an ambiguity[2] between the implication that these words are somehow quoted from the character concerned and the interpretation by the reader that there is a narrator giving her/his opinion or an omniscient narrator ostensibly presenting the 'truth'. Much FIS is, out of context, not unambiguously free indirect speech at all, so that the reader usually needs to draw on context to clear up this ambiguity:

10.7   He told the meeting that he had a good record from his time at the Treasury and said that he relished the idea of sorting out complex problems. He was the best person to lead the country out of recession in the prevailing economic climate.

10.8   History tells us that he had a good record from his time at the Treasury and that he relished the idea of sorting out complex problems. He was the best person to lead the country out of recession in the prevailing economic climate.

10.9   In my opinion, he had a good record from his time at the Treasury and he seemed to relish the idea of sorting out complex problems. He was the best person to lead the country out of recession in the prevailing economic climate.

In Examples 10.7–10.9, we have contexts that make the original utterance from Example 10.6 read as FIS in the first case, and as a narratorial opinion (impersonal and then personal respectively) in Examples 10.8 and 10.9. Note that FIS can become clearer if some aspects of the DS version are included. In Example 10.10 below, for example, the deictic form is changed to a proximal equivalent:

10.10   He was the best person to lead the country out of recession in the *current* economic climate.

Many examples of FIS from fiction are not clearly FIS for the reasons given above, but are 'seeded' with vocabulary that seems to belong more to the character than to the narrator. This can give an effect of the character's voice speaking through the narration.

10.4 **Ideological effects**

The potential for ideological effects of the presentation of speech and thought are many and varied. The analyst needs to take account of the perceived authority of the text producer, the context, and content of the text and the background and attitudes of the reader as well as the manner of speech and thought presentation. This section will give a few examples of the possible effect of the latter, but it should be borne in mind that the other factors may all influence the actual outcome in any one instance of reading. This does not invalidate the analysis of speech and thought presentation, which, like other tools of analysis in this book, is independent of interpretation and/or effect.

The extracts discussed here are adapted from real news reports and commentary and have a wide range of speech and thought presentation, some of which are highlighted in italics here. The reader may wish to read the extracts and think about the effects of this aspect of the texts before reading on:

10.11   It's a bizarre feeling, but *I've realised that* for perhaps the first time in my life, *I agree with Peter Stringfellow.* Appearing in front of a committee of MPs, the swinging 68-year-old *claimed that lap dancing clubs aren't erotic in the slightest. A visit to his 'gentleman's club', he said, was equivalent in terms of titillation to a trip to the disco, or looking at a picture of David Beckham in his undies.* His fellow *'adult entertainment'* mogul Simon Warr, owner of the Spearmint Rhino chain, *was equally adamant that his clubs were 'not sexually titillating', and that their purpose was 'to provide entertainment'.* Well, that's where we part company. *Warr and Stringfellow might be trying to play things down,* to make sure MPs don't place their establishments in the more restrictive category of *'sex encounter clubs',* but in the process *they've revealed an accidental truth.* Lap dancing clubs aren't erotic – but they aren't entertaining, either. They're awful, tawdry places, where what should be intimate becomes grimly transactional.

The opinion piece that is represented by the extract in Example 10.11 is written in the first person, and the ideology of the text is therefore clearly that of the journalist named in the by-line. This means that the two early presentations of thought (*I've realised that* (IT)...*I agree with Peter Stringfellow* (DT)) are believable because it is the writer himself that is reporting his own thoughts. This sets up the expectation that what is being reported is true, and because the thoughts themselves are surprising (agreeing with Peter Stringfellow is generally seen as a controversial thing to do), the reader is not only encouraged to read on, but is also possibly persuaded of the sincerity of the writer who is exposing a potentially embarrassing viewpoint, and may therefore be seen as honest to a fault. This sets up the experience of reading the rest of the text where the alleged agreement between the author and Stringfellow is shown to be from different ideological positions. The text represents Stringfellow's views with the IS: *claimed that lap dancing clubs aren't erotic in the slightest,* in which it is not entirely clear to what extent the verbiage is verbatim. A similar section of IS seems to be closer to verbatim as it has some fairly detailed points being made: *a visit to his 'gentleman's club', he said, was equivalent in terms of titillation to a trip to the disco, or looking at a picture of David Beckham in his undies.*

In fact, what we find is that the first of these sections of IS (*lap dancing clubs aren't erotic in the slightest*) is very far from being close to anything actually said by Stringfellow in his evidence to the Select Committee. We can demonstrate this since the original speech was given to a parliamentary committee and we therefore have a reasonably faithful transcript of Stringfellow's evidence, the only section of it which is close to being what is quoted in the commentary above is the following:

> From my many years of experience, of course it is sexually stimulating, so is a disco, so is a young girl flashing away with her little knickers showing. That is sexually stimulating. So is David Beckham laid out advertising Calvin Klein, he is sexually stimulating. So are the Chippendales, that is sexually stimulating. That is a great show, by the way,

I've been to see it. I was the only male there out of 3,000 females. It was a wonderful show. Of course it does have some form of sexual stimulation, but I think what my colleague over here is trying to explain is that it is not one hundred per cent sexual, 'My god, it's driving me mad, I'm going to get divorced and find a dancer to live with for the rest of my life'. It does not go on like that. In our environment, a dance lasts three minutes; clothes are on and off before you have blinked; it has a lot more to do with personality; it has a lot more to do with the ambience of the club and the male environment.

What is immediately striking is that the commentator in our extract (Example 10.11) is reading *behind* what Stringfellow actually said (*of course it is sexually stimulating*), which appears to be the opposite of what he is reported to have said (*lap dancing clubs aren't erotic in the slightest*). Nowhere in the evidence is the word *erotic* used, so we have to assume that *sexually stimulating* is the phrase that the journalist has latched onto, and he reads it as the opposite of what Stringfellow says because of the following comparison with a disco, which produces an implicature (see Chapter 7) that, since discos are not regarded as sexual encounter establishments, neither should a lap dancing club be. What this account misses, however, is the absolute nature of the reported speech, where the journalist has, it seems, gone for an exaggeration of Stringfellow's position by saying that he claimed *lap dancing clubs **aren't erotic in the slightest.***

The second section of the IS quoted in the extract (a visit to his 'gentleman's club', he said, was equivalent in terms of titillation to a trip to the disco, or looking at a picture of David Beckham in his undies) is, as predicted, closer to being verbatim, though the nature of this kind of reporting is to summarize to a certain extent, which leaves out some of the original detail. Note, however, that the use of a connotatively 'sexual' word, undies, is used in place of the original Calvin Klein, and this has a potentially stronger effect of making the image of Beckham in his boxers seem sexually stimulating, when the original, referring to his advertising this make of underwear, is less so. In addition, some of these more informal word choices imply (wrongly, as it turns out) that these might be the actual words used, and this results in a mild form of FIS, where the apparent 'voice' of the originator comes through the narrative style.

The extract I have used to illustrate the slippage between original speech and IS also includes some quotes from another nightclub owner, Simon Warr, which is worded as follows: *was equally adamant that his clubs were 'not sexually titillating', and that their purpose was 'to provide entertainment'*. What is interesting here is the use of short stretches of DS containing the most important parts of the propositions, so that the reader may well conclude that although there is some (understandable) summarizing going on, these stretches at least are verbatim. As we can see from the accurate records of the parliamentary archives, the first of these is indeed verbatim, though the second is not:

> Then you need to go to a club because the purpose of a club is *to provide entertainment*; it is to provide alcohol; it is a place of leisure. All right, the entertainment is in the form of nude and semi-nude performers, but *it is not sexually stimulating*.

The two highlighted sections here illustrate the editing process that goes on when a journalist is trying to represent the words of another. The order of the original points has been changed in 10.11, making the denial of sexual stimulation the focus. Not only that, but the word used, *titillating*, is also inaccurate, and very much more emotive than the neutral *sexually stimulating*. It may represent the original speaker as more seedy than he appears when using the neutral language that he actually employs. This may be the result of an unconscious desire to undermine his credibility with the readership, and whether or not you are in sympathy with this desire (as I am!), it is nevertheless more manipulative of the reader's viewpoint as a result of appearing to be verbatim language. The use of connotatively loaded words instead of their denotative synonyms is one common way of slanting the reporting of another's speech. It is relatively unusual to find such replacements in inverted commas, and thus implied as verbatim, but it is also true that where denotational equivalence is clear, the reader would not necessarily consider this a literal violation of honesty. The potential for abuse of DS reporting in non-fictional texts is thus quite alarming.

A final word on extract 10.11 relates to the use of what are often popularly called 'scare quotes'. They are used very frequently in the press, particularly the tabloid press, and they appear to have a range of possible meanings. Here, the following phrases are in inverted commas, and they could all be seen as scare quotes: *'gentlemen's clubs'*; *'adult entertainment'*; *'sex encounter clubs'*. The first of these appears in the middle of an IS section attributed to Stringfellow, and thus could be seen as a short stretch of DS. However, the framing of just this part of what he said with some degree of alleged accuracy in itself is a stylistic decision which the reader may well conclude has meaning of its own. In such a circumstance, the reader may conclude that the quotes are scare quotes because they imply a distance between the writer of the text and the words being quoted, and some element of disapproval. In this case, the inverted commas interpreted as scare quotes could imply the notion that something as sleazy as a lap dancing club should not be given the relatively dignified label of *'gentlemen's club'*. The other two examples are more clearly interpretable as scare quotes, with the first (*'adult entertainment'*) not clearly being quoted from anyone in particular, but implying that this is a euphemism for such men as Warr and Stringfellow and the second (*'sex encounter clubs'*) appearing to be a formal identifier (possibly from legal documents) with the scare quotes implying that this is not what the public would call them.

The following is an example of the kind of 'success story' that is published in women's magazines and slimming magazines. It is a very typical example of the merging of voices that tends to be the stylistic hallmark of these stories, which are presumably ghost-written:

10.12   At her first meeting, she was surprised at how much she weighed. 'The weight loss seemed quite daunting', she says. However, she was soon put at ease. 'Once my Leader explained everything I knew the *POINTS*® Plan would suit me.'

Suzanne classifies herself as a 'snacker', and likes to snack during the day and when she gets home from work. She could still snack, but changed her choice of snacks. 'Before I'd have a chocolate bar, now I'll have a piece of fruit or a snack bar.' She makes sure there are always snacks available – although she'll occasionally have chocolate so she doesn't feel deprived!

Things did become challenging just before she reached her goal weight. She spent about four weeks going back and forth with only ½lb to shift. 'I was so close, but the last little bit took a bit longer than I thought to shift!'

This extract includes a range of different types of speech presentation as follows:

- 'The weight loss seemed quite daunting', she says. (DS with reporting clause)
- 'Once my Leader explained everything I knew the *POINTS*® Plan would suit me.' (DS with no reporting clause. Called Free Direct Speech in earlier model)
- 'snacker' (Ambiguous. Probably scare quotes indicating a technical term from the organization promoting this story. Also possibly Suzanne's 'voice' coming through the narration.)
- She could still snack, but changed her choice of snacks. (FIS probably, as it changes the verb forms from previous sentence.)
- 'Before I'd have a chocolate bar, now I'll have a piece of fruit or a snack bar.' (DS with no reporting clause. Called Free Direct Speech in earlier model)
- She makes sure there are always snacks available – although she'll occasionally have chocolate so she doesn't feel deprived! Things did become challenging just before she reached her goal weight. She spent about four

weeks going back and forth with only ½lb to shift. (FIS because the information and the language it is given in are Suzanne's own.)
- 'I was so close, but the last little bit took a bit longer than I thought to shift!' (DS with no reporting clause. Called Free Direct Speech in earlier model)

What seems to me to happen in such stories is that the process of writing them, which is probably an interview and ghost-writing process, causes there to be a merging of voices, such that the narration includes words and phrases that might well be used by the subject of the text, and the apparent DS includes words that are more properly used by the narrator or writer. Here, the presence of some of the technical (pseudo-religious) vocabulary of weight loss systems (e.g. goal, leader) and even of a registered trade mark (*POINTS®*) in the DS causes the subject, Suzanne, to sound just like the company she is effectively advertising. Coupled with the use of a type of language which seems likely to be Suzanne's in the narration (*she could still snack; did become challenging; about four weeks; back and forth*), this means that there is little to distinguish the language of the narrator from that attributed through DS to the subject and what results is a kind of ventriloquism whereby the successful slimmer is made to mouth the words of the commercial organization.

10.5 Exercises

The following is an account of the inquest into the shooting and killing of an unarmed and innocent man, Jean Charles de Menezes, by police who mistook him for a terrorism suspect. It is full of different levels of speech and thought presentation. Try to work out what some of the cases could be categorized as. Are there any difficult cases, and how would you resolve or explain them? Most importantly, what are the ideological implications of any of the examples of speech and thought presentation? Keep in mind the possible viewpoint of the various people quoted (police witnesses etc.) as well as the reporting voice (newspaper journalist, editor etc.).

A POLICE marksman told today how his gun 'malfunctioned' at the critical moment he opened fire on Jean Charles de Menezes.

The highly-trained firearms specialist – using the code name C2 – said he was convinced the innocent Brazilian was a terrorist about to set off a bomb at Stockwell Tube station, south London.

But the Scotland Yard officer, who was accused of lying during evidence today, said his Metropolitan Police Glock pistol jammed as he fired at Mr de Menezes.

Mr de Menezes was shot seven times in the head by C2 and his colleague, C12, who both mistook him for failed suicide bomber Hussain Osman.

C2 also revealed he only shouted 'armed police' after deciding to shoot during the operation on July 22 2005.

When asked to explain why he fired six shots, C2 replied: 'At the time I fired I believed that I, and everyone else, was about to die'.

'From my position I knew that I could not access the brain stem. I could not be certain that of immediate incapacitation.

'I had to ensure that life was extinct also because of the fact I had a stoppage'.

'I could not be certain if I had lost rounds in the process.'

10.6 Further reading

The development of a comprehensive model for the presentation of speech and thought has largely taken place in the field of literary stylistics, and has demonstrated the potential for a writer to use a subtle range of voices in telling a narrative, including voices that merge the identity of characters, narrators, implied authors and the author her/himself. Leech and Short (1981: 320) make clear that it is too simplistic to claim that direct and indirect speech are just alternatives:

> This lack of fit between direct and indirect speech means that it is not possible for us to regard variants of speech presentation types as being merely syntactic variants of the same proposition. The 'equivalence' relation which holds between them is of a rather looser kind.

They proceed to investigate the different forms of speech presentation, and make a number of useful observations about the faithfulness of various types of presentation to the original words. In particular, they show how FIS is a fluid concept, defined as much by the lexical as by the syntactic features:

> Norman Page suggests that examples with subordination but which possess lexical or graphological features associated with the original DS are really IS with 'speech colouring'. In other words, he assumes that syntactic features alone determine the speech presentation category.

But this kind of account ignores the fact that the claim to faithfulness in sentences like those we discussed above seems to be the same as that found in more central examples of FIS, i.e. those where the marker of subordination is absent. We prefer to say that features from any of the three major linguistic levels might be instrumental in indicating that a particular sentence is in FIS. (Leech and Short 1981: 331)

This observation leads to Short's (1996: 289) view that 'Direct Speech and Indirect Speech are, in fact, only two places on a continuum, or cline, of speech presentation in the novel which blends the contributions of character and narrator, in different proportions at different points on the scale.' This is particularly useful when applied to non-literary texts, and where ideology and persuasion are of interest. The question of whose 'voice' one is hearing in processing a text is very significant as we may be misled about the words that someone uttered or be persuaded because of who we think uttered the words. The lack of clarity that may make a novel more interesting because of its unreliable narrator, may cause a reader of non-fiction to get the wrong end of the stick as a result.

Note that many of those who have applied speech and thought presentation analysis to literature have commented on issues that would be just as interesting when analysing non-literary texts. Here, for example, is McIntyre (2006: 32):

Genette then explains that mood may be further sub-divided into the categories of distance and perspective. These categories are not precisely explained by Genette, but it seems that distance refers to the extent to which a text exhibits narratorial mediation (or 'interference' as Leech & Short 1981: 324 describe it) and the extent to which that narratorial mediation is perceived by readers. This might be paraphrased as the extent to which readers are aware of the narrator in a text.

Such considerations may well be just as important to analysis of non-literary as literary texts, of course, because the extent to which the narrator (or journalist, commentator, advertiser etc.) is controlling what is said may be significant in how the message is received.

Note that the presentation of thought is described in many of the sources as being formally parallel to speech presentation, but functionally rather different. Simpson (1993: 23), for example, notes:

Clearly, the representation of thought requires an omniscience that is not necessary for the presentation of speech. Indeed, a parallel may be drawn between this situation and that of naturally occurring conversation where participants may report verbatim the speech of their co-participants. Reporting their thoughts in a comparable manner is, however, another matter.

This difficulty in directly experiencing others' thoughts, nevertheless, does not usually deter us from trying to represent them when it seems appropriate. This extends to the press, which increasingly seem to try and guess what is going on in the minds of politicians and other prominent people, and of course such techniques are widely used by advertising to suggest to the public what they might be thinking, and perhaps by implication what they ought to be buying.

The various models of speech and thought presentation each have something to recommend them, and the reasons why the model has evolved as it can be traced by the enthusiastic reader through Leech and Short (1981), Short (1996) and Semino and Short (2004) amongst others. Though Free Direct Speech has been abandoned now as a separate category, it is probably still worth identifying it at times, given that it does take a text to the extreme of faithfulness to the original speech, and thus has less interference from any narrator. Decisions about how exactly to use the model, then, remain for the analyst, and will depend on the nature of the investigation, the data and the purpose of the analysis itself.

Discourse presentation has been of interest to a range of scholars in different disciplines, and sub-disciplines. These include philosophers (e.g. Clark and Gerrig 1990), applied linguists (e.g. Baynham and Slembrouck 1999, Myers 1999), conversation analysts (Holt 1999, Holt and Clift 2006) and psychologists (Ravotas and Berkenkotter 1998). There is also a long tradition of studying discourse presentation within stylistics both qualitatively (e.g. Banfield 1973, Fludernik 1993, Leech and Short 1981, 2007) and quantitatively (e.g. Semino and Short 2004). Studies of discourse presentation in non-literary texts include Roeh and Nir (1990) and McKenzie (1987). So far, however, there is relatively little research which examines the ideological impact of the representations of others' speech.

11 Representing Time, Space and Society

11.1 Introduction

Much work has gone on in stylistics to define and analyse the ways in which writers of fiction, poetry and plays construct a 'world', now often called a 'text world' (Werth 1999) which the reader needs to understand to follow the narrative that is being played out. Recently, there has been a great deal of discussion about the cognitive aspects of this process whereby readers construct the world of the text in their minds (e.g. Semino and Culpeper 2002, Stockwell 2002), so that they can understand the developments in the narrative as they arise.

There has been less discussion of the cognitive aspects of texts which are not seen as constructing a fictional world, though many of the same processes must go on in order for us to understand texts. Indeed the general concept of text worlds may well help us to understand why it is that we believe texts can have a very strong affective impact not just when, for example, a poem makes you cry, but also ideologically, when texts can ensure that certain viewpoints may be readily assimilated as common sense by readers. Many of the textual practices in this book introduce the reader to aspects of the text world which may influence her/his outlook, but this chapter in particular deals with the textual processes by which the fundamental features of time and space are constructed for a text world and some of the parameters of the social world in which human participants act are set up.

We will look at a number of linguistic aspects of this construction of a time-space envelope for a text in later sections, but here it is worth considering the reasons why we are even interested in such matters. The following (invented) examples demonstrate different ways of explaining the role of the United States in world security:

11.1 We, the people of the United States, have the military power to go out into the trouble spots of the world and take democracy to the powerless and hungry there.

11.2   The United States has the military power to come into the trouble spots of the world and bring democracy to the powerless and hungry here.

11.3   The United States has the military power to enter the trouble spots of the world and give democracy to the powerless and hungry.

These three versions of essentially the same proposition, that the United States is all-powerful and can impose their version of democracy on whoever they wish, nevertheless each have slightly different points of view. Example 11.3 is probably the most neutral, as it does not seem to invite the reader to see the actions of the United States from any particular angle. There is a slight angle in the use of *give*, which emphasizes the direction of the influence, but this is unavoidable, given what the sentence is saying. The other two examples take a different slant on the sentence, Example 11.1 seeming to have the viewpoint based within the United States, since words like *go out*, deliver and *there* indicate that the recipients of their help are distant from the source of the power. Also, the use of *we the people* in addition to *the United States*, which then requires a first person verb (*have*) emphasizes that the point of view is from within that country. The other version (Example 11.2) takes a point of view from within the 'trouble spots' by using *come* rather than *go out*, *bring* rather than *take* and *here* rather than *there*.

Whilst these changes are linguistically quite small, the effect on the ideological basis of the sentence can be considerable. The context will, of course, often affect how a sentence is received, but the capacity to bring the reader into your point of view is one that may well be attractive to text producers, especially where persuasion is their aim. If the more slanted examples above were to have some more evaluative language added to them, as in the following versions, the effect of a point of view is much stronger:

11.4   We, the people of the United States, have the vision and military power to go out into the trouble spots of the world and take the gift of democracy to the powerless and hungry there.

11.5   The United States has the military power to barge into what they see as the trouble spots of the world and force their version of democracy on the powerless and hungry here.

In the next section we will examine the nature of the linguistic features that create such points of view, and this will be followed by more discussion of the ideological significance of such textual features.

11.2 A linguistic model of time, space and society

Though there are many possible ways of discussing the linguistic realizations of time, space and the human relationships that make up society, there is one linguistic model which brings them all together in a theoretical framework. This is deixis. The basic model of deixis developed from observations about how the perspective of the speaker was represented linguistically in face-to-face interaction. It was noticed that some linguistic items are less fully semantic than others, until they are placed into a context of use. These items have a shifting reference which relies on identifying the speaker or the speaker's position in space or time. Thus, for example, the personal pronouns *I* and *you* do not have the same referent throughout a conversation, but may shift each time there is a change of speaker, so that the speaker at any one time is the referent of *I* and the hearer is *you*. One of the reasons that adults often speak to little children in the third person (*Mummy is going to get your bottle*) is that it takes time for them to understand this shifting reference, whereby different speakers can be 'called' *I* or *you* at different times.

Here, we will consider the different aspects of deixis in language generally before considering its use to explain some of the effects of texts, whether literary or non-literary. The *general* effect of deixis is to construct a focus on the particular time, place and social circumstance of the interaction which is underway. Thus, at a simple level, the place where the interaction is occurring is *here*, and the time it is occurring is *now*, the speaker is *I* and the addressee is *you*. This focal position in time and space (we will come to *social* positioning later) is known as the 'deictic centre' of the speaker and the normal or default assumption for everyday interaction is that speakers are using the language in a way which assumes that they are at the deictic centre of their own speech, though they also recognize that others, including their addressees, are also at the centre of their own deixis. This ability to recognize the deictic centre of others is known as 'deictic projection' and is a significant human ability, allowing us to 'see' things from the point of view of others. It is, as we shall see in Section 11.4, also important for text processing, and can have ideological implications as a result.

The deictic system of English divides the context of interaction into those things (people, times etc.) which are close to the speaker, and those which are more remote from the speaker. Thus, place deictics use *here* for the proximal form (near to the speaker) and *there* for the distal form (further away from the speaker). This may seem simplistic, but it appears to work effectively in face-to-face conversation, so that we have a clear understanding when a speaker says *Take that chair to the dump, not this one* that s/he means the addressee to take the chair furthest away from the speaker and not the one nearby. Note that the distances are relative, and *there* may therefore refer both to the other side of the room and to the other side of the world, depending on the topic of conversation and the relative positions of the speaker and addressee.

The following are the main groups of deictic items in English, though the lists of examples are not comprehensive:

Place – adverbs (*here, there*), demonstratives (*this, these, that, those*), adverbial (often prepositional) structures (*on the right, opposite, further up the road*)

Time – verb tenses, adverbs (*then, now*), demonstratives (*this, these, that, those*), time adverbials (*later, tomorrow, afterwards, next, soon*)

Person – personal pronouns (*I, me, we, us, you*)

Social – titles (*Mr, Dr, Lord* etc.), address forms (first name, nicknames, formal names)

Note that the central examples in the lists above occur in proximal/distal pairings (*here/there; now/then*), but others are not so clearly distinguished. The general time adverbials, for example, are more or less proximal, with *soon* being more so than *later*, and *tomorrow* being (possibly, and depending on context) less proximal still. Social deixis, which was a late addition to the original model, uses address forms, titles and other referring phrases (*my dear*) to demonstrate the social distance or proximity between the speaker and addressee as well as the hierarchical relationship, if any.

Before we move on to consider the role of deixis in the processing of text as a reader or hearer, let us return to the notion of deictic projection which was introduced earlier. Though speakers assume a default deictic centre for most of the time, they may also imagine what it is like for their addressees to be at a different deictic centre, and this means that communication from different literal points of view becomes possible. Thus, for example, if a speaker is explaining how to get to his house, and knows which direction the addressee is coming from, then he can use terms like 'turn left' or 'keep straight on' or 'opposite the pub', from the point of view of the traveller, not himself.

It may be the case that deictic elements of language evolved to facilitate everyday face-to-face interactions and it may have contributed to, or been the product of, the empathy that human beings are capable of, in the form of deictic projection. However, the development of new modes and channels of communication where remoteness in time (e.g. writing) or space (e.g. telephones) or both (e.g. books) was possible, meant that the straightforward default deictic centre of the speaker was no longer the main form of point of view construction by language. This leaves the analyst with a question to answer: What is the role (if any) of deixis in these more indirect forms of communication?

The relevance of deixis to text processing is that the deictic elements which face-to-face interactants use to position themselves and each other can also be used to position the reader/hearer of a text in some kind of relation to the contents of the text. This may, for example, be by positioning the reader/hearer in the viewing position of the consciousness behind the text, whether that is the author or some kind of narrator. It may be by taking the reader on a 'journey' through a real or imagined landscape or cityscape. It may be that the reader/hearer is persuaded to take up a point of view that is time-related, such as in historical records or a historical novel. The deictic elements can help the reader to position her/his consciousness within the text concerned and this position will be the deictic centre of the text. Note that in order to position oneself at the deictic centre of a text, it is necessary to move from the default position of one's own deictic centre. If I am reading a text about the protestors against airport expansion who have been occupying Stansted airport as I write, I may find myself mentally leaving my study in Leeds, and imagining the scene on the runway in Essex. This will be aided by the deictic properties of the text, as we can see in the following radio report from the scene:

11.6   I am standing near the point where protestors cut through the perimeter fence of the airport early this morning. They are currently sitting on the runway, chained together to prevent their easy removal. Here in Essex, many families waiting to get away from the bitterly cold winter weather and businessmen in a hurry to get to meetings overseas are frustrated and angry. No one knows how long it will take to move them, but airport police are hoping to have the runway cleared before lunchtime.

Even if you are reading this months or years after the event, and even though I am writing about it one day later, the process of reading (or hearing) this report draws us into the here and now of the events themselves. The use of the first person (*I*), the present tenses (*am, are, knows* etc.), the proximal adverbs and prepositions (*here, near*) and the time reference (*lunchtime*) all create a point of view based on the reporter, and his time and place of speaking. Note that this is only reinforced by occurrences of distal deictics, such as *away from* and *overseas*, which by their very nature emphasize the proximal *here* of those stranded at Stansted.

   Some texts change the deictic centre or viewing position from time to time. In a novel, there may be frequent changes of viewpoint from character to character or from narrator to character, and in other texts too there are sometimes switches of viewpoint. Thus a news report may switch between narration and speech presentation, with the result that the reader is given a range of viewpoints on the topic concerned.[1] Some texts provide fewer clues to the viewing position of the text than others, but all texts construct (often a series of) what is known as a 'deictic field', which is the space/time envelope in which the events of the text occur. Although deictic fields have mostly been discussed in relation to the reading of fiction and other literature, we shall see that there is also a very useful application of this concept to non-fiction texts and their potential ideological impact.

What the deictic items do in texts, then, is to position the contents of the text in relation to either the real-world context (e.g. *Dear reader*) or in relation to the text world being constructed (e.g. *tomorrow* may refer to the day after the one on which the speaker is speaking in a fictional context for example). The reader of fiction is accustomed to placing him/herself psychologically in the appropriate position from which to view a fictional world and this is one of the attractions of the reading experience: the ability to 'lose oneself' in another world and identify with characters different from oneself. One way of explaining how it is that we are able to do this at all, given that we have our personal default deictic fields, is that we manage to place ourselves in the position of characters (places, times etc.) in a text because our deictic projection ability (to imagine the deixis of another) also enables to decode others' deixis in another context – that of reading.

Though reading a tax demand, a news report or a piece of propaganda is not identical to reading a novel, I would nevertheless suggest that a very similar process affects the reader of other texts, as we shall see from the examples in Section 11.4. Though there are indeed differences of detail and effect, it is first of all unlikely that the reading of fiction is a *completely* different process from reading non-fiction texts. Learning two different systems of reading and text interpretation would place a large cognitive burden on us human beings and the more likely explanation is that the process of decoding text is very similar whatever the content and context but that the effect or interpretation of the linguistic features will differ for all sorts of reasons, including the text's status as fiction or non-fiction.

Let us consider the deictic model a little more here, and in particular how it may construct certain kinds of time/space envelope. Note that together with the construction of alternative, hypothetical and indeed negated variants on 'reality' (see Chapters 8 and 9), deixis contributes to a cognitive theory of reading known as 'Text World Theory' (Werth 1999) which has been developed mainly in response to the question of how readers can envisage and understand the invented narratives of fiction and other literary forms. Here, we will consider just the deictic aspects of text world creation and their potential for naturalizing certain ideologies of time and space.

With respect to time and space, let us consider the options facing the producer of a text. These include, as a minimum:

- Deciding whether the text is primarily in the present or past tense, or whether it will project to the future.
- Deciding whether the text will focus on an individual's point of view, will aim for some kind of non-participant narrator, or will adopt an omniscient narrator style.

- In relation to the chosen narrator, deciding whether there will be an explicit or implicit preferred audience, or none.
- Deciding how to present the spatial and temporal world, and whether there will be any departures from default assumptions about norms.

These decisions will often not be made consciously, but they will be made nevertheless, and they will have effects on the reader/hearer. The textual consequences of such decisions are exemplified below, and ideological consequences will be explored in Section 11.4. Section 11.3 will explore the fact that, as with other tools of analysis in this book, there is no form-function unity in language, and as a result there is no definitive list of 'all' the deictic choices that can be made in English, and the analyst therefore needs to be constantly alert to other possibilities.

The first choice seems to be easy, how to structure the verb phrase tenses in a text. Thus Example 11.7 is the beginning of an invented news item in the past tense, whereas 11.8 is the text of an invented advert in the present tense:

11.7   Yesterday, the fourteenth victim of knife crime in a year died in St Mary's hospital. James Smith, a 15-year-old from the Putney area, was walking home from school when he was set upon by a gang of youths armed with knives.

11.8   You are in the middle of a long journey with the family when the car breaks down? What do you do? Panic? Run away? Call the local garage? Don't risk it, call the experts today and get protection for you and your family. National Transport Association. The experts in breakdown cover.

In each case there is a temporal deictic centre, which is the day of publication and assumed day of reading in the case of Example 11.7 as we can see from the use of the adverb *Yesterday*, which assumes a particular relationship between the day of the crime and the day when the report is being read. In Example 11.8, there is a time envelope of a hypothetical car journey and breakdown in the initial sentences, which may well be interpreted as generic present by a reader, and then the imperative final sentences (from *Don't risk it*) shift to the real present, with the intention of influencing the behaviour of the readers in the near future using the present tense.

To demonstrate the potential variants of personal point of view, we will consider just three alternatives for now, as the range of possibilities is rather large:

11.9   I promise you, the electorate, that I will work to improve health care.
11.10   I heard the candidate promise that she would work to improve health care.
11.11   The candidate promised that she would work to improve health care.

Here we have three of many possibilities and they demonstrate a first person (homodiegetic) narrative with an explicit audience (Example 11.9), a first person (homodiegetic) narrative from an observer, and with no explicit audience (Example 11.10) and a third person (heterodiegetic) narrative with no explicit audience (Example 11.11). There are many other possibilities, and they may have important effects, including an impact on the reader in ideological terms at times.

The other main deictic decisions a text producer is required to make, whether consciously or not, are those regarding the spatial and temporal dimensions and processes of the text world. This includes the decision not only about which pronouns to use, but whether the viewpoint will shift from person to person or remain constant; whether the viewpoint will reflect the point of view of a character, despite being in the third person; whether the shape and properties of places and artefacts will reflect the reader's own experiences and if/how the text will shift from one deictic centre to another. This notion, of the deictic centre shifting throughout a text may be important for ideological analysis, as the reader may be affected by the shifting point of view which results.

Another theory of understanding, coming out of philosophy, which works with deixis to achieve textual meaning is Possible Worlds Theory (see, for example, Ryan 1991), which has been elaborated upon by Text World Theory, but whose basic tenets remain the same. Section 11.6 will explore some of the work of those who have written on these subjects, but here I would like to introduce just one or two of the fundamental claims of Possible World Theory, so that the reader may be able to utilize them alongside deixis and deictic shift theory to explain some of the potential ideological effects of texts.

The theory of possible worlds was first conceived of to explain why it was not possible to draw any conclusions about the truth (or falsity) of utterances relating to fictitious or unknowable phenomena. Thus, the problem of how to deal with sentences such as *The Queen of the Elves is in my garden* or *God answered our prayers* is solved by hypothesizing a possible world in which there is a Queen of the Elves or God, and then establishing whether such a world would be likely to prove the truth of the sentences concerned.

Ryan (1991), then, developed a typology of such worlds as seen in texts. These include the Alternative Possible Worlds (APWs) which may represent the point of view of the participants in the narrative (whether fictional or not) and the subtypes, such as knowledge world, obligation world, wish world and intention world, each of which represents some kind of notional extension of the perceived alternative possible world of the relevant character or participant. We will consider the ideological significance of textually constructed alternative worlds in Section 11.4 below. Note here, however, that the sub-world categories have something in common with other tools of analysis that we have seen in earlier chapters. Thus, epistemic modality is one of the triggers that will construct a hypothetical or belief world in relation to the text producer, deontic modality may give rise to an obligation world and boulomaic modality can cause a shift to a wish world. Note that modality only triggers those worlds envisaged by the text producer, so other triggers will be the cause of such worlds in relation to other (third person) participants.

One of the concepts arising from Possible Worlds Theory is that of the Principle of Minimal Departure (Ryan 1991: 48ff) which suggests that in the absence of explicit information to the contrary, the recipient of a text will assume that the world of the text is identical in all respects to the actual world (that of the recipient him/herself). This principle is useful when we wish to explain how it is that science fiction or fantasy novels work, since the worlds they describe are assumed to be 'normal' until something unusual happens or is described. Thus, an opening sentence such as *Louise got up early that morning and fed her dinosaur before podding off to work in the translator* will challenge readers to accept a change in their notions of the world to the extent that dinosaurs can coexist with humans (as pets) and that there is probably some kind of a vehicle which is caused to move with the help of a translator. Other elements of the story such as getting up, feeding and going to work are familiar and the reader is likely to take them at face value. Writers of such fiction rely on the Principle of Minimal Departure to carry their readers along. A novel which was so dissimilar to the experienced world of the reader that nothing at all could be recognized would not be read, and the reader would have no way into its meaning. Here is the same basic sentence with less in the way of similarity to the Actual World we live in: *Lobee sleered surdly that ning and hud her dinosaur before podding off to farn in the reecher.* Even then, we recognize the grammatical words, like before and off to, so we still have a notion that time and space work much as they do in our world. If we got rid of all such links to our experience, there would no longer be any way of use accessing the meaning at all. We will see later that the Principle of Minimal Departure is useful for persuasion.

11.3 Form and function

Like the other chapters in this book, this one deals with a textual process (of representing time, space and society) which cuts across other form-function linguistic systems. Thus, we have already seen that modality can be associated with triggering an Alternative Possible World in a text, so that the textual function of hypothesizing and the one we are concerned with here clearly have some overlap. Nevertheless, deixis and possible worlds theory jointly help us to understand how texts produce a particular set of effects that construct a mental image of a world or worlds which will have some or all of its features identical to the one we inhabit.

Like other models we have encountered before, deixis is based on some core items which embody the notions of distal and proximal deixis, centred on the speaker (there/here, this/that, now/then etc.) and conceptualizing time and space in similar ways. The deixis of person is less symmetrical, though, as there are not only proximal (*I, we*) and distal (*you*) pronouns, but also what we might think of as 'more distal' ones (*he, she, they*).

The question of the meaning of deictic elements is also not straightforward, and the personal pronouns can be used to demonstrate this. We might expect the likely effect of proximal deixis would be to draw the reader towards the deictic centre of the first person speaker, thus making her/him susceptible to that speaker's ideology. However, readers are able to deictic shift within texts not only because of the deictic projection they constantly experience in everyday life. The other, more common, everyday experience is for us to interact with others, in the second person role from their point of view. Thus, we are able to identify BOTH with a first person speaking voice in a text AND a second person speaking voice. Compare the following examples:

11.12   I have seen these babies dying of cholera with mothers too weak to help them.

11.13   You should see these babies dying of cholera with mothers too weak to help them.

It is difficult to choose between these versions as far as the reader is concerned. We are drawn into such an emotive scene anyway, and the proximal use of *these* helps to confirm this effect. But there are two different ways of identifying with the producer (or narrator) of this sentence and they depend on deictic projection in Example 11.12, and the normal assumptions of interaction in Example 11.13, whereby the reader assumes identity with the referent of *you*. What is certainly clear, is that both of these options is more likely to cause the reader to abandon her/his own default deictic centre than the following, third person version:

11.14   She has seen these babies dying of cholera with mothers too weak to help them.

Even then, the use of *these* seems to imply the presence of the authorial persona in the same deictic field as the babies, and this draws the reader in. A final move away from reader-identification with the deictic centre of the sentence would involve changing this to a distal version:

11.15   She has seen those babies dying of cholera with mothers too weak to help them.

Though these examples are all similar in their proposition (that someone saw the scenes described), they can have rather different emotive effects, and this is one of the ways that the construction of point of view, and the drawing in of readers to identify with participants' viewpoints, is a powerful tool in the persuasive text producer's toolbox.

11.4 Ideological effects

The most important effect of deixis in ideological terms is the ability of a text producer to create a deictic centre that causes the reader to place him/herself mentally at that point in the deictic field created by the text. In some senses, this is an inevitable consequence of the normal functioning of language, as we saw in relation to deictic projection. The human ability to understand that someone facing him or her experiences concepts such as left or right in reverse underlies our ability to read texts about things which are not familiar to us, whether that is because they concern unreal things (e.g. science fiction) or real but unfamiliar things (e.g. a war overseas). This basic deictic ability, coupled with the ability to imagine possible worlds, allows us to process texts (both fiction and non-fiction) on a wide variety of topics that we may know little or nothing about. The Principle of Minimal Departure will fill in any gaps by assuming a default characteristic of the world being created in a text. However, it is interesting to note that many of the ideologically most interesting texts will be trying to convince their readers/hearers that they are representing the Actual World, when there is a clear possibility that some people would find the text's claims do not match their experience of the Actual World. Thus, the campaigning literature of pro-lifers or pro-choice supporters in the abortion debate, those in favour of, or against, fox hunting, those for and against nuclear weapons and so on would all be convinced that their version of the Actual World was correct.

Let us consider the following two examples, adapted from newspaper opinion columns:

11.16   So the real issue is not where our five million immigrants have come from, nor where they happen to be now.

The real question is whether we need another five million people on this island, adding to a population which is already at record levels.

11.17   Population shifts, increasing scarcity and the wanton consumption of arable land and natural resources (renewable and non-renewable) are pushing us ever closer to global disaster.

This is a crucial and sobering point in history. Despite setbacks and mistakes, progressive national and local governments are taking the initiative. There is still time for corrective action.

Our future is very much ours to decide. It will not ultimately depend on technology or the economy. What we leave to those that come after us will be determined by us, and whether or not we rise to the challenge we now face.

Notice that both of these extracts are written in first person and present tense formats, so that the reader's own deictic field will be bound in with the timescale, whether or not it is being read at or soon after the time of publication, or later still. The use of the inclusive *we* first person plural pronoun is particularly effective in causing the reader to shift into the viewpoint of the text. Note that we can be rather vague as to its precise meaning, so that in Example 11.16 it is presumably meant to refer to the population of Great Britain, whilst in 11.17 it refers more widely to the human race.

In addition to the tenses and pronouns, there is also some considerable use of deixis to create a deictic centre which the reader will identify with. In Example 11.16, there is the use of *come*, which indicates movement towards the deictic centre, the adverb *now*, emphasizing the present moment and the demonstrative *this*, placing the deictic centre firmly on the island of Great Britain. In Example 11.17, the use of *closer to* indicates movement away from the deictic centre, the demonstrative pronoun, *this*, focuses on the temporal centre, and *face* places the reader in the deictic centre of the text's narrating 'voice', facing towards the challenges of climate change.

Though it is one of the more subtle of the ideological tools of analysis in this book, deixis (and the effects of possible world construction) show how the reader/hearer is taken up by the text, relinquishing his or her own personal deictic centre to take up a mental viewing position from within the text. Evidence from psychological experiments on reading (Emmott 1999) seems to suggest that the longer a reader spends engaging with a textual deictic field, the more their own default centre fades, though of course it is possible to return to the Actual World at any moment when reading. Nevertheless, these theories together imply that lengthy engagement with textual deixis and the effect of deictic projection into viewpoints expressed in texts could have long-lasting effects on the viewpoint of the reader. Note that the reader of non-fictional texts, even if s/he is at odds with the text s/he is reading, may well have to temporarily suspend their deictic centre to see the world as the text sees it. This is surely one of the ways in which texts can affect our outlook on life.

11.5 Exercises

The following is the opening passage of the famous 'I have a dream' speech, by Martin Luther King. Comment on its use of deixis and the potential effect on the audience at the time of its delivery. How might a contemporary reader of this transcript relate to it?

11.18   I am happy to join with you today in what will go down in history as the greatest demonstration for freedom in the history of our nation.

Five score years ago, a great American, in whose symbolic shadow we stand today, signed the Emancipation Proclamation. This momentous decree came as a great beacon light of hope to millions of Negro slaves, who had been seared in the flames of withering injustice. It came as a joyous daybreak to end the long night of their captivity. But one hundred years later, the Negro still is not free. One hundred years later, the life of the Negro is still sadly crippled by the manacle of segregation and the chains of discrimination. (Martin Luther King)

My response to this extract can be found in the Appendix.

11.6 **Further reading**

Introductory texts, such as Chapman (2006: 122–4) and Jeffries (2006: 190–1, 229–30) in this series often give a brief overview of what deixis is, though for a more comprehensive account of the basics of deixis, Lyons (1977) and Levinson (1983) are helpful, the latter contextualizing deixis within Pragmatics and giving more detail than the former.

This chapter also touched on developments in stylistics which use deixis as a founding notion, and these include deictic shift theory, which is clearly explained by McIntyre (2006: chapter 4) in his book on point of view in drama, though the original discussion of deictic shifting can be seen in Duchan et al. (1995). Similarly, Text World Theory (Gavins 2007, Werth 1999) and Possible Worlds Theory (Ryan 1991) are dependent to a certain extent on textual features such as deixis for creating the conceptual worlds of the text concerned.

Appendix – Commentaries on Exercises

Chapter 2 Naming and describing

In Section 2.4, the following extracts from an adapted newspaper editorial were analysed and discussed in relation to their potential for ideological effects:

2.34   Barely a day goes by without more special pleading coming from a different part of the public sector.
2.35   But the real story of the credit crunch and the ensuing recession is the suffering being caused to the wealth-creating business sector.
2.36   Small companies and the self-employed have no bottomless pit of taxpayers' money to raid when the going gets tough.

The sentences below continue the text that was discussed in that section, and the exercises were aimed at continuing the analysis of naming practices in a similar fashion:

2.37   On the contrary, the tax authorities are famed for their lack of sympathy when a business hits cash-flow problems.

This sentence names something called the tax authorities as Subject, which may be a relatively common way of naming those involved, including, presumably, the Inland Revenue. But the more ideologically interesting noun phrase in this sentence is the one in the prepositional phrase beginning with for. The sentence as a whole is made up of Subject, Predicator and Adverbial (prepositional phrase) and it is the latter that contains an assumption worthy of investigation. The tax authorities are given no chance of answering the charge that they are unsympathetic to businesses in trouble, because their lack of sympathy when a business hits cash-flow problems is not a proposition, but a name. The sentence turns on whether they are (or are not) famed for this quality, and the reader is not invited to debate their lack of sympathy at all.

2.38 And the big banks, which have been advanced so much public money themselves, are prone to charging rip-off lending rates to business borrowers.

This sentence has a SPC structure, with the Subject and part of the Complement being named in ideologically charged ways. The Subject is as follows:

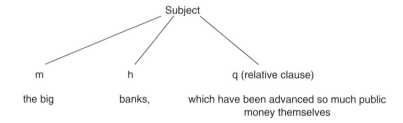

The existence of big banks may not be particularly contentious, but when the relative clause is included within the noun phrase, the reader is expected to accept the existence of not only big banks, but big banks which have been given a great amount of public money. This may be true, but it would also be possible to argue that the amount banks have been given is not a great deal (compared, say, with the cost of the military). However, the reader who may wish to argue such a case is not given the opportunity when the noun phrase incorporates this assumption.

2.39 Entrepreneurs are the life-blood of the economy. Operating without a financial safety net they generate the wealth and employment that keeps UK plc afloat.

Here, there are two sentences, the first of which is a straightforward proposition, using the verb to be surrounded by a Subject noun phrase (Entrepreneurs) and a Complement noun phrase (the life-blood of the economy). The proposition can be questioned, disagreed with or accepted, but the relationship between Subject and Complement is clearly asserted. In contrast, the second sentence here includes a noun phrase that names a phenomenon which is not so clearly up for debate. This is the Object the wealth and employment that keeps UK plc afloat. Note that in this case, the question of whether it is these people who generate the wealth and so on is also a proposition, and thus one we could theoretically argue with. The noun phrase, however, does not easily allow for contradiction and the notion that there is such a thing as wealth and employment and that it keeps UK plc afloat is assumed.

2.40 So, at a time when Labour is talking about indulging in another public spending binge, Tory leader David Cameron is right to focus instead on the needs of small firms.

In this sentence, there are two noun phrases which seem to incorporate ideologically motivated notions. First, there is the repeated ideology that spending public money is a wasteful and careless thing to do, which is captured by the phrase another public spending binge. Note, incidentally, that there is a logical as well as an existential presupposition included here, as another presupposes that there have been such binges before. Here, it is the choice of the head noun, *binge*, itself, which captures the negative evaluation of the writer towards the use of public money. The other noun phrase worth mentioning here is the needs of small firms, which may seem neutral, though it is cast as the opposite of the *binge* (see Chapter 4 on creation of opposites), and clearly sets out to name a phenomenon which readers are expected to accept together with the implicature (see Chapter 7) that their needs are valid.

2.41 If Britain wants to avoid a return to the mass unemployment of the early Eighties then paying heed to the essential interests of those who provide millions of people with highly productive jobs is absolutely essential.

In Example 2.41, the first noun phrase of any complexity is *a return to the mass unemployment of the early Eighties* which is reasonably factual, though of course the undesirability of unemployment is a naturalized ideology. Readers may be surprised by this thought, that unemployment in some possible version of the world, might be seen as desirable, but it only takes a moment's consideration to realize that economic activity, though it may bring us the lifestyle we are used to, also produces many of the problems of modern life as well, and that a society which divorced formal employment from the means of living (i.e. money) is at least possible to imagine, if difficult to achieve in practice. The other complex noun phrase in this example is similar to one discussed in relation to Example 2.39. In this case, it is *those who provide millions of people with highly productive jobs* which is co-referential with the small firms of the earlier example (2.40). Thus, we have a noun phrase as it were renaming small firms as those who provide millions of people with highly productive jobs. Again, it may be argued that this is factually true, that small firms do indeed provide many millions of jobs, but this would depend partly on one's definition of highly productive in relation to jobs, and the real point is that the truth or falsity of the relationship between the small firms (those who) and the provision of all these jobs is not open to debate here, as it is part of a simple naming practice.

Chapter 3 Representing actions/events/states

The following is an introduction to the discussion of capital punishment on the BBC's ethics website (http://www.bbc.co.uk/ethics/capitalpunishment/). Comment on the transitivity choices that have been made here, and what their ideological effects might be. How could you change the transitivity choices, and what differences in ideology would the changes produce?

3.44   The question as to whether or not it *is* morally acceptable for the state *to execute* people, and if so under what circumstances, *has been debated* for centuries.
The ethical problems *involved include* the general moral issues of punishment with the added problem of whether it *is* ever morally right *to deprive* a human being of life.

In the repeated version of the extract above, I have highlighted the Predicators (verb phrases), each of which represents a transitivity choice on the part of the writer. In the first sentence, the main clause has the Predicator, *has been debated*, which is a passive version of a Verbalization process. Thus, the fact of there having been a long-drawn-out debate is placed at the highest level of structure, with the subordinate clauses carrying Relational Intensive (*is*) and Material Action Intention (*to execute*) at first and second levels of embedding respectively. Here is a diagram of their relative levels, with some detail left out for clarity:

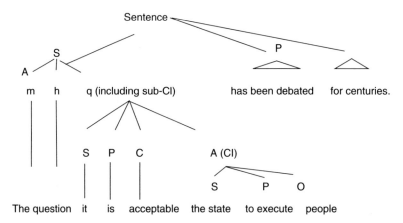

The BBC would probably defend its transitivity choices here, as this is intended to be a neutral introduction to an open debate, but it is interesting to see how the actual material action of killing people is at the lowest level in a three-level structure. The second sentence also has an interesting relationship between transitivity choice and level of structure (see Chapter 6 for more on levels of structure and prioritizing). In this sentence, the main Predicator is a rather general Relational verb, *include*, which tells us that the Object (everything from the verb onwards in this case) is part of the Subject (The ethical problems involved). Note that the Subject also has a transitivity choice (*involved*) which is also a Relational process. The really interesting part, though, is the Object, which consists of two conjoined noun phrases, the second of which has a very similar set of relationships to those in the first sentence:

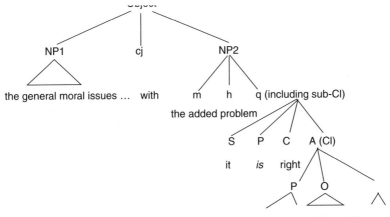

to deprive a human being of life.

So, both sentences in this extract demonstrate the same transitivity choices, and priorities, with neutral verbs in the main clauses (*debate*, *include*) followed at lower level structures by Relational Intensive verbs (*is*) within which the real question of the Material Actions concerned (*execute/deprive*) are embedded still lower. This reflects an ideology that is perhaps embodied by the BBC, in which discussion and debate is seen as the primary process of importance, followed by judgement (is acceptable/right) and only then by action. A political party, or perhaps a Charity or Action Group may well demonstrate different transitivity priorities in relation to similar topics.

The following is a passage adapted from accounts of Unidentified Flying Object (UFO) sightings. What do you think is the ideology of the writer? What transitivity choices has s/he made, and do they support the case being made? How could different transitivity choices affect this report?

3.45   Four passengers aboard a Boeing 737 *reported* a 'wingless projectile', *flying* underneath the aircraft as they *were taking off*, whilst on a flight from Gatwick to Hamburg, in June 1991. They *informed* the pilot, who then *reported* the incident to the Ministry of Defence and the Civil Aviation

Authority. Another report was made the following month by the crew of a 737 that *was descending* into Gatwick. The crew *described seeing* a 'dark, lozenge shaped object' *zooming* by the side of the aircraft. Air traffic control *confirmed* that they *had* a 'primary target' on their radar screens and *warned* another aircraft that *was descending* behind the 737 *to take* evasive action. This aircraft *had to take* a sharp turn *to avoid* the unidentified object, which *appeared to be heading* straight towards them, but then *turned* away.

The transitivity choices here demonstrate a tendency by this writer to choose the Verbalization processes as the main Predicators and other process types as subordinated Predicators. Thus, of the verb phrases in the extract (highlighted here), all except the final main Predicator are Verbalization processes, with sentence 6 presenting the action taken by the aircraft (had to take evasive action). The actions supposedly taken by the UFO are all at subordinate levels, and in some cases embedded two levels down. These are highlighted in the following table which shows all the Predicators in the extract:

Sentence	Main Predicator	Subordinate level 1	Subordinate level 2
1	reported	*flying*	were taking off
2	informed	reported	
3	was made	was descending	
4	described	seeing	*zooming*
5	confirmed warned	had, was descending,	to take
6	had to take	to avoid,	appeared, *to be heading, turned*

In the final sentence, the actions of the UFO are embedded below the already subordinate Mental Perception verb, appeared.

The choices made by this writer, then, indicate that s/he is not assuming that the reported sightings of a UFO are anything other than that – reported. S/he chooses to indicate that these are not her/his own sightings by telling a story based mostly on the reports of others. This would indicate that the writer has an ideology with some level of scepticism since all the supposed activities of the UFO are dependent on someone else's reporting.

Chapter 4 Equating and contrasting

The following sentences, adapted from a range of sources, each construct some kind of unconventional opposition. Write a paragraph on each one, using the previous section as your model, and commenting both on the technical way in which the opposition is constructed and also on the ideological implications of the resulting semantic relationship. The parentheses after each example give a context in which you might find the sentence:

4.18   I'm not a manipulator, I'm a manager. (spoken by a spin-doctor)

This sentence uses a pair of parallel structures to juxtapose two words which have phonological similarities since both are multisyllabic and both begin with the phoneme /m/. In addition, there is negation in the first and not the second clause, resulting in the clear contrasting of the two words, *manipulator* and *manager*. Both refer to people and the way they deal with others who may be under their control. Though these are not normally opposites in English, the context makes it clear that we are to see them as opposed here, and that the second (*manager*) is to be seen as the preferred of the two. Although some readers might normally react adversely to the idea of managers who are seen in some circles as unproductive and intrusive, the text forces even such a reader to see the difference between manipulating and managing in a different light, with managing seen as benign compared to the underhand and self-serving connotations of *manipulator*. The ideology of the speaker, then, is one of seeing politics as a simple question of organization, and not driven by personal ambition or philosophy.

4.19   There is real enthusiasm for Labour. It's not just loathing for the Tories. (written by a political commentator before the General Election in 1997)

Here, the contrast is made by the near-parallel structures, though note that the larger part of the structure is different. However, the *X for Y* frame also contains two relatively conventional opposites within the British electoral system, *Labour* and *Tories*, which encourages the reader to see the other parts of the parallel structures also in oppositional terms. These are *enthusiasm* and *loathing*, which although not conventional opposites, certainly contain positive and negative evaluation respectively as part of their semantics. The ideology of the writer, that there was something about New Labour that appealed to the electorate in 1997, is thus underlined by this opposition.

4.20   Marina says she hopes for a natural birth, 'though I'll probably start off with whale music and end up with an epidural!' (Reader's story in a pregnancy magazine)

This example demonstrates the extremes of potential in textual creation of opposites. Here, there is a trigger which might be seen as similar to those called 'transitive' by Davies (2008), and which marks out the two possibilities, and the switch from one (*whale music*) to the other (*an epidural*). The reader may be confused at first as to why a kind of communication system of one of the Earth's largest mammals should be contrasted with a drug administered during labour. The context of advice to pregnant women may start to unravel the mystery, and some may know that certain forms of relaxation, including listening to whale music, have been recommended by experts in natural childbirth. So we find that what these two share is their aim, which is to help a woman cope with the pain of childbirth, and their salient difference is that epidurals would be seen as high tech and interventionist, whereas whale music would be seen as natural, though of course some might argue that this is an evaluative view of the two.

4.21   Publishing 12 indifferent cartoons a few weeks ago was justified. In today's climate, it is plainly wrong. (Tabloid newspaper editorial)

Example 4.21 is another case of near-parallel structures, at least to the extent that the two have *X is Y* at their centre. The first sentence has a SAP structure, and the second has a ASPC structure, so only the position of the Adverbial (a *few weeks ago/in today's climate*) is different. Note, however, that even these adverbials help to set up the opposite, since they amount to a *then-now* conventional pairing, albeit in different words. The writer holds back from using the conventional opposite in the evaluation, since that would force him/her to use *right* in opposition to *wrong*. Instead s/he uses *justified* as the opposite of *wrong*. The subject of each sentence, of course, has the same referent, the publishing of the cartoons, and this helps to underline the opposition in Complement position, since we are expecting the judgement to change from one to the other.

The following is an extract from the 'I have a dream' speech on civil rights by Martin Luther King. Examine the opposition-creation in this text. What ideological issues are raised by it?

4.22   This is no time to engage in the luxury of cooling off or to take the tranquilizing drug of gradualism. Now is the time to make real the promises of democracy. Now is the time to rise from the dark and desolate valley of segregation to the sunlit path of racial justice. Now is the time to lift our nation from the quick sands of racial injustice to the solid rock of brotherhood. Now is the time to make justice a reality for all of God's children.

This extract, as in so many political speeches, uses parallel structures to provide a framework and also a kind of rhythmic musicality to the text. The repetition of the SPC structure, Now is the time, as the opening of each sentence after the first allows the remainder of each sentence to be expanded by means of a subordinate clause:

- to make real the promises of democracy
- to rise from the dark and desolate valley of segregation to the sunlit path of racial justice
- to lift our nation from the quick sands of racial injustice to the solid rock of brotherhood
- to make justice a reality for all of God's children.

These sentences form a list of actions which the speaker is proposing as the opposite to the potential inactivity that he fears would undo the progress that the Civil Rights movement had already made:

- This is no time to engage in the luxury of cooling off or to take the tranquilizing drug of gradualism.

This initial sentence is negated, so that with the positive forms of the same structure in the rest of the passage, it triggers an opposition where on the one hand there is lack of activism (*the luxury of cooling off*) or only small steps of progress (*the tranquilizing drug of gradualism*) and on the other there is the list of actions in the following sentences. Note that even within the first sentence, there is an opposition trigger in the conjunction or. So, as well as contrasting relative inaction with activism, he is also contrasting in a smaller context complete inaction (*the luxury of cooling off*) with slow progress (*the tranquilizing drug of gradualism*). This creates a kind of hierarchy of opposition, which is the scaffolding of his argument at this point:

Inaction	vs.	**Action**
complete vs. relative		make real the promises ...
		rise from the valley ...
		lift our nation ...
		make justice a reality.

This passage, then, uses parallel structures and negation to create the overarching opposition between political action (positive and therefore desired) and inaction (negative and therefore not desired). Within inaction as a concept, we also find a contrast between the two kinds of inaction that he sets up between doing nothing and doing something but so slowly that it has no effect. This effectively answers those who were arguing that the Civil Rights movement was somehow overreacting and that things were anyway moving in the right direction. Within action we find not another contrast but a list of actions which sum up his vision. Chapter 5 deals with questions of listing versus apposition, and if I was completing an analysis of this passage I would wish to discuss to what extent this list consists of different items, and to what extent they are all rewordings of the same basic concept. For now, I will simply note that any text analysed in the way described in this book will usually draw on a range of linguistic features to construct ideological content.

Chapter 5 Exemplifying and enumerating

Look at Examples 5.20 to 5.24 and consider the enumeration/exemplification/listing issues that they raise. Start by describing what they contain, using the commentaries in the previous section as your model. Then consider whether they raise ideological issues for the reader, and what kind of issues these are. Generic contextual information is given in parentheses after each example.

5.20   The role of the organization is to assess on a *comprehensive, objective, open and transparent* basis the *scientific, technical* and *socio-economic* information relevant to understanding *the scientific basis of risk of human-induced climate change, its potential impacts* and *options for adaptation and mitigation*. (A scientific organization's website)

This single, rather long, sentence contains three lists.The first is the list of adjectives used to modify the noun *basis; comprehensive, objective, open* and *transparent*. As a four-part list, this appears to indicate not a symbolic completeness, as you would find with a three-part list, but a real list of genuine options. However, it is interesting to note that the difference between the final two items, *open* and *transparent* is more apparent than real, and that the writer may possibly have made the mistake of overdoing the emphasis on the good qualities of the organization to the extent of effectively repeating the last one. As a critical reader, this may well alert me to the organization's evident desire to be seen as *open/transparent* which is a naturalized ideology in our society. This in turn may lead to enquiries about the truth of such assertions. In other words, as with the overuse of strong epistemic modality (see Chapter 9), the emphasis may undermine its credibility.

The next list is a three-part one, also a list of adjectives modifying a noun: *the scientific, technical* and *socio-economic information*. Here, the organization asserts its coverage of all the factors affecting climate change, and the three-part list serves the symbolic function of indicating that all options are included. Note that there are other possible ways of covering the same ground, since scientific and technical are not always necessarily separate;

social and economic could be separated, and there may be other factors not included here (political):

- the scientific and socio-economic information (two-part list)
- the scientific, technical, social and economic information (four-part list)
- the scientific, technical, social, economic and political information (five-part list).

However, the important point about the use of a three-part list is that it is not normally questioned by readers, and will serve as a general indicator of completeness without being comprehensive. The problem with four- or five-part lists is that they begin to make the reader think in more detail, and this may lead to her/him coming up with other aspects that the writer has forgotten to include. It is far easier, then, to use a three-part list and let it stand for completeness.

This is also the argument which explains the use of another three-part list in this extract: *the scientific basis of risk of human-induced climate change, its potential impacts and options for adaptation and mitigation*. This time, it is a list of three complete noun phrases, which together appear to cover the three main questions about climate change: what is it, what will it do and how can we deal with it. Note, however, that there is an implicit four-part list here, since the final part divides into two (*adaptation and mitigation*) which are actually potential opposites. Whether we just get used to climate change or find ways to mitigate its effects could be seen as not just contrasting, but also contradictory strategies, but these are rolled into a single item in the list. There is an underlying naturalized ideology here, as the assumption that we will find ways to cope with climate change by variously adapting and mitigating its effects are presented as concurrent rather than options. The assumption that climate change may be avoided by more drastic action now is altogether ignored here, in favour of an assumption that it will happen and that a range of reactions will be required.

5.21   local and regional agencies should use existing planning powers to bring partners together to tackle the underlying economic causes of decline *by tackling worklessness, promoting enterprise, and giving people the skills to progress.* (A government ministry's website)

This extract uses a three-part list of subordinate clauses which sum up the ministry's view of how to tackle the underlying economic causes of decline. The three options here, include a rather general one (*tackling worklessness*), which possibly incorporates the others as well as other options that are not listed here. The ones that are listed in the second and third items indicate the current ideology of independence and self-reliance that is the aspiration for all members of society so that they should be given skills and encouraged to be enterprising, whereas other ideologies at other times and in other places might have listed here things like creating socially useful jobs in the public sector, supporting alternative forms of lifestyle not reliant on traditional employment and so on.[1]

5.22 We humans are by and large pretty obsessed with how we look and take any measures available to ensure we *appear as good as possible* at all times. Such measures can be as simple and everyday as *a new hairstyle, new clothes, make-up, tattoos and so on.* (A website advertising cosmetic surgery)

This extract lists a number of *simple* and *everyday* measures for looking good, in a five-part list. It is taken from a website advertising measures that are anything but *simple* and *everyday*, so it presumably aims to reassure potential customers that there are times when drastic measures are also desirable. The interesting aspect of the five-part list, which would normally indicate that it is a real list of genuine options, is that first of all it has a last part which is open-ended (*and so on*), indicating that after all it is not complete. Second, it includes items that for my generation, gender and background would not be a normal part of *simple* and *everyday* measures: tattoos. The tattoo has, it appears, now joined make-up and clothes as a normal (naturalized) part of beauty ideology.

5.23 We would all like to be part of a *safe, prosperous and healthy* community. A community where everyone has the right to the same *opportunities, freedom and respect.* Somewhere we can be proud of. (A government ministry's website)

Governments wish their citizens to believe that they are in tune with their desires and this example is typical of the kind of statement that often precedes policy statements and manifesto promises. There are two three-part lists, each one symbolic in nature, indicating that all options are covered. No doubt we could think of other adjectives in the first case and nouns in the second, which could be added just as appropriately:

- a safe, prosperous, happy and healthy community
- the same opportunities, freedom, wealth and respect.

Note that once you start to make four-part and longer lists, the real meaning of the included items becomes more salient and readers may begin to think more carefully about the implications of those listed. Thus, to believe that citizens wish for happiness or wealth (my added items) might cause difficulties for governments that cannot deliver the first and would have to espouse communist policies to deliver the second. It is much safer, then, to assert that what people want is the generic contents of a three-part list which is likely to be skimmed over in the reading process, rather than considered in detail.

The following is a more extended passage from the home page of the Communities and Local Government Office of the British government in 2008. Write an analysis and interpretation of the enumeration and/or exemplification that is to be found in this text, and the potential ideological effects of these.

5.24   Communities and Local Government is working hard to create *thriving, sustainable, vibrant* communities that improve everyone's quality of life. To achieve this we are:

- *building more and better homes – and reducing homelessness*
- *improving local public services*
- *regenerating areas to create more jobs*
- *working to produce a sustainable environment*
- *tackling anti-social behaviour and extremism*

Communities and Local Government sets policy on *local government, housing, urban regeneration, planning and fire and rescue.* We have responsibility for all race equality and community cohesion related issues in England and for *building regulations, fire safety and some housing issues* in England and Wales. The rest of our work applies only to England.

(http://www.communities.gov.uk/corporate/about/ 27/10/08)

The initial sentence in this extract includes a symbolic three-part list of adjectives modifying the noun communities: *thriving, sustainable, vibrant.* Like Example 5.23, this appears to cover all the options of the kind of community that citizens might desire. Note, however, that *thriving* and *sustainable* are quite close in meaning when applied to communities and vibrant might mean full of lively young (but possibly drunken) people which is not conducive to family life and is thus not automatically desired by all citizens, some of whom crave a quieter existence. After this opening sentence, the extract appears to become far less symbolic in its use of lists. The bullet points, for example, look like a set of action points or areas of strategy, and may well be so. However, it is noticeable that these are relatively vague in setting out what they really involve, so that the reader may be forgiven for not being clear about what precisely is involved in working to produce a *sustainable environment* or *tackling anti-social behaviour.*

The highlighted features in the paragraph below the bullet points seem more real and include a five-part list (*local government, housing, urban regeneration, planning and fire and rescue*) and a three-part list (*building regulations, fire safety and some housing issues*) both of which appear to be complete and uncomplicated by other potential members or vagueness. These are most likely statutory obligations of the ministry, and thus not open to manipulation. There may be an interesting lesson for the critical reader in this passage, which is that the combination of real and symbolic lists could make the latter more difficult to discern, and ideological influence harder to detect as it takes place.

Finally, consider another passage from the 'I have a dream' speech by Martin Luther King. The italicized part looks like a list. Is it a simple enumeration? What are the issues raised by this listing?

5.25   And when this happens, when we allow freedom to ring, when we let it ring from every village and every hamlet, from every state and every city, we will be able to speed up that day when *all of God's children, black men and white men, Jews and Gentiles, Protestants and Catholics*, will be able to join hands and sing in the words of the old Negro spiritual, 'Free at last! free at last! thank God Almighty, we are free at last!'

This passage includes a list of types of people which appears to combine apposition and listing. Although it looks like a simple list, the first item appears to be the summary of the others, and thus stands in apposition to the others. So, *all of God's children* is then exemplified by the three sets of opposites *black men and white men, Jews and Gentiles, Protestants and Catholics*. These are not, clearly, the only religions in the world, and one could also argue about whether black and white covers all skin types. However, the context in the United States of the 1960s meant that these were three of the main causes of division at the time, and he was attempting to unite them by incorporating them into the description *all of God's children*. The fact that he ends up with a three-part list of items means that he appears to symbolically include everyone, though from our perspective in the twenty-first century, this may not seem to be the case. Note that another leader, Barack Obama, uses a similar tactic in his inauguration speech as the first black US president, in 2009:

We are a nation of *Christians and Muslims, Jews and Hindus, and non-believers*. We are shaped by every language and culture, drawn from every end of this Earth.
http://www.nytimes.com/2009/01/20/us/politics/20text-obama.html?

In the world constructed as West versus Islam by his predecessor, George Bush[2], President Obama uses a three-part list evocative of King's by mentioning five belief systems (including non-believers), but in a three-part structure. He does this for the same reason – symbolic completeness of his coverage. Whilst it is easy on reflection to think of all the world religions which are left out (e.g. Buddhist, Sikh), this is not the point. Obama simply wants to indicate all the US citizens in one simple list, and his precise choice of terms reflects the reality of twenty-first-century politics and US foreign policy whereas Dr King's reflected his own times.

Chapter 6 Prioritizing

The following extracts are versions of texts concerning police accountability, repossession of homes, debt management and injury claims respectively. They have been changed in some details, to make the analysis clearer. Think about how they have prioritized different parts of their content over others, and write commentaries explaining their structure, perhaps by pointing out some of the alternatives. Then comment on the ideological significance of the prioritizing choices that have been made.

6.19   What this also relates to is *the tradition of the police being allowed to collaborate on crafting a story, a commonly agreed version of events*, whereas members of the public would be questioned separately to establish facts and veracity of testimony. So with the police proving themselves to have no superior morals or professional standards they should have to follow *the same rules of investigation that are applied to everyone else*.

The focal points of these two complex sentences are highlighted above. In the first case, the focus is on the fact that the legal system allows the police to operate as a unified team in producing evidence against defendants, and this is prioritized over the description of the witnesses whose treatment is included in an optional Adverbial clause (*whereas members of the public would be questioned separately to establish facts and veracity of testimony*). What makes this particularly interesting ideologically is that the writer is clearly trying to represent police practice in a negative light, and the language used in this focal clause element is emotively charged with the use of *collaborate* (pejorative connotations), *craft* (reminiscent of crafty?) and *story* (connotations of fiction). The relatively low focus on what happens with the public is accompanied by a neutral choice of vocabulary which sounds almost technical and is connotatively formal by comparison (*questioned separately to establish facts and veracity of testimony*).

The second sentence has its focus on the desired outcome of this debate, which is that police witnesses should follow *the same rules of investigation that are applied to everyone else*. The fact that this is the focus means that there is more scope to question it on the reader's behalf. But it is also the case that a relatively low priority subordinate clause at the beginning of the sentence is thereby glossed over in the process of reading: *with the police proving themselves to have no superior morals or professional standards*. The ideology is assumed here, that the police are flawed and human, rather than being individually as well as corporately superior to the general public. Prioritizing, then, brings focus, and it also necessarily backgrounds some content which might otherwise be questioned.

6.20   Remember that a large number of properties get repossessed because the borrower was just too frightened to fight it, not because they could not afford to pay back the debt.

The question of prioritizing here is tied up with transitivity. The main clause has the Predicator *remember* in imperative form, so the top level of proposition is about encouraging the reader to perform a mental cognition process. This means that the remainder of the sentence is, superficially at least, assumed (presupposed – see Chapter 7) to be known already. There may be a persuasive function in this kind of prioritizing; the writer wants to suggest to the reader that they already know all this information, and are just trying to help them take the brave step of fighting repossession, rather than accepting it too mildly. The structure here avoids the writer accusing the reader of being frightened or weak, by transferring this message to a third person narrative at a lower level of structure.

Note that the Actor of the repossession (the bank or the building society) is not mentioned because the passive transformation has applied to the relevant clause (get repossessed). This leaves the home owner as the sole human participant mentioned in the extract, and lays the responsibility firmly on their (already burdened) shoulders. The ideology of self-help which underlies many such texts is pervasive in our society, and may in many cases be helpful to those concerned. On the other hand, the arguments about why the situation is unfair in the first place, or which of the relevant authorities might be charged with improving fairness, are thereby de-prioritized.

6.21   If your financial circumstances change for the better or the worse, you may adjust payments in the debt management programme accordingly. This will give you the chance to regain control of your finances.

This extract contains two sentences, with the first giving an illusion of control to the debtor by the main clause having him/her as the Actor (*you*) in a Material Action clause (*may adjust*) and the fluctuating debt situation being downgraded to a subordinate clause (If your financial circumstances change for the better or the worse). The second sentence makes such control explicit, but in a differently prioritized structure, where the main clause is an Event process (*This will give you*) and the control is downplayed within a noun phrase (*the chance to regain control of your finances*). The noun phrase is focused around its head noun, *chance*, which is key to the whole passage. As with the previous example (6.20), the onus is on the debtor to take the chance and the fault if it fails is also with the debtor.

6.22   We are the most experienced personal injury specialists in the UK and have helped hundreds of thousands of people by putting them in touch with our nationwide network of specialist personal injury solicitors who will work hard and fast to win your case.

The priority in this sentence is given to the two conjoined main clauses explaining who the company is (*We are the most experienced personal injury specialists in the UK*) and what they have done (*have helped hundreds of thousands of people*). The lower priority is given to the detail of how the latter is achieved, which is put into the subordinate Adverbial clause containing a Relative clause which is highlighted in the following: *by putting them in touch with our nationwide network of specialist personal injury solicitors who will work hard and fast to win your case.* The emphasis, then, is put on the assertions of experience and success in helping people, and less priority is given to the means by which this is achieved which amounts to putting people in touch with solicitors. Even lower than this in priority terms is the question of what these solicitors will do, and this makes sense for the advertisement itself, as it is the contact service which is being provided here, not the actual legal work. However, the unwary reader may well read this as offering a complete service including the prospect of a successful outcome, which is at the lowest level of all, within the Relative clause (*to win your case*).

Chapter 7 Implying and assuming

The following examples have either presupposition or implicature adding to the surface meaning of the text. In some cases, there is more than one. Write a short commentary on each one, explaining what it is that they are assuming and/or implying, and how you know this. Comment on the ideological effect.

7.38   After yet another of their ideas fails to fly – when will they replace unworkable plans with serious leadership for the long-term good of the country.

The first clause here has a logical presupposition triggered by the iterative adverb *yet* and noun *another*, which presuppose that there have been earlier ideas which failed. This contributes to the ideology of scepticism about political effectiveness in Britain. The second clause includes an existential presupposition in the definite noun phrase *unworkable plans* which are presupposed to exist, and thus contribute to the atmosphere of criticism of the government. The next noun phrase, serious leadership, contrasts with the *unworkable plans* which together form a created opposite triggered by the transitional verb replace (see Chapter 4). *Serious leadership*, thereby, becomes presupposed not to exist currently and contributes further to the ideological viewpoint that is critical of the government.

7.39   Mr Brown's irresponsible plans are not a way forward. They're a return to the dark old days of spiralling deficits and capital flight that are the hallmark of every Labour government to have ever held office.

Similar to 7.38, this example also espouses an ideology critical of Labour governments in general and the present one in particular. This ideology is embedded in the existential presuppositions evident in the two definite noun phrases *Mr Brown's irresponsible plans* and *to the dark old days of spiralling deficits and capital flight that are the hallmark of every Labour government to have ever held office*. The latter in particular demonstrates the power of the noun phrase to incorporate a range of ideological viewpoints in a single naming practice. Thus, the presuppositions include the proposition that the *old days* (of Labour) were indeed *dark* and were marked by *spiralling deficits* and *capital flight*.

7.40   It is a pity that the people who run this country only read newspapers such as the *Times, the Guardian and the Telegraph*.

What is happening in this sentence is that the main clause (and thus the proposition of the sentence) is that something is a pity. That something is then incorporated as the subordinate noun clause *that the people who run this country only read newspapers such as the Times, the Guardian and the Telegraph*. This clause creates an existential presupposition that the situation described is indeed true: that politicians only read the broadsheet newspapers. In turn, the pragmatic knowledge of the reader will be used to fill in the gap left by the text (i.e. why such a situation should be a pity) and this leads to the implicature that they are elite and more highly educated than the population generally. This implicature, then, is produced by under-specificity, or a flouting of the maxims of relation (why is this relevant?) and quantity (there is not enough information provided).

7.41   St John's Wort plant as effective as Prozac for treating depression.

This advertisement for a 'herbal remedy' uses a comparative trigger to produce the logical presupposition that Prozac is effective for treating depression. Note that comparatives are not watertight producers of presuppositions, and may be defeased relatively easily. Thus, a reader with a bad experience of Prozac might retort that this is not much of a recommendation for St John's Wort. In fact, this advertisement risks undermining itself within its own terms. The reason for comparing itself with the chemical equivalent is to imply that the natural product will be less harmful than the drug-based one. However, the basis of the comparison is one of similarity, not difference, in this sentence, and this could lead to implicatures that they are similar not just in efficacy but also in side effects.

7.42   Helen Mirren: why I stopped taking cocaine.

The change of state verb *stop* here produces a logical presupposition that Mirren took cocaine in the past. Whilst a report on this topic could also include a proposition about this (Mirren took cocaine), building it into a presupposition somehow underlines the shock because it seems to configure the earlier situation as normal, and the new situation (being drug-free) as a new departure. This is contrary to the public's assumptions about the very famous actress who has a respectable reputation and plays high-ranking police officers in her work.

7.43   In addition, the real reason for their development has not been to end world hunger but to increase the stranglehold multinational biotech companies already have on food production.

This comment on genetically modified food products (GM) includes two presuppositions, the first triggered by the adjective *real*, which assumes that there has been talk of reasons which are *unreal* or *untrue*. The second is an existential presupposition produced by the definite noun phrase *the stranglehold multinational biotech companies already have on food production*. This includes the evaluative head noun *stranglehold*, which demonstrates the writer's negative view of the companies concerned and the effect they have on food production.

7. 44   Food is not just food, and milk is not just milk. (from an anti-milk campaigning website)

One of the pervasive food ideologies in our society is that milk is good for you. There is increasing evidence that cow's milk, being suited to calves rather than humans, can be harmful to some people. In addition, campaigners against the exploitation of animals by human beings see milk production as harmful to cows. The message in this example is carried by implicature since the surface structure of this sentence appears not to be contradictory and thus appears to flout the maxim of quality, and to the extent that readers will try to reconstruct a reason why it is not untrue, it then flouts the maxim of relation, in not explaining the apparently contradictory propositions.

Chapter 8 Negating

The examples below each contain one or more negated elements. Comment on the ideological effect of these forms in their context, using the concepts of negating as your reference point. What kinds of ideas do these examples have the potential to conjure up in the mind of the reader, and why?

8.18   National Accident Helpline specialise in making *no win no fee* accident compensation claims easy and straightforward, with *no hidden costs*.

This advertisement uses negation to conjure up a hypothetical situation in which the company fails to win compensation for the client (*no win*), which is clearly not particularly attractive, but in this worst case scenario, the question of whether it will cost anything to try is also answered negatively (*no fee*). Although this is not the most positive message to give, it may well be a strategy that works, since the idea of trying to win a civil damages court case, which is generally viewed as a difficult thing to achieve, is made worse by the notion that it might cost the client even to fail. This message is emphasized by the final phrase *no hidden costs*, which ought to go without saying in any agreement on service provision. There is an implicature created by the unnecessary inclusion of this phrase, which arises from the flouting of the maxim of quantity, and suggests that others may perhaps be guilty of such unethical practices, so that somehow to be able to claim in a double negation that you *don't do* something unethical becomes the best form of advertising possible.

8.19   Where we have really fallen down is, we have *lacked* the ability to be relevant to people's lives.

This example could come from many sources but actually originates from a political statement of failure. The negation is embodied in the semantics of the word *lacked*, which can be paraphrased as a negative (*didn't have*) and indicates a situation which has not been achieved but is clearly desirable; *the ability to be relevant to people's lives*. The way in which this admission might work ideologically is that it conjures up in the reader an alternative reality in which politicians are relevant to people's lives, and the honesty of the negation, coupled with an ability to see what is needed might then be credited to the producer of the text.

8.20   Nearly £2bn owed by absent parents should be written off as *uncollectable*, according the organisation that will replace the Child Support Agency.

This example reports on the problems of collecting money from absent parents, and uses morphological negation (*uncollectable*) to describe how it is being seen by those about to take over responsibility for this task. In using this negative, they achieve two things. Firstly, they manage to argue for a clean start for their organization, without having to take over the problems of the Child Support Agency which failed to collect the £2bn. Secondly, they create an expectation on the part of the reader that there is an alternative reality – the one that they will create – in which these payments are indeed collectable.

8.21   The Queen yesterday called the global financial crisis 'awful' – and asked why nobody had seen it coming.

The financial crisis which began in 2008 is here reportedly characterized by the Queen as a complete surprise, as many described it at the start. Her use of a negated form (*nobody*), however, allows the reader to envisage a situation in which someone did see it coming, and question who that someone might have been. This allows the reader to speculate on whether indeed there were those who knew what was likely to happen, but who kept silent. The apparently innocent question, then, hides an implicit accusation against those who were in a position to warn the rest of us and/or take evasive action.

8.22   HBOS and Lloyds TSB last night created a monstrous new banking entity safe in the knowledge that nothing can possibly go wrong.

This example, also relating to the financial crisis, may or may not be intended ironically, but the negated form (*nothing*) and the knowledge of what had gone wrong already, may lead the reader to envisaging a situation in which even a giant bank with huge assets could still be affected by the recession.

Chapter 9 Hypothesizing

The examples below each contain a modal form. Comment on the ideological effect of these forms in their context, using the concepts of negating or hypothesizing as your reference points. What kinds of ideas do these examples have the potential to conjure up in the mind of the reader, and why?

9.28   Organic farming 'could feed Africa'.

This is typical of news reporting of others' words, where the use of short stretches in quotation marks gives an impression of faithfulness (see Chapter 10), but the responsibility for the truth of what is being stated is allocated to the original speaker, not the journalist. Here, in addition, the quotation includes a weak epistemic modal verb (could), which undermines the confidence of both speaker and journalist in the possibility of achieving such a huge task (feeding Africa) by such a means, when organic farming is often presented in the press as expensive and not very productive.

9.29   The consequences of a credit crunch could be dire for both their public and corporate sector. This would ultimately stall the last engine of growth on which the world economy relies. (Experts comment on the situation in emerging markets such as India and China)

The problems of the world economy have been much commented upon in late 2008 and early 2009. The lack of certainty over the future is evident in many aspects of these texts, but one noticeable feature is the frequent use of weak epistemic modality, as we see here (could, would). Whilst wanting to comment on the situation, economists are aware of how wrong they have been in the recent past, and are therefore hedging consistently in case they are proved wrong. In the case here, there seems to be an ideology of growth as the only economic aim, since the world is here said to rely on it.

9.30   No barbed wire ... it might hurt the thieves, allotment holders told.

This example shows a modal form (might) used in reported discourse, where the 'authorities' are the target of complaint by the report concerned, at least implicitly, for protecting the prospective thief over the legitimate possessions of allotment holders. There is, of course, an implicature here, that the rule on not protecting one's possessions on the allotment is unjust and ridiculous, and this implicature arises from the flouting of the maxim of manner. But the use of the modal to present a possible world in which a thief is harmed by the barbed wire as he attempts to steal vegetables or tools, is also aimed at ridiculing what is seen as an absurd position, not least because the situation in itself is unlikely. Thus, here the ideology of the right to protect your own possessions is being implicitly supported by the ridiculing of what is presented as an extreme case of health and safety awareness 'gone mad'.

The delaying of the reporting clause here (allotment holders told) allows the shock of the absurdity to hit the reader before it becomes clear that it is not the newspaper's own view that is being put forward. This technique – of attributing speech to someone after the indirect speech has been narrated – is used in other situations too, as we see in Chapter 10.

9.31   Emperor Akihito of Japan *should follow* the example of Germany in making a genuine gesture of contrition for his country's wartime aggression in Asia, Lee Myung Bak, the South Korean President, has said.

Example 9.31 is slightly different, but it illustrates a very common feature of news and other reporting, where the main verbalization process (*has said*) is left until late in the sentence, so that the verbiage (*Emperor Akihito of Japan should follow the example of Germany etc.*) appears at first sight to be the opinion of the text's producer. This merging of the voices of the text producer and some of the participants in the narrative is one way of influencing the readers/listeners without any danger of being accused of misrepresentation. This delaying of the reporting clause in a sentence based on a verbalization process is explored in more depth in Chapter 10 on speech and thought presentation.

Chapter 10 Presenting others' speech and thoughts

The following is an account of the inquest into the shooting and killing on the London Underground of an unarmed and innocent man, Jean Charles de Menezes, by police who mistook him for a terrorism suspect. It is full of different levels of speech and thought presentation. Try to work out what some of the cases could be categorized as. Are there any difficult cases, and how would you resolve or explain them? Most importantly, what are the ideological implications of any of the examples of speech and thought presentation? Keep in mind the possible viewpoint of the various people quoted (police witnesses etc.) as well as the reporting voice (newspaper journalist, editor etc.).

A POLICE marksman told today how his gun 'malfunctioned' at the critical moment he opened fire on Jean Charles de Menezes.

This opening sentence of the passage represents the speech of an unnamed police witness mostly indirectly, but with one word (malfunctioned) in quotation marks. The effect is potentially two-fold. On the one hand, the inclusion of a small amount of apparently 'faithful' text, may carry over the image of faithfulness to the indirect speech. On the other hand, it could be seen as representing scepticism on the part of the journalist, who is emphasising the fact that the police officer is claiming his gun didn't work, and may be implying that this could be untrue.

The highly-trained firearms specialist – using the code name C2 – said *he was convinced the innocent Brazilian was a terrorist about to set off a bomb at Stockwell Tube station, south London.*

This sentence carries the speech of the police witness as indirect speech (italicized). Whilst there is some claim to faithfulness in this fairly standard form of indirect speech presentation, there are aspects of the language used which are unlikely to belong to the police officer. If we try to recast this sentence as direct speech, this may become evident:

The highly-trained firearms specialist – using the code name C2 – said '*I was convinced the innocent Brazilian was a terrorist about to set off a bomb at Stockwell Tube station, south London.*'

It seems unlikely that the police officer would use the phrase *innocent Brazilian* in a case where he was being asked to justify his actions. This is more likely the journalist reminding the reader of the man's innocence. It also seems unlikely that the police officer would say the whole of *Stockwell Tube station, south London.* Possibly the last phrase, south London, also belongs to the journalist, informing readers with little or no knowledge of London. These may be relatively minor additions from the journalist in the spirit of clarification, but there may be ideological consequences. The inclusion of *innocent*, for example, within the witness's indirect speech, is a reminder that the police were being accused of overreacting and that they killed an innocent man. Thus, the reader is not given a clean version of the witness's words, but one seen through the prism of the journalist's viewpoint.

But the Scotland Yard officer, who was accused of lying during evidence today, *said his Metropolitan Police Glock pistol jammed as he fired at Mr de Menezes.*

This sentence also presents the officer's words as indirect speech (italicized) but the parenthetical relative clause (*who was accused of lying during evidence today*), as in the previous sentence, reminds us that the officer is implicated in the death. Note that this clause does not tell us who accused him of lying, nor about what part of the evidence. This makes it redundant in the context of this sentence, since we cannot be sure of its link to the indirect speech presented here. The only remaining function of this narrative report of speech act here is as stated above: to remind the reader that this may be an unreliable witness.

> Mr de Menezes was shot seven times in the head by C2 and his colleague, C12, who both mistook him for failed suicide bomber Hussain Osman.

There is no speech presentation here, though one could conclude that the reporting of a mental perception process (mistook) is thought presentation which must have been based on speech during the inquest, though this is unclear.

> C2 also revealed he only shouted 'armed police' after deciding to shoot during the operation on July 22 2005.

This sentence presents more indirect speech from the police witness, in which he reports his own speech at the time of the shooting directly ('*armed police*'). Again, this implies faithfulness, but the inclusion of the phrase *during the operation on July 22 2005*, brings the journalist's voice into the context and makes the strands of individual voices more difficult to pick out. Note also that it is not clear whose contribution the word *only* might be. The police officer may well have stated that he shouted *armed police* after making the decision to fire, but he would have been unwise to use the evaluative adverb *only* which implies that he ought to have shouted sooner.

> When asked to explain why he fired six shots, C2 replied: 'At the time I fired I believed that I, and everyone else, was about to die'.
> 'From my position I knew that I could not access the brain stem. I could not be certain that of immediate incapacitation'.
> 'I had to ensure that life was extinct also because of the fact I had a stoppage'.
> 'I could not be certain if I had lost rounds in the process.'

Most of this extract is direct speech, and thus likely to be considered faithful to the original by readers, though it is unclear whether the sentences presented on each new paragraph are consecutive or whether there was other speech in addition that has been excluded here. There is considerable evidence of uncertainty in the weak epistemic modality in the above (*could not be certain*) which gives the impression of chaos and lack of confidence.

However, it may be that the sentences chosen to quote here emphasize that aspect more than the whole of what was said by the witness.

Chapter 11 Representing time, space and society

The following is the opening passage of the famous 'I have a dream' speech, by Martin Luther King. Comment on its use of deixis and the potential effect on the audience at the time of its delivery. How might a contemporary reader of this transcript relate to it?

11.18   I am happy to join with you today in what will go down in history as the greatest demonstration for freedom in the history of our nation.

Five score years ago, a great American, in whose symbolic shadow we stand today, signed the Emancipation Proclamation. This momentous decree came as a great beacon light of hope to millions of Negro slaves, who had been seared in the flames of withering injustice. It came as a joyous daybreak to end the long night of their captivity. But one hundred years later, the Negro still is not free. One hundred years later, the life of the Negro is still sadly crippled by the manacle of segregation and the chains of discrimination. (Martin Luther King)

The importance of political speeches is in their moment of delivery, their place of delivery, the character of the audience and the political context of that speech generally. They are performed, therefore, at the archetypal deictic centre. However, the good (and sometimes the bad) ones also have resonances beyond their place, time and participants, and Martin Luther King's is one famous example of this phenomenon. As with many political speeches, this one is in the first person singular[3] (*I*) and refers to proximal addressees in the audience (*you*) as well as using proximal space (join with) and time (*today*) references to locate the deictic centre of his speech. The temporal centre is emphasized in the next sentence by the reference back in time (*Five score years ago*) which can only be understood now by the reader re-centring him/ herself in the time of the speech to get the perspective of the 1960s looking backward 100 years to the end of slavery. The use of the proximal demonstrative this in the following sentence (*this momentous decree*) encourages the reader to see the continuing relevance of the Emancipation Proclamation to the Civil Rights movement, and perhaps has the effect of prompting the question of whether it remains relevant in twenty-first century, causing the contemporary reader to momentarily re-centre in the present. The final two sentences of the extract relocate us in the 1960s and remind us that King was effectively still fighting the emancipation battle. He uses one hundred years later with present tense verbs (*is*) to show that he is locating his views in the present, but with a strong distal connection to the past. Perhaps most surprising in this extract is his use of the third person in these last two sentences (*the Negro/the life of the Negro*), rather than the first person. He is, perhaps, effectively stepping outside history, and outside his own skin to declare the truth as he saw it.

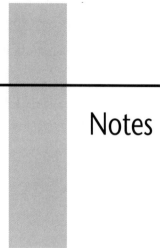

Notes

Chapter 2 Naming and describing

1 Note that the terminology arises from different theories of grammar with 'phrase' belonging more to the structuralist and generative approaches and 'group' to the functional and systemic approaches. For my purposes here, there is no significant difference, and the point is the same.

2 Note that noun phrases often occur in English within prepositional phrases and whilst one might wish to make further ideological analysis about the role a noun phrase plays in the higher clause structure, the basic points being made here apply to all noun phrases, irrespective of their syntactic function.

3 Please note that I am avoiding the term 'original', in line with other commentators on textual intervention (Pope 1993). This is because it may imply some kind of superiority for the first version of a text, and I am not wishing to prejudge this issue.

Chapter 3 Representing actions/events/states

1 See, for example, McCarthy and O'Dell, 2004.

Chapter 4 Equating and contrasting

1 'It is difficult to see how even a conservative estimate of English vocabulary could go much below a million lexemes. More radical accounts, allowing in all of scientific nomenclature, could easily double this figure' (Crystal 1995: 119).

2 See Jeffries (2006: 115–6) for discussion of noun phrases in apposition.

3 Though the original lexical relations of synonymy and opposition are semantic (i.e. context-free), those being described here are at least co-textual and in some cases contextual in the non-linguistic sense. Thus, this textual function draws on semantic meaning to create pragmatic meaning, and is at the cusp of the interface between these two kinds of meaning.

4   Davies (2007): 'A classic example of a "situational or context bound antonymy" would be the much quoted response by George W Bush to the attack on the World Trade Centre in 2001 when he announced, "Every nation, in every region, now has a decision to make. *Either* you are with **us** *or* you are with the **terrorists**".'

Chapter 5 Exemplifying and enumerating

1   David Crystal's blog on his website (http://david-crystal.blogspot.com/) provided a very early stylistic analysis of Obama's speech and I am grateful to him for pointing out the relative lack of rhetorical flourishes in the thanking section of the speech.
2   Though of course, I may have missed something.

Chapter 6 Prioritizing

1   The main initial publications setting out the case for a transformational generative grammar are Chomsky (1957: 29–65) but if the reader wishes to read an introduction to TG grammar, it might be best to start with Radford (1988).

Chapter 8 Negating

I wish to acknowledge Lisa Nahajec's work on the textual importance of negation which alerted me to the need to include it as one of the tools of analysis in this book. Nahajec (2009) sets out her approach to the subject.

1   For a brief discussion of this phenomenon, see Glucksberg (2001: 47).

Chapter 9 Hypothesizing

1   See Palmer (2001) for a detailed description.
2   The concept of 'semantic prosody' first discussed by John Sinclair, and later examined copiously by Bill Louw (1993) is one example of the way in which connotative features of lexical items may be investigated through corpus linguistic methods.
3   Though of course the ideology of women's bodies is also both triggered and reinforced by non-linguistic texts such as photographs as well.
4   Interestingly, the ground on this has shifted between the drafting (September 2008) and the revising (November 2008) of this paragraph! The media view is changing as I write, in reaction to the way in which the government are dealing with the recession which is widely predicted. This in itself is also, of course, a creation of textual ideology, since the stock market is so responsive to opinion, rather than anything tangible. I decided to leave this 'moving picture' of public opinion on the British government as it was, to demonstrate the fast pace of ideological change that is possible with the media's help.

Chapter 10 Presenting others' speech and thoughts

1 There was an early version of the model that went a step further with a Free Direct Speech (FDS) category, where the words stood alone with no reporting clause ('I'm terribly sorry'). This has now been rolled into a single category with other direct speech, because FDS gives no extra claim to faithfulness.

2 The reason I suggest that this is ambiguous (rather than, for example, simply vague) is that there is a clear 'switch' that is needed to move from a narrative interpretation to a FIS interpretation. Try looking at Example 10.6 from each of these points of view in turn, using the contexts provided in Examples 10.7 and 10.8 to help you. I hope readers will 'feel' the transition between two rather different meanings of this utterance.

Chapter 11 Representing time, space and society

1 Note that the switching between narration and quotation is not necessarily straight-forwardly representative of the two points of view, as we saw in Chapter 10.

Appendix – Commentaries on exercises

1 Note that the naturalized ideologies of the free market, enterprise and self-reliance are so ingrained in our society today that even as someone with non-standard political views, I had to think extremely hard to come up with some alternative items for this list. This demonstrates to me the power of the naturalized ideology and the difficulty of being a critical 'reader' of society.

2 Amongst other things, in a joint session of Congress on 20 September 2001, George Bush said, *Either you are with us, or you are with the terrorists*. This and other similar comments are seen by many commentators as having exacerbated the conflict of ideologies between the West and Islamic fundamentalism.

3 Though note that Barack Obama has used more first person plural (we) than others.

Bibliography

Atkinson, M. (1984) *Our Masters' Voices: The Language and Body Language of Politics*. London: Routledge.

Banfield, A. (1973) 'Narrative style and the grammar of direct and indirect speech', *Foundations of Language*. 10: 1–39.

Barthes, R. (1977) 'The death of the author', *Image-Music-Text* (trans. Stephen Heath). London: Fontana, 142–8.

Baynham, M. and Slembrouck, S. (1999) 'Speech representation and institutional discourse', *Text*. 194: 439–57.

Beard, A. (2000) *Language of Politics*. London: Routledge.

Bloor, T. and Bloor, A. (1995) *The Functional Analysis of English. A Hallidayan Approach*. London: Hodder Arnold.

Butt, D., Fahey, R., Feeze, S., Spinks, S. and Yallop, C. (2000) *Using Functional Grammar – An Explorer's Guide*. Sydney: Macquarie University Press.

Caldas-Coulthard, C. and Coulthard, M. (eds) (1996) *Texts and Practices*. London: Routledge.

Carter, R. and McCarthy, M. (2006) *Cambridge Grammar of English: A Comprehensive Guide: Spoken and Written English: Grammar and Usage*. Cambridge: Cambridge University Press.

Carter, R. and Nash, W. (1990) *Seeing through Language: A Guide to Styles of English Writing*. Oxford: Basil Blackwell.

Chapman, S. (2005) *Paul Grice. Philosopher and Linguist*. Basingstoke: Palgrave Macmillan.

Chapman, S. (2006) *Thinking about Language: Theories of English*. Basingstoke: Palgrave Macmillan.

Chomsky, N. (1957) *Syntactic Structures*. The Hague: Mouton.

Chomsky, N. (1965) *Aspects of the Theory of Syntax*. Massachusetts: MIT Press.

Clark, H. and Gerrig, R. (1990) 'Quotations as demonstrations', *Language*. 66: 764–805.

Cook, G. (1994) *Discourse and Literature. The Interplay of Form and Mind*. Oxford: Oxford University Press.

Coupland, N. (1988) *Dialect in Use: Sociolinguistic Variation in Cardiff English*. Cardiff: University of Wales Press.

Croft, W. and Cruse, D. A. (2004) *Cognitive Linguistics*. Cambridge: Cambridge University Press.

Cruse, D. A. (1986) *Lexical Semantics*. Cambridge: Cambridge University Press.

Crystal, D. (1995) *The Cambridge Encyclopedia of the English Language*. Cambridge: Cambridge University Press.

Davies, M. (2007) 'The attraction of opposites: The ideological function of conventional and created oppositions in the construction of in-groups and out-groups in news texts', in Jeffries, L., McIntyre, D. and Bousfield, D. (eds) *Stylistics and Social Cognition*. 79–100.

Davies, M. (2008) 'The attraction of opposites: The ideological function of conventional and created oppositions in the construction of in-groups and out-groups in news texts', unpublished PhD Dissertation. Huddersfield: University of Huddersfield.

Duchan, J., Bruder, G. and Hewitt, L. (eds) (1995) *Deixis in Narrative: A Cognitive Science Perspective*. Hillsdale: Lawrence Erlbaum Associates, Inc.

Emmott, C. (1999) *Narrative Comprehension*. Oxford: Oxford University Press.

Fairclough, N. (1989) *Language and Power*. London: Longman.

Fairclough, N. (2000) *New Labour, New Language?* London: Routledge.

Fairclough, N. (ed.) (1992) *Critical Language Awareness*. London: Longman.

Fludernik, M. (2001) *Narrative Voices – Ephemera or Bodied Beings New Literary History*. 32(3), Summer 2001, 707–10, The Johns Hopkins University Press.

Fludernik, M. (1993) *The Fictions of Language and the Languages of Fiction*. Routledge: Taylor and Francis.

Fowler, R. (1991) *Language in the News: Discourse and Ideology in the Press*. London: Routledge.

Fowler, R. (1996) 'On critical linguistics', in Caldas-Coulthard, C. and Coulthard, M. (eds) *Texts and Practices*. London: Routledge. 3–14.

Fowler, R., Hodge, R., Kress, G. and Trew, T. (1979) *Language and Control*. London: Routledge and Kegan Paul.

Gavins, J. (2007) *Text World Theory: An Introduction*. Edinburgh: Edinburgh University Press.

Glucksberg, S. (2001) *Understanding Figurative Language*. Oxford: Oxford University Press.

Goatly, A. (2007) *Washing the Brain: Metaphor and Hidden Ideology*. Amsterdam: John Benjamins Publishing Company.

Grice, H. P. (1975) 'Logic and Conversation', in Cole, P. and Morgan, J. (eds) *Syntax and Semantics 3: Speech Acts*. New York: Academic Press, 41–58.

Grice, H. P. (1978) 'Further notes on logic and conversation', in Cole, P. (ed.) *Syntax and Semantics 9*: Pragmatics. New York: Academic Press, 113–28.

Halliday, M. A. K. (1971) 'Linguistic structure and literary style: An inquiry into the language of William Golding's The Inheritors', in Chatman, S. (ed.) *Literary Style: A Symposium*. New York and London: Oxford University Press, 332–4.

Halliday, M. A. K. (1985) *An Introduction to Functional Gramma*r. London: Edward Arnold.

Halliday, M. A. K. (1994) *An Introduction to Functional Grammar*, 2nd ed., London: Edward Arnold.

Hidalgo-Downing, L. (2002) 'Creating things that are not: The role of negation in the poetry of Wislawa Szymborska', *Journal of Literary Semantics*. 31, 113–32.

Holt, L. (1999) 'Just gassing: An analysis of direct reported speech in a conversation between employees of a gas supply company', *Text*. 194: 505–37.

Holt, L. and Clift, R. (eds) (2006) *Reporting Talk: Reported Speech in Interaction*. Cambridge: Cambridge University Press.

Horn, L. (1984) *A Natural History of Negation*. Chicago: The University of Chicago Press.

Huddleston, G. and Pullum, K. (2002) *The Cambridge Grammar of the English Language*. Cambridge: Cambridge University Press.

Jeffries, L. (1993) *The Language of Twentieth Century Poetry*. Basingstoke: Palgrave Macmillan.

Jeffries, L. (1994) 'Language in common: Apposition in contemporary poetry by women', in Wales, K. (ed.) *Feminist Linguistics in Literary Criticism*. London: Boydell and Brewer, 21–50.

Jeffries, L. (1998) *Meaning in English*. Basingstoke: Palgrave Macmillan.

Jeffries, L. (2000) 'Don't throw out the baby with the bathwater: In defence of theoretical eclecticism in Stylistics', *PALA Occasional Papers*. 12: 1–15.

Jeffries, L. (2001) 'Schema affirmation and White Asparagus: Cultural multilingualism among readers of texts', *Language and Literature*. 10: 325–43.

Jeffries, L. (2006) *Discovering Language: The Structure of Modern English*. Basingstoke: Palgrave Macmillan.

Jeffries, L. (2007) *Textual Construction of the Female Body. A Critical Discourse Approach*. Basingstoke: Palgrave Macmillan.

Jeffries, L. (2009) *Opposites in Discourse*. London: Continuum.

Jones, S. (2002) *Antonymy: A Corpus-Based Perspective*. London: Routledge.

Justeson, J. S. and Katz, S. M. (1992) 'Redefining antonymy: The textual structure of a semantic relation', *Literary and Linguistic Computing*. 7(3): 176–84.

Kress, G. (1985) 'Discourses, texts, readers and the pro-nuclear arguments', in Chilton, P. (ed.) *Language and the Nuclear Arms Debate: Nukespeak Today*. London: Frances Pinter, 65–87.

Leech, G. and Short, M. (1981, 2007) *Style in Fiction*. London: Longman.

Levinson, S. (1983) *Pragmatics*. Cambridge: Cambridge University Press.

Louw, B. (1993) 'Irony in the text or insincerity in the writer? The diagnostic potential of semantic prosodies', in Baker, M., Francis, G. and Tognini-Bonelli, E. (eds) *Text and Technology*. Amsterdam: John Benjamins.

Lyons, J. (1977) *Semantics*. Cambridge: Cambridge University Press.

McCarthy, M. and O'Dell, F. (2004) *English Phrasal Verbs in Use: Advanced*. Cambridge: Cambridge University Press.

McHale, B. (1978) 'Free indirect discourse: A survey of recent accounts', *Poetics and Theory of Literature*. 3: 235–87.

McIntyre, D. (2006) *Point of View in Plays: A Cognitive Stylistic Approach to Viewpoint in Drama and Other Text-Types*. Amsterdam: John Benjamins.

McKenzie, M. (1987) 'Free indirect speech in a fettered insecure society', *Language and Communication*. 7(2): 153–9.

Mettinger, A. (1994) *Aspects of semantic opposition in English*. Oxford: Clarendon Press.

Mindt, D. (1995) *An Empirical Grammar of the English Verb; Modal Verbs*. Berlin: Cornelsen Verlag.

Murphy, L. and Andrew, J. M. (1993) 'The conceptual basis of antonymy and synonymy in adjectives', *Journal of Memory and Language*. 32: 301–19.

Murphy, L. (2003) *Semantic Relations and the Lexicon*. Cambridge: Cambridge University Press.

Myers (1999) *Ad Worlds*. London: Arnold.

Nahajec, L. (2009) 'Negation and the creation of implicit meaning in poetry', *Language and Literature*. 18(2): 109–27.

Nørgaard, N. (2007) 'Disordered collarettes and uncovered tables: Negative polarity as a stylistic device in Joyce's "Two Gallants"', *Journal of Literary Semantics*. 36(1): 35–52.

Pagano, A. (1994) 'Negation in written texts', in Coulthard, M. (ed.) *Advances in Written Text Analysis*. London: Routledge, 250–65.

Palmer, F. R. (2001) *Mood and Modality*, 2nd ed., Cambridge: Cambridge University Press.

Quirk, R., Greenbaum, S., Leech, G. and Svartvik, J. (1985) *A Comprehensive Grammar of the English Language*. London: Longman.

Radford, A. (1988) *Transformational Grammar*. Cambridge: Cambridge University Press.

Ravotas, D. and Berkenkotter, C. (1998) 'Voices in the text: The uses of reported speech in a psychotherapist's notes and initial assessments', *Text*. 182: 211–39.

Roeh, I. and Nir, R. (1990) 'Speech presentation in the Israel radio news: Ideological constraints and rhetorical strategies', *Text*. 10(3): 225–44.

Ryan, M. (1991) *Possible Worlds, Artificial Intelligence and Narrative Theory*. Bloomington and Indiana: Indiana University Press.

Ryan, M. (1998) 'The text as words versus the text as game: Possible world semantics and postmodern theory', *Journal of Literary Semantics*. 17(3): 137–63.

Semino, E. (1997) *Language and World Creation in Poems and Other Texts*. London: Longman.

Semino, E. and Short, M. (2004) *Corpus Stylistics: Speech, Writing and Thought Presentation in a Corpus of English Writing*. London: Routledge.

Semino, E. and Culpeper, J. (eds) (2002) *Cognitive Stylistics. Language and Cognition in Text Analysis*. Amsterdam: John Benjamins.

Short, M. (1988) 'Speech presentation, the novel and the press', in Van Peer, W. (ed.) *The Taming of the Text: Explorations in Language, Literature and Culture*. London: Routledge, 61–81.

Short, M. (1996) *Exploring the Language of Poems, Plays and Prose*. London: Longman.

Simpson, P. (1993) *Language, Ideology and Point of View*. London: Routledge.

Stockwell, P. (2002) *Cognitive Poetics: An Introduction*. London: Routledge.

Thomas, J. (1995) *Meaning in Interaction, an Introduction to Pragmatics*. London: Longman.

Tottie, G. (1990) *Negation in English Speech and Writing. A Study in Variation*. San Diego: Academic Press.

van Dijk, T. A. (1996) *Discourse Studies: A Multidisciplinary Introduction.* London: Sage.

Werth, P. (1999) *Text Worlds: Representing Conceptual Space in Discourse.* London: Longman.

Widdowson, H. (1998) 'The theory and practice of Critical Discourse Analysis', *Applied Linguistics.* 19(1): 136–51.

Willners, C. (2001) *Antonyms in Context. A Corpus-Based Semantic Analysis of Swedish Descriptive Adjectives.* (Travaux de l'institut de linguistique de Lund 40). Lund: Lunds universitet.

Index

This one's For Sam